Eccentric
Propositions

Also by Jane Miller

Many Voices: Bilingualism, Culture
and Education

Eccentric Propositions

Essays on literature and the curriculum

edited by
Jane Miller

Routledge & Kegan Paul
London, Boston, Melbourne and Henley

First published in 1984
by Routledge & Kegan Paul plc
39 Store Street, London WC1E 7DD, England

9 Park Street, Boston, Mass. 02108, USA

464 St Kilda Road, Melbourne,
Victoria 3004, Australia and

Broadway House, Newtown Road,
Henley-on-Thames, Oxon RG9 1EN, England

Set in 10/12 Times
by Hope Services, Abingdon
and printed in Great Britain
by St Edmundsbury Press Ltd
Bury St Edmunds, Suffolk

Library of Congress Cataloging in Publication Data

Eccentric propositions.
Includes index.
1. English literature – Study and teaching – Addresses,
essays, lectures.   2. Literature – Study and teaching –
Addresses, essays, lectures.   3. Children – Books and
reading – Addresses, essays, lectures.   4. Creative
writing – Study and teaching – Addresses, essays, lectures.
I. Miller, Jane, 1932–
PR37.E26   1984   820'.7'1   83-24691

British Library CIP available

ISBN 0-7100-9987-8 (pbk.)

Contents

Contents

Acknowledgments

I would like to thank many people and acknowledge their help. There are all the English teachers with whom I have worked in different ways during the last fifteen years. This book came out of my recognition that without them my students would have a hard time becoming good teachers. The book is dedicated to all students and probationary teachers, in the hope that it will inspire and reassure them. The book could not have come about without the work of the ILEA English Centre and its remarkable publications, in particular *The English Magazine*. Thanks are due to the Editors for permission to reproduce chapters 3, 8 and 11, which first appeared there. Chapters 9 and 13, by Maureen Worsdale and David Jackson, first appeared in *English in Education*, Spring 1982, and a version of Paul Hoggart's chapter (number 10) appeared in *Media, Culture and Society*, 1981, 3, and the Editors of these publications also receive my thanks. I would also like to thank the following: Gerard Benson, for permission to reproduce 'The White Mouse' in chapter 7; Jonathan Cape Ltd, for permission to reproduce some lines from 'Crusoe's Journal', from *The Castaway* by Derek Walcott and for permission to reproduce some lines from 'Out, Out –', from *The Poetry of Robert Frost* (ed. Edward Connery Latham); Oxford University Press, for permission to reproduce four lines from 'Calypso', from *Rights of Passage* by Edward Kamau Brathwaite (1967); Laurence Pollinger Ltd and the estate of Frieda Lawrence Ravagli, for permission to reproduce two lines of verse by D. H. Lawrence in chapter 8; Sidgewick and Jackson Ltd, for permission to quote from 'Romance' by W. J. Turner in *Come Hither* (ed. Walter de la Mare, 1923). 'Men Made Out of Words', by Wallace Stevens, is reprinted by permission of Faber and Faber Ltd from *The Collected Poems of Wallace Stevens*. Two lines from copyright 'The Message' by Grandmaster Flash and the Furious Five are used by kind permission of Four Hills Music Ltd/Heath Levy Music Ltd.

I would also like to thank the following authors and publishers for allowing us to use extracts included in articles reprinted from *The English Magazine*. They are H. D. Carberry and the Oxford University Press, for 'Nature'; Brian Patten and Allen & Unwin, for 'The Projectionist's Nightmare'; B. Phythian, the Editor of *Considering Poetry* and Hodder & Stoughton; Patricia Hubbell and Atheneum Publishers Inc., for 'Chant of the Awakening Bulldozers'; and Charles Malam and Holt, Rinehart & Winston, for 'Steam Shovel'.

I should also like to thank my colleagues in the English Department of the University of London Institute of Education. That department has, for many more years than I have been a member of it, exerted a powerful influence on English teachers through the pioneering work it has done on both reading and writing. I have been involved, as have most of the writers here, with the *London Association for the Teaching of English* (LATE), the *National Association* (NATE) and with the *National Association for Multicultural Education* (NAME). Many of us have also met and worked together on the *Language and the Inner City* project and the *Schools Council Language for Learning* project.

Without the advice and support of Shyama Iyer of the English Department at the Institute and of Mike Raleigh of the ILEA English Centre the book would have remained one of those ghostly 'good ideas'. Finally, I owe the 'good idea' to my students, the ones who are becoming teachers and the ones who are already experienced teachers. They have not stopped asking awkward questions yet; nor has my son, Sam, who helped me with the index.

Contributors

Paul Ashton taught English during the seventies at Woodberry Down Comprehensive school in Hackney and at Tollington Park Comprehensive School in Islington. He was an Advisory Teacher based at the ILEA English Centre for four years, and is now an Education Officer with the BBC. He is co-editor of *Our Lives* (1981), a collection of school-students' autobiographies, and editor of *City Lines* (1982), a collection of poems from London schools. He has also contributed articles to *The English Magazine*.

Andrew Bethell is currently Head of the 16–19 Section at Stoke Newington School. He has taught English and media studies for over ten years in various London schools. At the ILEA English Centre he helped to produce *The Visit* and *Choosing the News*, as well as *Ourselves* and *Macbeth*, a study guide. He has written articles for *Screen Education*, the *Times Educational Supplement* and was a founding member of *Teaching London Kids* magazine. Other publications include: *Viewpoint* (with Thames Television) and *Eyeopeners One* and *Two*. He now edits *Act Now*, a series of original plays for young people.

Tony Burgess is a lecturer in the English Department of the University of London Institute of Education. He has worked as an English teacher in secondary schools and as research officer on the development of writing and on language diversity. He has been interested in school-based teacher training and is co-founder of the Institute's Alternative Course, located in a number of inner-London secondary schools. He is currently working, within an ethnographic perspective, on the realization of understandings about language and learning within classroom settings. He is co-author of *Understanding Children Writing* (1973), *The Development of Writing Abilities 11–18* (1975) and *The Languages and Dialects of London Schoolchildren: an Investigation* (1981).

ix

Contributors

Mary Collins was educated at state schools and at University College London, where she gained a First in English. She went on to research the work of poets publishing in small press format. She became a lecturer in English and Communications at South East London College, where she specializes in language provision on Access courses for students from ethnic minorities. She also teaches for the University of London Extra-Mural department and has published poems and stories.

Maura Docherty is a tutor in the Language Division of ILEA's Centre for Urban Educational Studies. She is involved in the in-service education of teachers, running courses which focus on language issues relating to the multi-cultural classroom, particularly the education of young bilingual children.

Richard Exton has been teaching in London comprehensive schools since 1967. In 1971 he became Head of English at Tower Hamlets School and Leader of the Local English Centre there. Recently he has been working with teachers on the implications of literary theory and the devising of practical applications for the classroom. He was involved for some years in the Schools Council Humanities Curriculum Project. He is now an ILEA District Inspector for English. He teaches a University of London Extra-Mural film studies course and has served on the editorial board of *Screen Education*. He is also on the board of *The English Magazine*, which has published some of his articles. He was involved in creating the BFI pack entitled *Teaching Coronation Street*.

Terry Furlong has taught in London schools since 1967 and has been Head of the English Department of Holland Park School since 1973. From 1975 he was also warden of the Local Centre for English at the school and was seconded as a full-time local adviser from 1979–81. He has been secretary of the London Association for the Teaching of English (LATE) since 1978 and is currently an officer of the National Association for the Teaching of English (NATE). In 1979 he was elected chairman of the English panel of the LREB (the London Regional Examination Board) and shortly afterwards chairman of the group working on the 16+ examinations being developed by the consortium centred on the University of London Schools Examinations Board. At present he is Head of the Faculty of Languages and Humanities at the new Holland Park School formed from the amalgamation of Ladbroke, Isaac Newton and Holland Park schools.

Marion Glastonbury has taught English in a variety of schools, universities and colleges of further education, and has worked with overseas students both in Britain and abroad. Her son and daughter, now in their teens, have fostered her interest in children's literature. She is a regular contributor to radical, educational and feminist journals, and her study of the domestic life of nineteenth- and twentieth-century writers – *Inspiration and Drudgery* – is published by the Women's Research and Resources Centre (190 Upper Street, N.1).

Judith Graham is a lecturer in the English Department of the University of London Institute of Education. Until recently she combined this with teaching English and reading at Clissold Park School in Hackney. Before that she taught at Hornsey School for Girls and at Risinghill. She has three teenage children. She is one of the joint authors of the recently published *Achieving Literacy*.

Gerry Gregory taught English in three inner-London comprehensive schools, and in Brazil, before joining Shoreditch College of Education to teach English and Education. He has published articles on literature and on English teaching and reading material for older literacy students. He is currently researching into working-class writing and community publishing and has published articles in this field in *The English Magazine*. He is now a lecturer in Education at Brunel University.

Paul Hoggart has been teaching in secondary schools and colleges since 1975, in England and in Kenya. He is researching into popular literature and education at the University of London and has taught on the Open University course on Popular Culture. He has been teaching on widely varied English and Communications courses at Kingsway-Princeton College of Further Education in London since 1980.

David Jackson is a teacher at Toot Hill comprehensive school,

Bingham, Nottinghamshire, and co-ordinator of Nottingham School-Based Action Research Group in English. His *Continuity in Secondary English* was published in 1982 by Methuen.

Heather Kay has taught at St Christopher School, Letchworth, the Central School of Speech and Drama, Goldsmiths College, Kings College and, currently, at the Institute of Education. Alongside her teaching of English and Drama she has always been a professional verse speaker and for many years has been a member of the Barrow Poets. She also writes operas for children with her husband Peter Kay and works with him on Opera Workshops for schools.

John Lee taught for two years in a Lancashire Primary school, then for thirteen years in Primary and Secondary Schools in East London. In 1982 he became Senior Lecturer in Multi-Ethnic Education at Bristol Polytechnic.

David Marigold is English and Drama Adviser for the London borough of Harrow. Before that he taught for twenty years in ILEA and Haringey. He is co-author of *The English Department Book*, published by the ILEA English Centre and he is author/editor of a series of fiction for children, to be published by John Murray.

Sue May worked as a film editor and scriptwriter in Sydney and London before becoming a teacher. She has been a primary school teacher for twelve years, working with all ages from middle infant to the oldest classes in primary school, and she has held posts of responsibility for language and literacy across the curriculum. She is now Deputy Head of a large First and Middle School in Surrey.

Jane Miller is a lecturer in the English Department of the University of London Institute of Education. Before going there in 1976 she taught English for several years at Holland Park School in London. She is the author of *Many Voices. Bilingualism, Culture and Education*, which was published in 1983 and has written articles about literature and about education in, amongst others, *The New Review*, *The Times Literary Supplement*, *The Times Educational Supplement* and *The London Review of Books*. She is currently working on women writers and their representation of men.

Bob Moy has taught for eighteen years in London comprehensive schools and has been an ILEA advisory teacher for the last five years, working with primary and secondary teachers on in-service courses and acting as the co-ordinator of ILEA involvement in the 'Schools Council Reading for Learning Project'. His speciality is all aspects of reading. Recently he has been looking into the possibilities of using microcomputers to help children work on dense and difficult text.

Mike Raleigh did postgraduate work in literature before training to be a teacher. He taught in Leicestershire before becoming Head of English at Ladbroke School in London. He now works at the English Centre, a teachers' centre serving secondary English teachers in the ILEA.

Peter Traves was brought up in Longbridge, Birmingham and educated at Meadows Primary School, Five Ways Grammar School and University College of Swansea. After a first degree he spent two more years working on a thesis on the seventeenth-century writer, Lancelot Andrewes. From there he moved to the University of London Institute of Education. He has worked for nine years at Hackney Downs School, where he is now Head of Humanities. In September 1983 he will become an Advisory Teacher for two years with ILEA.

Maureen Worsdale left school at fifteen, worked in industry, produced three children and resumed her education in her thirties, taking a B.Ed, followed by an MA in Education at London. She is now Head of English and Drama at a large comprehensive, King John School, in Essex. She is secretary of the South Essex branch of NATE and its journalistic offshoot, *The Essex Review of Children's Literature*, and is a member of the Secondary Committee of NATE. She spends her leisure time jogging and feeding spaniels.

Introduction

Jane Miller

This is a book about literature – the reading and the writing of it – in school. It is written by teachers for teachers, and it represents just a fraction of some remarkable work done during the last ten years or so; years, it should be added, when it has been fashionable to blame teachers for many of our social ills, from rioting to soaring unemployment. Most of these teachers have worked in schools and colleges in inner cities: crumbling places, as we know, where poor housing, unemployment and falling rolls weigh heavily on schools. No one would deny that children who live in such places come to school with problems. If the children are black they will have suffered from racism. If they are becoming bilingual they will have been treated as stupid, languageless or both. If they are working-class they may know, before they even get to school, that they are not expected to do well there. If they are girls they may have discovered that girls bring up families, for which no educational qualifications are required. Schools may add to those problems, but they do not create them. Indeed, most schools and most teachers know that it isn't children who are the problem.

So many bad things have been said and done to state education in the last few years that it might amaze some people to discover that they have also been years of massive and exhilarating innovation. If some of that innovation – mixed-ability teaching, new syllabuses and modes of assessment, the involvement of teachers in research and in educational theorising – is cheaply dismissed as making the best of a bad job, I hope that these examples of developments in the teaching of literature will scotch all that. Changes in pedagogy and in curriculum and learning theory, which may have crept into teaching under such rubrics as 'mixed-ability teaching' or 'education for a multicultural society' or 'language across the curriculum' or 'examination by course-work' or 'gender and schooling', have only borne fruit when it

1

could be demonstrated that serious attention to their principles delivered better ways of working with *all* children.

English teachers have always been in the vanguard of educational change and have not been afraid to see their work as inevitably political. This collection of essays by English teachers charts some of the most important changes, brought about by teachers themselves, in the way literature is read and written in schools. All the work described here assumes the cultural, racial and linguistic diversity of British society, just as it assumes that schools need to respond to that diversity whether their own populations are homogeneous or mixed. So we are not, first of all, talking about bits and pieces, tinkering, insertions into the curriculum to pacify or beguile particular groups of pupils. What we are talking about is a creative enriching of pedagogy and content for all children, and we are suggesting that the recognition of diversity releases teachers and pupils into new possibilities of what is studied and how.

The book aims to do four main things. First, it concentrates on real classrooms, real lessons and real children, and in doing so it sets out to show how particular ideas can be put into practice. Second, both explicitly and implicitly it suggests the theories of learning and the theories of literature, of culture and of school which underlie such practice; and in doing so it makes a case for the centrality of literature and of literacy to the curriculum. Third, the chapters themselves, and the notes to them, provide resources: books to read with children and books for teachers to read for themselves to deepen their understanding of the ideas and their confidence in adapting them for their own classrooms. Fourth, the book is constructed round the necessary continuities of English teaching: continuities between life and literature, between reading and writing, and between learning to read, becoming better at it and studying literature. It suggests too the need for continuity between reading and writing as creative activities and the examinations, which must be able to encourage such activities through their methods of assessment if they are to acquire the least credibility.

The book begins with two-year-old Theo in Maura Docherty's account of a child learning from books as he learns to read, and ends with Gerry Gregory's consideration of how the writing of working women and men, produced by community publishers, could be used productively in schools. Sue May examines the relation between the stories primary school children read and the ones they write. Books told Marion Glastonbury about the double-edged destiny of growing up a girl, providing her with society's expectations and the means to explore and resist those expectations. Tony Burgess looks at a first-year classroom in a secondary school, where the reading and the making of literature contribute to a culture built on expectations of opportunity and choice. Richard Exton uses ideas from structuralist theory to work on poems and stories with a second-year class, and Judith Graham shows that inexperienced readers need the same things from literature as the rest of us. Heather Kay, Paul Ashton and David Marigold consider a variety of activities, from improvised drama to games and writing, which make for good poetry lessons in the lower years of the secondary school, while Maureen Worsdale suggests ways of helping young people to write about the books they read as exams begin to loom. Paul Hoggart's piece reminds us of the need to know what children read – comics and magazines, particularly – outside school and for pleasure. The chapter by Bob Moy and Mike Raleigh delves into the extraordinary traditions and practices called 'comprehension' in school, and suggests alternatives, while Terry Furlong takes some of these alternatives into a fourth-year class, where a group of boys are reading a poem together. David Jackson shows some O level pupils developing ways of working on *Great Expectations*, and Andrew Bethell looks at the strengths of formal analysis as it has grown within media studies. The last four chapters are about young adults. John Lee shows some black 17-year-olds making sense of black literature for their CEE coursework and Peter Traves writes about the A level proposal his school made to an examination board, and what happened to it. Mary Collins discusses the uses of literature on some new courses in further education, and Gerry Gregory returns us to the classroom with the possibility that kinds of adult autobiography would add productively to what young people read in school.

I have said that this work rests on ideas about learning and ideas about literature and culture. I shall need to start autobiographically if I am to suggest a little of how teachers develop their theory and their practice. On Friday afternoons in December and January I often interview young English graduates who want to teach

English in London schools. It is harder these days for them to get as far even as a training, and it is harder for me to decide whom to accept. I want to know what has made them think they will enjoy teaching and I want to know too whether, in answering that question, they have any ideas about what English teaching is, or might be, in a large inner-city comprehensive school. Most of them have been reading for years, and some are experienced and confident writers. A good many are pleased to have had the chance to study literature; and they often use words like 'instil' to suggest how they might share their own enthusiasm for literature with children. They usually know that that is a difficult thing to want, let alone do. That confusion may emerge from another one: the relation between their own histories as readers and the sorts of reading and writing and thinking they've been engaged in during their three years 'doing English'. An encouraging number mention a particular teacher they had, usually in the sixth form, who did instil or awaken, or at any rate support, their growing interest in reading and writing. A few remember English lessons, and, of course, English lectures and seminars, as no more than a distraction from the plays they were directing, the novel they were writing or the poems they performed or listened to.

This part of our conversation may peter out. I cannot quite bring myself to ask how they intend to go about 'instilling' things into all those lively and intelligent young people who have resisted, sometimes with outstanding success, the blandishments of a procession of teachers, all of whom loved literature. A gap is growing between the classroom in my head and the glorious communications in theirs. I may, a little petulantly, move on from there to ask why reading and writing should be thought so important anyway, and we will steer ourselves precariously through the rocks of acquiring a 'critical sensibility' or getting 'pleasure from language' or encountering 'other experiences'. Often things get better at the end when we talk about something one or other of us has read recently, perhaps a book written for children.

Yet the teachers writing here have, I am glad to say, kept the optimism of those nervous candidates and their uneasy interviewer. None of them has lost the capacity to wonder on occasions why they are doing it or how it might best be done. Good teachers know that they have to live without simple answers to either of those questions. A 'good' lesson raises almost as many queries as a spate of bad ones, and 'good' teachers have had a lot of 'bad' lessons: ones where children yawned or varnished their nails or turned the poem they'd been given to read into a neat round ball or a dart. They are different from bad teachers because lessons like that have not made them despair of children or of literature. They are optimists, and their optimism is valuable for coming out of experience and the realities of classrooms and of the lives lived in them and outside them.

There was a time when F. R. Leavis would have been invoked to explain that optimism. It may be worth rehearsing some of the reasons for his now being blamed for those principles embodied in English examinations and some course books which have seemed crippling to the literature curriculum in schools. His brand of 'elitism' has been held responsible for attitudes to what is read in school as well as to how it is read. It is worth remembering that just as he was importantly countering another sort of elitism, for which he was horse-whipped, so has his been replaced by other kinds of study and criticism, which are no less exclusive. In a marvellously characteristic lambasting of Ezra Pound[1] Leavis apologizes ironically for his 'descent into pedagogy', reminding us that it was above all as a teacher, a trainer of sensibility, that he took up arms. 'Everything must start from the training of sensibility' he wrote, and later, 'Armed in the ways suggested with a technique of reading, a trained sense for the significant, and types and analogues for dealing with further experience, the student may be left to educate himself (otherwise he is ineducable).' Then, 'having trained one's sensibility and grasped firmly the significance of "tradition" and "a literature" in the literature of one's own language, one is equipped to profit by incursions into other literatures'.

Leavis was, of course, proposing a 'training' programme for university students, many of whom he was bound to regard as 'ineducable', though elsewhere in the same piece he sketches in the only very slight modifications needed for such a programme to be viable in schools. The systematic and military nature of the enterprise, with its hints of remediation, might, in rosier times, have commended the programme to the MSC. Teachers who find this position objectionable would do well to resist it on grounds broader and deeper than that it is elitist. It was meant, none the less, to show that all but a tiny minority of the population had no sensibility and were not likely to acquire one. Also, a version of that position, sadly unbuttressed by Leavis's surely very powerful insights into the nature of poetic language, filters into classrooms *via* literature examinations issuing from the universities. Then all that 'training' and 'arming' has done much to deny the value of those infinitely heterogeneous experiences of reading from infancy onwards which contribute to the development of powerful readers. The best moments for most of us as readers are those when we come unawares, with surprise, but also with a most complex sense of recognition, upon ideas and impressions for which we have *not* been prepared. A beady anticipation of the 'significant' is the very opposite of how we would want children to approach literature and to account for the meanings they make and the importance they attribute to them. Leavis and his training put readers of all ages and kinds into a relationship with literature and its 'tradition', which left them powerless to do more than exclaim and agree that yes, *that* probably is why Shakespeare, or Conrad, is so good. Leavis also wanted, and rightly, to insist on a 'living tradition', which meant for him the recognition of new work as valuable by virtue of its organic rootedness in the best of the old. Whether 'great' or 'living' it was a tradition defined by its inaccessibility to the 'ineducable' majority. The teachers writing here would want to redefine that 'living tradition' as carrying the ways by which all readers and all writers actively engage with written and spoken language and by doing so enrich and develop the tradition and their own powers of negotiating its offerings and difficulties.

There are real readers and writers in this book and all of them *are* actively engaged in making sense of written language for purposes they are learning, through that process, to distinguish and define. Theo at two, in the first chapter, is already asking questions of stories, demanding coherence, moralities and kinds of truth from them. Trevor is eleven and a 'bad' reader, yet Judith Graham shows how a good story, even a complex one, rather than one cobbled together for 'bad' readers, teaches him to read by confronting him with the stuff which makes being able to read worthwhile and even vital. No one is helped by the belief that very young readers or 'bad' ones or simply inexperienced ones need something quite different from the rest of us. That will be one of the continuities of the book: that 2-year-olds ask the same things of literature as 20-year-olds or old-age pensioners, and that the support or interventions of adults – especially, but not only, of teachers – are not about 'training', nor about sifting the good from the bad. They are to help children to take on the task for themselves by focusing on experiences of reading which children can see are exciting and full of promise. Teachers are not there to conjure up pious reverence for those, now and in the past, who have written well and lastingly. They are there to make it possible for children to do it themselves and to learn from that how writing can make its own worlds and allow you some control over other people's as well as the one you inhabit.

Carolyn Steedman, in her remarkable[2] study of three 8-year-old girls who wrote a story together called 'The Tidy House', a fiction which both contained and commented upon their own experience of family life, suggests how important the process was for these children:

> what writing 'The Tidy House' provided Carla, Melissa and Lindie with was a powerful notion of change. The idea of change functioned in several ways, the simplest and most accessible being the children's understanding that as writers they could alter the words on the page, cross them out, start again. They were able to alter the sequence and effect of events witnessed in the real world by constructing a fiction. By writing, and particularly by making use of dialogue, they were able to analyse the way in which the words of adults altered events and to envision for themselves possible changes in circumstances. It is probable that children who are illiterate are quite unable to make these analyses or perform these transformations.

'The idea of literature as a training-ground for life is servile', Raymond Williams[3] wrote many years ago, and of course that carries in it a riposte to Leavis and his trainers of sensibility. Reading neither gives us reality nor prepares us for it. It does, though, allow us to understand that all our realities are constructions of the imagination and of language. Wallace Stevens, in his marvellous 'Men Made Out of Words' (and his 'Men' must be permitted here in its inclusively generic sense) exultantly demonstrates that for us:

What should we be without the sexual myth,
The human reverie or poem of death?
Castratos of moon-mash – Life consists
Of propositions about life. The human
Reverie is a solitude in which
We compose these propositions, torn by dreams,
By the terrible incantations of defeats
And by the fear that defeats and dreams are one.
The whole race is a poet that writes down
The eccentric propositions of its fate.

More recently a group of English teachers asked Raymond Williams[4] what he thought their task, and his, should be, and he replied, 'to relay literature as active'. That will do as a description of another of this book's continuities. Children make stories and poems and pictures and the world they live in *mean* something, and they make that meaning through negotiating between what they already know, what they are coming to know and what writers and story-tellers have made for them. The *making* is active and must continue to be. We are not asking children to consume literature passively, but to use it and resist it too, through their understandings of what it is and through their own writing.

Two-year-old children draw and write. Their first efforts at both may be indistinguishable to most adults, but they are increasingly differentiated by the children themselves, as forms which they can use to represent and to transform their reality and their language in similar but different ways. Vygotsky[5] described it as learning that 'one can draw not only things but also speech'. That process of differentiation is continuous and makes it possible for children to work with the notion that what is perceived is a construction determined by kinds of imaginative representation. Very young children talking to themselves have been heard[6] to teach themselves bits of language, play with sound and meaning, tell the story of their day, or a part of it, and rehearse possible and probable future events. That happens anyway. Stories, nursery rhymes, songs, acting out and games feed and lead the process, and, as Edward Blishen[7] has put it, 'From books . . . a child leaps miles ahead of himself in terms of general understanding.' Literary forms are not arbitrary, but continuous with social practices and the language which frames and explains them to children.

Yet literacy and literature do not, of course, just 'rub off' on children. They are mediated by what might be called the discourse of learning to read, a characteristic item of which might be, 'I'm not allowed to read that until I've finished Book 3.' Yet learning to read will only work for children who regard that discourse as quite marginal to the business of moving (often physically) into stories and forcing them to yield up their worlds and points of view. For Sue May, the most sophisticated understandings of written narrative, its structures, its possibilities and its constraints on writer and reader, are learned by children from reading stories and writing ones of their own, which they expect, as all writers do, someone else to read, understand and enjoy.

At a time of economic and political crisis schools are doubly vulnerable. Starved of funds and support, they are also expected to produce goods, like any manufacturing industry. The advice and admonishment of experts is harder to resist when it is accompanied by a government's need to blame unemployment on the unemployed and on their inadequate educators. Teachers are becoming wary of some of that advice, not least when it comes from the specialisms of university research, which will rarely seem to address the complexities even of a classroom, let alone of whole schools and whole-school careers of children. Linguists, for instance, may advise English teachers to drop story-writing with children because 'Accurate (sic), competent fiction requires great technical control, and this fact should not be obscured by the occasional random success' (of some children, that is).[8] So we don't want children to acquire 'technical control' apparently and shouldn't be giving children difficult things to do. A concentration on what are called 'language skills' by some, hierarchically arranged and directed towards 'the world of work' (an apparently unproblematic concept), is often proposed nowadays. Those 'skills' – and they are the ones like spelling and punctuation, for the most part, which are easier to isolate - can sit with a notion of literacy so barren as to undermine any complaints schools might make about their reduced budgets for books. From other quarters come homilies about reading being particularly good for you if there is no other obvious route to an encounter with 'the best that has been thought and known in the world'. Most of such advice depends on a view of learning as something which just happens, as a sort of layered accretion of knowledge and habits, provided that teachers listen to their betters about what that knowledge should be and what are the best habits to acquire. Teachers know that it isn't like that. This is not special pleading, not some covert hint that the children *they* teach either cannot or will not learn. The reverse. They know that children make progress and engage with their work when they are in classrooms where cultural and individual diversity are assumed and relished: ones where debilitating certainties about both learning and literature, which have served to define most readers as 'ineducable', are seen to be demonstrably untrue.

When Gabriel Josipovici[9] writes that 'symbolic systems, including novels, are not repositories of meaning but invitations to take part in certain kinds of activity' he is not condescendingly privileging 'certain kinds of activity' as against others, nor is he determining either the nature of the activity or the benefits which might accrue from it. He is pointing to the social nature of reading and of writing to their inevitably shared nature as activities. Theo at two, creeping into his parents' bedroom to whisper urgently, 'Read a book, daddy', knows that already. That, it might be said, is what has been 'instilled'. For too many other children it is their inadequacy as readers and writers, their ineligibility as critics, their immaturity in matters of taste and discrimination which are so laboriously 'instilled'.

The pedagogic dilemmas issue partly from those other dilemmas about what literature is. If it is a special sort of written language, which requires particular kinds of response and understanding which must be learned, it may simply be that we are talking about literature as 'art'. In which case why aren't children being taught to perform in it as they would be in dancing or drama or painting or music lessons? Of course, even with those 'arts', examination syllabuses are springing up which deflect from the doing of them to the writing about them, whether critically or historically. Suzanne Langer[10] believes that,

> the reason why literature is a standard academic pursuit lies in the very fact that one can treat it as something else than art. Since its normal material is language, and language is, after all, the medium of discourse, it is always possible to look at a

literary work as an assertion of facts and opinions, that is, as a piece of discursive symbolism functioning in the usual communicative way.

Perhaps Suzanne Langer, as a philosopher of aesthetics, is too emphatic in insisting on what is universally special about other kinds of artistic representation, rather than on the continuities as well as the dislocations between all forms of imaginative symbolic activities and the social practices in which children participate from birth and through which they learn who they are and where. By this I mean that narrative, metaphor, dramatization are embedded in the discourses which children enter at birth and which, in their turn, frame their understandings and perception and define their choices.

For instance: following a wonderful account of what Trabb's boy in *Great Expectations* could be said to be doing when he swaggers past Pip with the words, 'Don't know yah!' Harold Rosen[11] writes, 'Representation of action and speech through the use of our own bodies and speech is the birthplace of drama.' Drama at its most elaborated and heightened is not the same thing as Rosen's example of a little girl putting on a long cloak from the dressing-up basket and declaring 'apparently to no one, "I am a queen and I am outrageous".' But the connection between them, like the connection between a child's first single-sentence story – 'She crying' – and *The Golden Bowl* is what makes literature (the oral as well as the written kind) recognizable and intelligible, and intrinsic to human development. Nor, of course, is language the only way for human beings to abstract and organize their experience. The game an infant may invent for herself with two saucepan lids and an egg-whisk contains the beginnings of that active and formal transformation of the world, by acting on it, which is characteristic of thinking and of learning. As Vygotsky[12] puts it, 'From the point of view of development, creating an imaginary situation can be regarded as a means of developing abstract thought.'

Of course, there is a danger that by insisting on the everyday bases of literary forms one is taken to be suggesting that the process of moving towards the making or receiving of complex, dense text is a natural one. Frank Smith[13] – and there are echoes of William Morris in what he says – has recently made the case for that process being a good deal more natural than most teachers will allow it to be. That may be an extension of Chomsky's 'ideal speaker', and with its insistence on the universally creative potential of all children it does some useful redressing of the balance. In practice teachers know that it doesn't happen quite like that. By emphasizing the connections between elaborated literary forms and kinds of everyday social practice I mean only to invoke the vital resources which even the youngest children bring to reading and to writing and the importance of helping children to use these consciously and confidently as they learn to read. They still have a lot to learn and they will learn a good deal of it from reading and from writing. Because adults have come to enjoy reading alone they may forget that classrooms, other people and teachers, have a function in relaying 'literature as active'. There is the need to develop attention and the ability to reflect on one's own and other people's strategies for understanding text. There is a need to learn what sort of thing written language is, what can be done with it, how all kinds of literature bear their own cultural and institutional histories, and stand in different relations to people's lives in different cultures; so that literature can tell us something (but not everything) about those cultures in a variety of ways.

Children need experience of literary forms and they need to be encouraged to bring to bear consciously on what they read their knowledge of the world and of language. They may be helped to understand the nature of literature as an institution, and to resist its blandishments, by the kinds of formal analysis proposed by Richard Exton and Andrew Bethell, for this will enable them to understand that they are considering not just what a poem or a television news item 'means', but how it means it, the meanings and messages of form. The progress teachers look for in the children they teach are towards kinds of awareness: of what writers can and cannot do with language and with experience, and a conscious control of their own writing and their own understandings in the context of collective wisdoms and beliefs. Turning this into practice is an extraordinary challenge. That is why we need to hear from teachers who are working creatively to meet that challenge.

Notes

1 F. R. Leavis, 'How to Teach Reading', in *Education and the University*, Chatto & Windus, London, 1943.
2 Carolyn Steedman, *The Tidy House*, Virago, London, 1982,
3 Raymond Williams, *Culture and Society 1780–1950*, Chatto & Windus, London, 1958.
4 Raymond Williams, 'Making it Active', an interview in *The English Magazine*, Spring 1979 – 1.
5 L. Vygotsky, *Mind in Society*, Harvard University Press, 1978.
6 A superb example of this is Ruth Weir, *Language in the Crib*, Mouton, The Hague, 1962.
7 Edward Blishen, a review of Dorothy Butler's *Cushla and her Books* in the *Times Educational Supplement*, 4.1.80.
8 J. McH. Sinclair, 'The integration of language and literature in the English curriculum', in R. Carter and D. Burton (eds), *Literary Text and Language Study*, Edward Arnold, London, 1982.
9 Gabriel Josipovici, *The Modern English Novel*, Open Books, London, 1976.
10 Suzanne Langer, *Feeling and Form*, Routledge & Kegan Paul, London, 1953.
11 Harold Rosen, 'The Dramatic Mode' in Phillida Salmon (ed.), *Coming to Know*, Routledge & Kegan Paul, London, 1980.
12 Vygotsky, op. cit.
13 Frank Smith, in a lecture, 'Reading, Writing and the World in the Head', given at the University of London Institute of Education on 24 March 1983.

1   That's not right. Look!
There's no Daddy in this book

Maura Docherty

When Theo was three months old, I, one of his hearing parents, was quite sure he was deaf. It transpired that he was not. Strangely, I have had no such fear about Theo as a potential reader; I have never been anything but perfectly certain that he would learn to read and come to enjoy literature. Given the number of children who never learn to read at all, or not to a level to satisfy their personal needs, and those others who can read but don't, my unwarranted confidence and high expectation probably grow out of my own love and high regard for literature and my strong hope that this activity – reading – will occupy as large a place in Theo's life as it does in mine.

Until the time when I was able to observe a very young learner in a home setting my experience of early reading had been limited to working with young children who had to start the first round of learning to read in a formal school setting, or with those children who came to school able to read and who then developed their skills in the classroom.

I have always felt that because of the nature and the conditions of conventional classroom instruction the first of these two groups had a very difficult task, while the second group often had to progress as readers in a far less congenial and stimulating language environment than they had probably experienced in their pre-school years. I believe this applies to whatever stage the children were at in their physical, cognitive and linguistic development. School is a very strange and difficult place to learn to read. Most children succeed despite the constraints, but few are left with any strong love of literature.

Margaret Clark,[1] in her study of young children who had learned to read before going to school, dismissed the idea that they were merely a group of unusually intelligent children or that their precocious reading development was simply attributable to parental pressures or expectations. She saw the more important factor as the stimulating language context in which reading stories took place in their pre-school family life. Most of the children had an interested adult to talk to and read with, access to good reading material at home and from the library and very few had 'suffered' any formal teaching. Many schools may try to simulate these conditions, but most teachers have not the time nor the resources nor the confidence to support their children in this way.

Bettelheim notes,

> The worst aspect of the way reading is presently taught is the impression the child receives during his earliest years in school that skills like decoding are what reading is all about. There is nothing wrong with teaching a skill as long as it is not done in ways that do damage to the purposes for which the particular skill is needed or desirable. But the teacher's emphasis on decoding and word recognition – and these are all she can emphasise since *the utter emptiness of the text does not permit her to stress meaning* – gives the child the idea that these are all-important.[2]

Like Bettelheim, I believe that the learning of real literature should begin in the home and continue uninterruptedly through school. What I wanted to see through my study of Theo in his home environment were generally applicable features of this home reading which might make me a better teacher of literature in school, and might increase my understanding of the learning process. 'The way the learning to read is experienced by the child will determine how he will view learning in general, how he will conceive of himself as a learner and even as a person,' says Bettelheim. If this is so, the experienced reader-support has a huge responsibility to build up in the child positive attitudes towards himself as a learner.

Closely observing Theo learning to read has allowed me to understand better the complementary role the experienced reader has in supporting the efforts of the learner to carry out his own task of learning to read, a task he can come to through reading with another interested reader, and, most importantly, the crucial part real literature plays in the whole process.

What I shall describe here is the early progress of one pre-school reader in order to indicate his ability to control and phase his development towards becoming a reader (in the conventionally held sense of the word). I will present this in the context of shared high expectation of pleasure from both the experienced reader-support and the learner, a familiarity and confidence with books, and a constant supply of stimulating and varied stories. Jane and Peter have never been invited.

Margaret Meek[3] says that 'children learn to read by discovering what to do and making the most of the help they are given. . . . . There is only one rule: avoid frustration and enjoy the time that you spend together and the books that you share.' Reading, she says, is whole-task learning, right from the beginning. 'From first to last the child should be invited to behave like a reader, and those who want to help him should assume that he can learn and will learn, just as happened when he began to talk.'

I needed to find out what was going on in order to chart the development of my case-study towards literacy. I decided to set down anything significant as it occurred, placing his reading development in the context of his general language development. I made frequent video recordings of Theo sharing books with his father or with me, audio tapes of his conversations, and noted in a journal any particular items which I took to be especially significant as they occurred in these sessions, particularly features I recognised as growth points in his development. I looked for and noted any readerly behaviour, observable indications of his comprehension of what a book was about and how he approached reading as an activity.

For instance, I noted his movement from 'Read a book' (1.6) to 'Read a story' (2.2) to 'Read *Postman Pat's Rainy Day*', and an occasion when he picked up a book with pictures but no words, *The Snowman*, and said 'Can you say words?' (3.0). I also noted when book language and ideas intruded into his life, such as when he was eating his soup and remarked 'It's just right' (*Goldilocks and the three bears*), and when he took to chanting 'Why should I?' (*The Tale of Thomas Mead*), or 'The wind blows me up and up' (2.9 *The Wind Blew*), and when on a shopping trip he called out 'I see an avocado pear and I mash it up to eat' (3.0 *Avocado Baby*).

Theo's world of books was supporting not just his linguistic development but the development of his ideas and concepts, and broadening his experience in the way books can at a very early stage, helping him to become a reader and explore the real world through its representation in his books at the same time.

Seeing a dog with a sharp-pointed nose one day he said, 'Look, Mammy, a fox', his experience at that time not being wide enough to tell him that a dog on a lead was unlikely to be a fox (2.2). Six months later, and after many more stories, his reaction to a large dog which had entered the garden was a more tentative 'Mammy, is that a wolf?' His further reading was making him aware of greater possibilities, as were TV and trips to the zoo, and he was striving to reconcile these different types of information in his everyday life. Children come to an understanding of their world by reflecting on their own experiences and relating them to any new information they encounter in books.

I also looked carefully at the interaction between adult and child and the nature of the collaboration from which I expected Theo to move through literature to literacy. The study began when Theo was two. He is the only child of working parents, for both of whom reading is an important part of life. As Bettelheim says, 'we read regularly for both enjoyment and meaning and from a feeling that reading enriches our experience', and we probably inevitably offer Theo this view of reading, underlining it by always looking for stimulating literature for him, and on our trips to the library letting him choose appealing stories. Reading together is an experience we all enjoy very much and at any time, not simply at bedtime, often hearing an urgent whisper at dawn – 'Read a book, Daddy'.

Theo's familiarity with books has given him great confidence in handling them, and he has developed certain rituals, such as removing the dust-wrappers, examining the endpapers, noting his name if it is written in, and, most recently, looking for a 'contents' page. He usually repeats the title and the author's name; a few seem to have appealed to him particularly, such as John Burningham and Helen Oxenbury, and he often points to a book and says the name of one or the other (though not always correctly). From an early age he has adopted a kind of classification system of his own. 'Pictures' and 'no pictures', 'Daddy's/Mammy's book' and 'Theo's book', again usually distinguished by the presence or absence of pictures, Theo's always having pictures in them.

From the start of his reading life we have always encouraged Theo to choose what he wanted to read from our own wide selection of children's literature. In his first two years Theo was given lots of glossy hardboard books, designed for very young children. Many had single illustrations on each page, usually with the name printed in large letters underneath – farm animals, etc. – but Theo seemed to lose interest in most of these at a very early age, though a few have remained favourites, Helen Oxenbury especially, and the Zebby books, which each contain a little story. Rather incomprehensibly, the Ahlbergs' *A Place to Play* became an early and enduring favourite, possibly because it contained so much detail in the illustrations.

This last example seems to suggest that children's literature cannot be successfully 'staged' according to age groups, as the Ahlbergs' book was aimed at a much older level than Theo was at when it attracted him. For Theo there was no graduated series of simple–harder–harder material. He chose what he wanted from the bookshelf and we simplified or improvised at first until he became familiar with the pictures and layout and then gradually we supplied closer and closer approximations of the actual contents, as he asked for them, eventually reaching the word by word reading. Ultimately he exerted control, in that if we tried to go too fast or got too involved he would lose interest.

Theo dictated the stages for himself; but his criteria were quite different from those of publishers who produce simple books for very young children. They clearly see the process as starting with a simple picture, later with a one-word or one-sentence caption, building up to more complex stories. What could a young child get from a picture of a multi-coloured ball on a bright yellow background compared with a detailed view of the Brick Street Boys at the swimming baths being ordered out for playing football in the water? (in *A Place to Play*).

Where he was interested enough to stay with the single picture per page type of book, he negotiated with the reader-support until he was satisfied with the label for the particular object. This extract shows Theo looking at *My First Picture Dictionary* and a picture of a hen:

F: Now . . . what's this?
T: A cock-a-doo . . . a cock-a-doodle-doo.
F: It's a hen, actually.
T: A chicken.
F: OK.

The movement from cock-a-doodle-doo to chicken and hen was

clearly negotiable. At no time did the experienced reader insist on the correct spoken equivalent for the printed word 'hen'.

Again with *My Amazing ABC*; looking at a picture of a woodpecker:

F: What have we got here?
T: That pigeon . . . that robin.
F: What is it? A Robin?
T: Yeh.
F: Well he's got a red head. I suppose that's what misled you. He's actually called a woodpecker.
T: Oh!
F: Woodpecker, but he's got a red head.
T: Robin, robin.
F: A robin has a red breast. A robin is red . . .
T: A robin . . . red.

Looking at a picture of a lobster:

F: What is it?
T: A quack quack.
F: Well, it's a lobster, actually.
T: Eh?
F: Rather eccentric to make it a quack quack.
T: Quack quack.
F: Well, perhaps we'll let you have artistic license.
T: Quack quack.
F: Let you say 'quack quack' if you wish.
T: Quack.

Notice how Theo draws on his own understanding of how things are and look to him to make sense of the pictures of the lobster and the woodpecker.

With a simple caption book, *Bedtime*, looking at a picture of a pair of pyjamas and a lamp:

M: Darling, *Bedtime*.
T: Bedtime.
M: Mm . . .
T: 'jamas (pointing to the book), 'jamas (pointing to his own which he is wearing).
M: Pyjamas.
T: 'jamas (pointing at the book).
M: Yes, like yours.
T: Yes, girl 'jamas (second page shows girl wearing the pyjamas) . . . zip . . . zip, zip . . . zip (tracing line of zip up and down).
M: Yes, has yours got a zip?

T: No, . . . no zip (pointing to his own pyjamas) . . . go to sleep . . . light on, light off (with actions of pulling a light switch on and off) . . . I pull light off . . . all gone.

This room for negotiation, agreed between the adult and child, may not be thought appropriate in a formal school setting or within the more conventional view of what is allowed as reading. In the *Bedtime* example, Theo's whole body is working to an understanding of the text through comparing his own pyjamas, which have no zip, and through this demonstration of what a zip is feeling his way to the pyjamas of the text in a much fuller way. So too for the lamp, the physical movement of switching the lamp on and off in the air adds a fullness to his reading of lamp, and, incidentally, builds up his understanding of things called lamps.

Negotiation over the words was also important. Theo was quite sure the woodpecker was a robin because of its red head, and that the lobster was a quack quack. The connections he was making seem fairly obvious and at that point he was classifying much of his world in terms of sameness, so there was the general term 'birds', but 'differences' also took his attention as in duck, robin and owl being 'named' birds. They were special in that we fed ducks in the park; owls featured in many of his stories, and were also 'different' in their physical flatness and wide eyes, generally viewed face on, so tended to stand out separately from the others. The robin was also specially different because of its red colour and its frequent occurrence in stories. So, having a finer discrimination in his categorising of birds, he then, in this extract, over-generalises the redness to the red-headed woodpecker, and from the beak of the bird to the beak-like shape of the lobster's claw.

While in reality the possibility for negotiation has been lost by the author's choice of 'lobster' and 'woodpecker', I regard this confidence and decisiveness as important in the development of a sense of power over the written form and in banishing fear of books. I am not saying that children do not need to recognise a word such as robin, whatever the context, or the inadequacy of the picture clue, but at that stage I think the working out of an agreed understanding between Theo and his parents was vitally important.

The next stage in his development towards stories came through pictures. He did not want a story sequenced with the pictures, but would pore over a single picture and we would tell a complete story from it and then go on to the next one. In one story, *The*

Trunk, which is a visual and verbal pun on tree trunk and elephant's trunk, we assume the trunk to be a tree until the last page, when animals which have run up it appear sitting on the elephant's back. Theo has only recently understood the joke (3.1). Though he was familiar with 'trunk' in both meanings he was unwilling to follow the sequence as the author intended, and even after a second and third reading would only see that at the end of the book the animals were now out of the tree and on the elephant's back. Yet in reading the picture of the swimming pool in the Ahlbergs' *A Place to Play* he could sequence the events of the incident fairly easily; that the Brick Street Boys' ball had hit the instructor and he had said 'out you go' and had blown his whistle and the boys had to leave.

He later moved towards the story sequence with no apparent need for exact reproduction of the story or particular details or exact sequence. The experienced readers told the story from the picture in a sequence. In the two extracts that follow the same story is told by M and F. Theo makes no demands for exact or even similar renderings though he has heard the story several times before.

M's telling of the story

M: 'Goldilocks and the Three Bears' (T: 'Daddy one, mammy one and Theo one')
M: 'Yes, once upon a time there was a girl called . . .' (T: 'Oggy')
. . . Goldilocks and . . . (T: 'What's this . . . a swing?') . . . and one day she didn't want to play with her sailor doll, didn't want to play with her rocking horse, didn't want to read a book . . . (T: 'No chalk') . . . Not to chalk . . . (T: 'No 'phant') . . . not her elephant, not her jester; she didn't want to play with her teddy and she didn't want to play with her . . . (T: 'What's that?') . . . umbrella, her umbrella . . . (T: 'Not that') . . . and she didn't want to play with her doll. Her mammy said "Go and play in the garden . . . but don't go in the woods", so Goldilocks went out of the house into the garden and across the stream and into the woods. She ran in among the trees. Soon she found herself in parts of the wood she didn't know at all. She was a little bit frightened, and then came to a . . . (T: 'Locked key') . . . she came to a . . . what's

this? (T: 'A wood') . . . She came to a house but it's the three bears' house, and could she get in? . . . (T: 'No') . . . Why not? . . . (T: 'No, couldn't get in') . . . No, couldn't get in, could she? So what did she do? She went in the window . . . (T: 'Yeh') . . . and whose house was it? The three bears' house . . . (T: 'I don't like it') . . . She sat on Daddy Bear's chair, and she said "I don't like it" . . . (the story continues until) She tried Daddy Bear's *soup*.'

F's telling of the story

'Right, Theo, Goldilocks and the three bears. Goldilocks lives in this house near the forest . . . (T: 'A swing') . . . yes, a swing in the garden. Then she gets bored with the swing . . . (T: 'Backwards and forwards on the swing?') . . . What does she do with the swing? (T: 'Backwards and forwards') Yes, backwards and forwards. She goes back in the house. She plays with the little doll dressed as a sailor, with the picture on the blackboard, with the animals, with the elephant, with the teddy bear, with her rocking horse, but in the end she gets fed up with these.

What can I do? What can I do different? One day her mammy goes to the shop and she says "Whatever you do don't leave the house until I come back. Don't leave the house." But as soon as her mammy has gone to the shops Goldilocks goes through the front door and . . . she's left it open, can you see? She's left it open . . . down the path, across the stream, over this little bridge, which is really just a tree trunk. She walks across there very carefully. She goes deeper and deeper into the forest. Then she comes to this little house deep in the forest. Nobody's in it at the moment, and the door is locked . . . see this big lock on the door . . . so she climbs through the window, and when she gets in she sees three chairs . . . (T: 'I don't like it') . . . (the story continues until) Three bowls of *porridge*. . .'

He was able to retell even the stories he had heard only once. The following extract is of his retelling a story he had heard while his daddy was out. The story was *Red Riding Hood*, retold by Tony Ross.

F: Did you read that one (picking up the book)?
T: Yes, the wolf eats her . . . I don't like wolves eat Theos.
F: Did he, the rotter?

T: The wolf eat Riding Hood.
F: The wretch.
T: Yes, and the woodcutter bang and shook and shook. Riding Hood
  came out and Grandma came out, everything out.

Now he has begun to read *Where's Spot?* as a reader does. The book traces a journey a mother dog makes looking for her puppy. Everywhere she looks she finds another animal hiding, and to questions like 'Is he under the bed?' the animal-occupier always says 'No!' The story does not depend on a particular order of events, but Theo has begun to indicate his developing sense of a permanent sequence and a permanent text. He reads the question and reply, and knows if a page has been missed out, ending the story with a flourish and the mother's words 'Good boy, Spot, eat up your dinner'. This is an important development since, in Frank Smith's[4] terms, readers need to be able to predict what is coming next or there would otherwise be far too many alternatives for them to choose from. This must be particularly crucial for emergent readers. Smith claims that this skill

> tends to distinguish skilled readers from beginners or from anyone having difficulty with a particular piece of reading. In fluent reading the eye is always ahead of the brain's decision, checking for possible obstacles to a particular understanding. Readers concerned with the word directly in front of their nose will have trouble predicting and they will have trouble comprehending.

Theo had shown now that he was ready for the story as written and could hold the sequence. This would support him when he came to retell and later re-read the story. His play has for some time indicated his interest in behaving like a reader, and as Holdaway[5] describes: 'Attracted by the familiar objects with which he has such positive associations the infant picks it up (i.e. a favourite book), opens it and begins attempting to retrieve for himself some of the language and its intonations. Almost unintelligible at first, the reading-like play rapidly becomes picture-stimulated, page-matched, and story-complete.' This early extract shows Theo reading his 'play people' a story from a book. The story is *Eat up* by Helen Piers. Theo was 2.6.

T: One day . . . One day . . . One day (with a beginning of story-

intonation) . . . eating a banana . . . monkey eating a banana . . .
bunny likes cabbage. One day . . . eat a bone . . . what's that? One
day mouse eating cheese. One day . . . getting pigeon . . . squirrel
eating nuts. All gone, all gone. Finished that one.

M: Did they like that story?
T: Liked that story . . . get another book.

Notice Theo's skill in turning this factual book into a story.

For some time Theo had been reading nursery rhymes. These
became his first known texts, and through these we hoped he
would get a sense of himself as a reader. Through reading these
poems and rhymes he knew in different books he came to know
that the texts stayed the same whenever they were read. Though
he was often surprised by the lack of constancy in the pictures, he
has read several versions of *Humpty Dumpty*. In one of the
pictures Humpty Dumpty is shown broken into pieces and in
another sitting on the wall. 'Where's the break?' he asked me
(2.6). His expectations from print are very high. The title of one of
his books, *On Friday Something Funny Happened* led him to look
in the book for the something funny that happened. He found
something funny that hadn't happened on Friday, a child losing a
wellington boot as she played on a swing. The story is an adult
joke. Theo put the funniness into it for himself without realising
how he had been cheated.

The titles of his books now have to have meaning related to the
content:

What happened at Rita's Party became 'The Birthday Cake',
which is basically what the book is about; *Cakes and Custard*
became 'Cakes and Pudding', a memory miscue, but indicating his
meaning orientation; *Helpers* became 'Washing Up'.

Recently, the story as written has become very important, and
he recognises changes in the text. In *Postman Pat's Difficult Day*,
Postman Pat hurts his hand, Alf asks if he is all right and Postman
Pat says 'No, I think I've sprained my wrist.' For fun, I read 'Yes,
I'm fine, thanks.' Theo was indignant. 'No, no, he sprained his
wrist, look! Mrs Thomson bandage it.'

Again, recently, after reading *Peter Rabbit* for the first time, I
asked Theo what had happened to Peter's daddy (made into a pie
by Mr McGregor). Theo was again quite certain. 'That's not right.
Look! There's no Daddy in this book'.

For Theo now, books hold their truth, but their lessons can be generalised. In *Little Red Riding Hood* Theo was upset by the wolf's behaviour: (The text reads 'For wolves are no friends of theirs'). Theo said: 'I don't like wolves too. Wolves eat Theos.'

In a reading year, Theo has taken on his own learning, pacing it to satisfy his personal needs, recreating texts now to indicate his understanding of the story. Holdaway may well be right when he says,

> Children with a background of book experience since infancy develop a complex range of attitudes, concepts and skills predisposing them to literacy. They are likely to continue on entering school with a minimum of discontinuity. They have developed high expectations of print, knowing that books bring them special pleasures which they can obtain in no other way.

Gordon Wells's[6] findings in Bristol showed that 'the best single predictor of attainment in literacy after two years of schooling was the extent of the children's own understanding of the purposes and mechanics of literacy at the time when they started school.' These things may be true and very encouraging.

What I have learnt from Theo is not just about good preparation for future gains but more about the rewards that are available for him whenever he reads, rewards which are not only linguistic and cognitive but also psychological and emotional. What I would like to think is that I could create these conditions in schools to predispose young children towards literacy, and by that means towards literature. I believe this means very much more parental involvement in schools, so that home reading can continue uninterruptedly in schools.

Notes

1 Margaret M. Clark, *Young Fluent Readers*, Heinemann, London, 1976.
2 B. Bettelheim and S. Zelan, *On Learning to Read: The Child's Fascination with Meaning*, Thames & Hudson, London, 1982.
3 Margaret Meek, *Learning to Read*, Bodley Head, London, 1982.
4 Frank Smith, *Understanding Reading: a Psycholinguistic Analysis of Reading and Learning to Read*, Holt, Rinehart & Winston, New York, 1977.
5 Don Holdaway, *The Foundations of Literacy*, Ashton Scholastic, 1979.
6 Gordon Wells, *Learning Through Interaction*, Cambridge University

Press, 1981. In particular, Chapter 7, 'Language, Literacy and Education'.

Children's books

John Cunliffe, *Postman Pat's Rainy Day* (from BBC series), Hippo Books (Scholastic), London, 1982.

Raymond Briggs, *The Snowman*, Hamish Hamilton, London, 1978.

Goldilocks and the Three Bears, traditional story in *Award Classic Fairy Tales*, 1980.

Pat Hutchins, *The Tale of Thomas Mead*, Bodley Head, London, 1980.

—, *The Wind Blew*, Picture Puffin, Harmondsworth, 1978.

John Burningham, *Avocado Baby*, Jonathan Cape, London, 1982.

Helen Oxenbury, *Friends, Playing, Dressing, Working, Family*, Baby Board Books (Methuen/Walker), London, 1981.

—, *Bedtime, Shopping, Helping, Holidays, Animals*, Board Books (Methuen/Walker), London, 1982.

Binette Shroeder, *Zebby Gone with the Wind, Zebby's Breakfast, Shop Zebby Shop, Run Zebby Run, Zebby Goes Swimming*, Methuen/ Walker Books, London, 1981.

A. and J. Ahlberg, *A Place to Play* (The Brick Street Boys), Picture Lions, 1976.

My First Picture Dictionary, Dean & Sons, London, 1981.

Robert Crowther, *The Most Amazing Hide and Seek Alphabet Book*, Kestrel/Viking, Harmondsworth, 1977.

Bedtime, Brimax Books (Show Baby Series), Harmondsworth, 1973.

Brian Wildsmith, *The Trunk*, Oxford University Press, 1982.

Eric Hill, *Where's Spot?*, Heinemann, London, 1980.

Helen Piers, *Eat Up*, Methuen (Methuen Chatterbooks), London, 1981.

John Prater, *On Friday Something Funny Happened*, Bodley Head, Lions, London, 1976.

Petronella Breinburg, *What Happened at Rita's Party*, Kestrel Books, Harmondsworth, 1976.

Children's Rhymes chosen by Brian Alderson, *Cakes and Custard*, Heinemann, London, 1974.

Shirley Hughes, *Helpers*, Bodley Head, London, 1975.

John Cunliffe, *Postman Pat's Difficult Day* (from BBC series), André Deutsch, London, 1982.

Beatrix Potter, *The Tale of Peter Rabbit*, Frederick Warne, London, 1902.

Little Red Riding Hood, retold by Tony Ross, Picture Puffin, Harmondsworth, 1978.

2   Story in its writeful place*

Sue May

Let us suppose, for a moment, that you are attending a course on some aspect of language in education, and that this evening your tutor has the bright idea of getting you to do some writing. 'I would like you,' she says, 'to write the first paragraph of a boy meets girl story. Choose whether you want your story to appear in *Jackie*, *The Times*, *True Confessions*, *Woman's Own*, or to be seriously considered for the Booker Prize.' Since you are a co-operative student and are attending the course because you know, or hope, that it will Do You Good, you pick up your pen and after a brief pause for thought begin to address your chosen audience. You assume that there is some reasonable purpose behind the exercise, and that it is not a matter of testing your ability to write True Romances.

The purpose, you later find, is to get you to address the question, 'How do you know how to do it?', not 'How well do you do it?' or 'Could you make a living doing it?', but 'How do you know how to do it *at all*?' Since you are a teacher, or intend to be one, the question is of the sharpest relevance, because your perception of how you yourself learnt to write coherent English is likely to be a deep and abiding influence on how you go about teaching children to do so, and because you are surrounded by a great deal of noise and heat generated by people, many of them outside education altogether, who think that they know best how children acquire competence in writing.

On one side there are the advocates of 'skills' teaching, armed with a vast paraphernalia of worksheets, exercises, tests and grades, glossily and convincingly packaged to appeal to teachers and at the same time be 'teacher-proof'. On the other side are ranged the supporters of the view that writing is first and foremost communication; and their chief concerns are with expressing meaning, providing an audience and linking early writing with the child's own speech. Teachers are divided amongst themselves as other people are about which theory is of most benefit to children, and widely divergent practices occur in the classrooms of teachers holding one of the polarised points of view.

Between the two, the activity you were asked to engage in, story-writing, sits uneasily. That it takes place in almost every primary classroom, irrespective of whether every other writing activity is 'skills' oriented or 'communication' oriented, is confirmed by both the recent HMI surveys of primary schools.[1] Typically, HMI did not comment on whether they approved or disapproved of the activity, or whether the results were worth the effort. There must be a risk, though, that if the main emphasis in a classroom is on learning to write by means of exercises and worksheets, and story-writing merely makes an occasional appearance in the weekly double period of 'creative writing', many children will form such an aversion to written work that their stories will prove only that children are not very good at writing them. Story-writing as a sop to liberalism is not an adequate rationale for doing it. There is also a risk attached to story-writing in the classroom where the teacher's view of learning to write has its origins in the Plowden[2] Report and its later elaborators, since Plowden comments that children's stories are 'imitative . . . derivative of second-rate material' and recommends that most children should be discouraged from writing them most of the time. Where this view lingers children will be allowed to write stories if they insist, but the activity is likely to be ranked lower in the teacher's esteem than expressive writing from 'direct experience'. A situation of some irony thus appears to exist, whereby story-writing is tolerated in all classrooms despite otherwise opposing approaches to learning to write, yet nowhere is it regarded as vital or central. In this context it becomes instructive to wonder how it is that story-writing remains so prevalent, so resistant to contrary winds that blow, and this line of thought leads us back to the idea that how people now teaching were themselves taught to write is at least as powerful a determinant of their own practice as any theory developed since.

When the compilers of Plowden castigated children's stories as 'imitative' and 'derivative' they were not merely having a sideswipe at stories in particular, but mounting a forceful and general attack on the view of learning which characterised the whole primary curriculum of the time – that learning took place chiefly by imitation – and attempting to substitute for it a view of learning through 'personal growth'. In so far as their efforts succeeded in freeing some teachers and children from a whole array of boring and trivial tasks, and in so far as they laid to rest the notion that children only needed to be shown a suitable model and they would henceforth be able to copy it, we have all good reason to be grateful to Plowden. However, as with all revolutionary statements, Plowden showed some tendency to throw the baby out with the bath-water, and nowhere more so than in its treatment of children's stories. For although the idea that children learn to write simply through imitating suitable models seems laughably simplistic now, the theory did have one very solid advantage over both the theories which face each other across the barricades today. It did assume that if children were to write well by imitating other good writers they would first need to encounter their work. In other words, the experience of literature was central to the business of learning to write. Since for the younger children the experience of literature was taken to mean, very largely, the experience of hearing, reading, acting, retelling, and rewriting traditional tales, there is a good chance that for many teachers now in service story was more central to their own experience than it is to the children they teach.

It may well be that this is how you learned to write, and how you knew, when asked to write the first paragraph of a boy-meets-girl story, how to go about it. It may also account for the persistence of story-writing in primary classrooms despite the clashes on other grounds, and for the vague but persistent belief still held by many teachers that the stories children hear and read are the most influential factor in learning to write. This belief gains its most emphatic support, among contemporary 'experts', from Frank Smith,[3] who argues that 'Reading and writing are in an asymmetric relation with one another . . . reading can do without writing, but writing cannot do without reading.' The truth of the first part of this statement is well attested both historically (King Alfred learnt to read when he was seven, but did not master writing till he was twenty) and by the large number of handicapped people who learn to read but are physically disabled from writing. Smith expands on his idea of an asymmetric relation as follows:

Reading is the essential source of information about writing, from the conventions of transcription to the subtle differences of register and discourse structure in various genres. No one writes enough to get all this information from editing and correction of their own writing, and very little of it can be imparted by direct instruction.

While endorsing every word of this, one would want to add that since, given a reasonable chance, children who are too young to have gained much information about written language from their own reading can none the less write, we must say that the information comes from reading *and* from hearing written language read aloud. It's not too difficult to prove this point. The five-year-old who writes, 'Onec a prinss livd in a crssll', has learned more about the conventions of transcription and about the genre of fairy story than her teacher can have taught her, and more than she can have learnt through reading. Since, for the majority, listening comprehension remains ahead of reading comprehension throughout the primary years, there is a good case for ensuring that listening time and writing time are more closely linked in the school day than is generally the case. The HMI 5–9 survey[4] reports that most listening to stories takes place in the last twenty minutes of the day: this is clearly not the most useful time to associate listening with writing. Moreover, important though the information that leads to competence in writing is, that is not the only contribution story heard offers to story writing. Few of us – in particular, few children – live sufficiently interesting and exciting lives to provide us with enough raw material to write only from our own experience. The 'virtual experience' we gain through stories read and heard fill out our experiences and widen our horizons. As Rosen and Rosen[5] put it some years ago,

> The receiving of stories is part of a child's cultural inheritance, providing the models, patterns and symbolic figures for personal story making. If the stories he hears are sufficiently compelling, not only will they help him to make sense of his world, but offer him the raw materials for the complementary process of composing.

Hence it is not only in the structure of the writing but in the content that children's own stories will stand in a close relationship to the stories they hear, and if one believes that this is desirable one will agree with Margaret Meek,[6] who insists that we must 'associate children's literature with the whole business of becoming literate . . . because if we don't, the natural story-telling of children will be dissociated from the art of the storyteller'. The danger is that unless the nature of the relationship between stories heard and stories written is thoroughly explored and articulated, the stories children write can still be dismissed as 'imitative' and 'derivative' when they reveal their connectedness to other stories, and this misconception of what children are really doing can lead to story-writing being regarded as merely peripheral to learning to write. These ghosts of Plowden need to be laid to rest, and that can best be done by facing them, by asking the question, What are kids really doing when they appear to be merely imitating?

The clearest example of what might be taken to be mere imitation is the retelling, in whole or in part, of a story the child has heard. There is mounting evidence, from studies of children's oral and written stories, that retelling is a characteristic response, between four and seven, and that, far from being 'mere imitation' it fulfils some important needs at this age. It is, for a start, one way of saying 'I like this story', a beginner's version of lit. crit. As C. and H. Rosen observe, 'One way of appreciating a story is to tell the same story, or one very like it.' Another excellent reason for retelling a story is that by those means we are able to make the story our own: we cannot really say that we 'know' a story unless we can retell it, and part of our interest as listeners or readers is our need to be able to recall it at a later date, to retell it to ourselves or to others. In an oral culture, the only way to recommend a story to others is to be able to retell it; children under the age of seven live in a predominantly oral culture – most of their information comes from speech – so their interest in retelling can be said to be similar to that of non-literate people of all ages. With the acquisition of literacy, and the assumption of literacy in others, our interest in retelling shifts to an interest in knowing the story well enough to generalise, to comment, to criticise, to review, and thus encourage others to read it for themselves. None of these advanced literary activities are possible unless we can retell the story first.

Good retelling is not easy. There is a case for suggesting that the *need* for story is a universal human characteristic and perhaps innate, that the worldwide tendency to put some structural bounds, such as beginnings and endings, climaxes and episodes, on the otherwise undifferentiated ebb and flow of events, is a response to some inborn patterning of the human psyche. However, the actual *form* of stories is at all times and in all places culturally derived, and learnt within a culture. Once learnt, the form of story current in one's culture is fixed. As Sancho replied when asked by Don Quixote to speed up his storytelling, 'I tell it you as all stories are told in my country, and I cannot tell it any other way . . . nor is it fit I should alter the custom.'

The young child retelling a story is not in Sancho's position – rather, she is in the business of learning how 'all stories are told in my country', and her success at learning is entirely dependent on a rich experience of hearing how stories *are* told. However, not all stories are of equal value in teaching children how stories are told. The most useful stories to an apprentice reteller are stories which other people have found it possible to retell, which have acquired their present form precisely because of the ease with which they can be retold, and which would have continued, had not print petrified them at a certain point in their evolution, to have passed, their form intact, to future generations of retellers. Traditional tales, and modern stories which preserve the form of a traditional tale, have a special appeal to children between the ages of five and eight, and part of that appeal lies in the developing interest of children at this age in being able to retell the tale. Many of these retellings will be oral. Some children will begin to attempt written retelling from the age of five, and be adept at the art by seven. Others will begin later; but if they begin too late the consuming interest in retelling may pass before competence is achieved. An opportunity has been missed which may be difficult to make good later.

The point here is that retelling, although a perfectly reasonable end in itself, is also the 'way in' to other means and other ends. In learning how stories are told in her country, the reteller is learning important things about stories in general and about the linguistic structures through which the story is brought into existence, and these structures are not exclusive to story. For example, the conventional structure of a beginning, placed more or less arbitrarily somewhere in the flow of events, is central to story but also to accounts of scientific experiments, whose real beginnings may stretch back hundreds or even thousands of years. The chronological sequencing of events is also common to both genres, as is the assumption of a conclusion, or resolution, of some problem or hypothesis. The one important distinction is that we assume the scientific experiment actually took place, whereas we can make no such assumption about a traditional tale. Otherwise, we can reasonably describe the recounting of a scientific experiment as the story of what took place. Structurally, it *is* a story.

However, a story worth telling is never simply a structural framework imposed on events. There is a built-in assumption that there is a reason for selecting these particular events, that there is something about the events which makes them worth telling. That is, somewhere in the story is a proposition. It may be a philosophical proposition: good ultimately triumphs over evil. It may be moral: poverty is a virtue. It may be plausible, or it may be highly implausible but entertaining: elephants have trunks because of the 'Satiable Curtiosity' of the Elephant's Child. What we as readers or listeners actually do with the propositions in stories, whether we agree or disagree, decide to act on them, disregard them, or simply enjoy them, is one part of the total act we call, for want of a better word, 'response'. One thing we might want to do with a proposition we first encounter in a story is elaborate on it, not necessarily in the form of story. Sermons – and indeed all writing on the subject of religion – are an obvious example of discourse which is not itself story but whose roots are firmly fixed in story. Or take political or economic discourse. If the propositions explored and examined in such writing are not firmly linked to events, past, present and future, which could be related in the form of story, the propositions would hardly be worth examining. Hence we can say that story is a narrative about a proposition, while discursive prose is a proposition about a narrative, and thus that understanding the first half of the equation is half-way to understanding the second. Understanding what a story is to the extent that one can retell it with its structure and propositions intact is, therefore, as good an apprenticeship as one could devise for all other forms of discourse.

Once we accept that retelling stories is a valuable, even vital, means of learning important things about written language in general, we can begin to look more professionally and critically at what children's retellings reveal about their progress in understanding writing, and make suggestions about the needs of individual children. Oral retellings will obviously be fuller in the early stages than written ones, but the latter can, from a surprisingly early age, provide some very useful indicators. Here, for example, are three 5½-year-olds, who chose, in a period of 'free choice' to retell the story of 'How the Tiger Got His Stripes', which they had recently heard read by their teacher.

John: The tigers slept in the jungle The tiger played with the flies The tiger looks at the monkeys the tiger played with bumble bees.

Robert: Once upon a time there was a tiger he slept in the sun all day he slept under a tree and the sun made him stripey all over.

Paul: Lazy tiger slept in the sun too much and when he woke up he was stripey his mum told him to wash it off but he couldn't.

It is clear that John has simply linked together the events in the original which appealed to him, and not focused at all on the proposition in the story. Nor has he attempted to structure the events in the form of introduction/episodes/conclusion, nor has he retold the events in a way which reveals the fundamental means/ends relationship between sleeping under a tree and the sun producing stripes. It may well be, of course, that in an oral retelling John would manage very much better, or that he found this particular story difficult: one would certainly not want to judge a child's understanding of story on the basis of one written retelling. None the less, if this pattern were found to be typical of his retellings, if he persistently focused on details which appealed to him rather than on details salient to the structure of the story, it would be reasonable to suggest that as yet his understanding of story is very limited and he needs lots of opportunities for listening and for retelling.

By contrast, both Robert and Paul have linked sleeping/sun/stripes in a causal chain and have thus retained the form of the original. Robert focuses more on time and place (once upon a time, all day, under a tree), while Paul is more aware of what caused the events (the tiger was lazy) and final results (the stripes were there for good). However, one gets, from their writing, a strong impression that both boys not only understood that particular story but are probably reasonably adept at receiving and retelling stories in general. One way of describing what they can do is by saying that, through the experience of hearing stories, they have acquired a 'framework' in memory which helps them to interpret new stories they hear and to retell them. John, maybe, has not had enough experience of hearing stories to build up such a framework, and is thus more likely to tell fractured stories with important elements missing. It will be noted that in terms of length there is little difference between the three boys' writing, possibly as a result of expectations in their own class and replicated in many other 'middle infant' classes. Given different expectations (and another year in school) the competent reteller is at a tremendous advantage over one still struggling to construct a 'framework'. Here is Caroline, aged six and a half:

> Once upon a time there was a King and a Queen they had 20 children and the King and Queen had a nanny. the nanny looked after the children. one hot day the nanny whet to the childrens bedrooms and she said I will take you to the woods and you can play and I will watch you. But when they got there she fell asleep the youngest child was a girl and she was the most beautiful of them All when the nanny fell asleep. A big bear came and he took the yongest Because he wasn't very well. When the nanny woke up the counted them she found there were 19. the bear had a big Houes the girl lived there a Long time and she Loved the bear one day it was so hot the girl whet out in the garden. The bear was still ill. he was outside too. Suddenly he fainted the girl was very sad so she kissed him. at that moment he turned into a handsome prinss so they were married and they lived Happily ever after.

At six, Caroline knows that for a retelling to be complete it has to be quite long. Below the level of consciousness she is grappling with that difficult proposition which gives *Beauty and the Beast* its power: that someone must be loved before they can be lovable. Not that she's quite sure that one could love a really horrible beast, but a bear is a fair compromise.

By contrast, here is Russell, at the same age, retelling *The Magic Horse*.

> Once there was a man and one night the little horse came to the cornfield and the man cord his three boys one boy was cord Mickul and one boy was cord Gouje and one boy was cord jon and there daddy said to Mickul you are going to watch out for the little horse. There is a queen living on a rock the first boy took a sword and he didn't catch the little horse and the third boy he climd the rock.

It is not, of course, that Russell has not listened, nor that he is careless. On the contrary, he took great care with this writing and was rightly proud of the results. However, he has still not had enough experience to have internalised the structure of even an archetypal traditional tale like *The Magic Horse*, with all its trebling of moves and predictive possibilities, to be able to reproduce the order of events in a written retelling. A full retelling would need to be twice as long as Russell's: there was no time limit set on his writing, and he is not 'lazy'. He wrote less because he knew less.

Although our concern here is with writing rather than with reading, it is worth noting at this point that Robert, Paul and Caroline, who showed evidence of having acquired enough information about stories to be able to retell them, are all able to read some stories for themselves at an independent level, while John and Russell are making slower progress. In this connection, the finding of the Bristol longitudinal study of 1500 children,[7] that the most important factor in the acquisition of literacy was the amount of listening to stories done in the pre-school years, is pertinent.

So far we have concentrated on retelling and its importance to the beginning writer, but from the earliest stages children use the stories they hear as the raw materials with which to construct stories of their own. However, just as 'imitative' is a gross simplification of what is happening in a retelling, similarly 'derivative' is a misleading description of how children make other stories form part of their own. Since story-writing which draws heavily on other stories is extremely common among junior-age children, taking over from retelling as the dominant form at around the age of seven, we need to know something about what is happening if we are to give the activity our full support.

Left to their own devices, children of junior age will include so many elements from so many different stories – large numbers of which will be unfamiliar to us and thus unrecognisable – that investigating what is going on can be rather difficult. A useful way to make our investigations easier is occasionally to follow reading of a story to a class with a request to write one. One can vary the circumstances – encourage or discourage discussion of the story heard, for example – and compare what happens. In my experience elements from the story they have heard reappear in the stories of about two-thirds of the class, and there is a strong tendency for the most use of the original to be made by children whose experience of story, as far as can be judged by their reading habits, is likely to be greatest. It is a reasonable guess, therefore, that children who were competent retellers at a young age are liable to make the most use of a story heard when writing one of their own soon afterwards. It is, of course, a strictly non-statistical exercise, since the possible variables are beyond control. The story read makes a difference; its relative appeal to different children in the group affects subsequent use, the interval between hearing and writing, or an intervening unrelated activity, reduces use of the original very sharply. Age seems to be of some importance: 11-year-olds generally use the model more than 7- or 8-year-olds. None the less, some important generalisations can be risked.

It is virtually certain that the feature of the original most likely to reappear in the children's stories is the type, or genre, of the model. Read a ghost story and almost everyone will write a ghost story; and for some children this will be the end of their involvement with the model, particularly if it does not fit in with their ideas of the genre of ghost stories. If your story does not contain creaking cupboards, severed heads, moving armour, cobwebs and so forth, the children will make good your omission. Assuming that their perceived audience is each other, and maybe you, they will set out with the intention of telling the most spine-chilling ghost story they can, and will put in every detail they deem to be appropriate to that genre. One group of 9-year-olds included in their stories seventeen haunted houses, five haunted castles, ten slamming doors, twelve clammy cobwebs, five clanking chains, three damp cellars, and fifteen mysterious noises, although the story they had heard did not contain any of these.

One response to this kind of work is, of course, to dismiss it as derivative of second-rate material and suggest that children should be discouraged from writing it. Another is to say that these children's experience of the genre has been heavily influenced by stories in comics and on television which rely on conventional images, and resolve to introduce them to something with rather more to it. The story you just read them may be the first ghost story they have ever heard which did *not* include clanking chains. They are quite reasonably exploring the genre, and catering for the audience as they perceive its needs to be. A variation on this possibility, particularly common among the younger juniors, is to adopt the genre, but to introduce events and characters from stories in other genres. An eight-year-old group who heard the same ghost story introduced far less conventional images from other ghost stories. They introduced four minotaurs, four Sherlock Holmes, St George, Lady Godiva, Captain Pugwash, Goldilocks, and a large gallery of other unexpected intruders into the ghostly genre. Although the results were inevitably of more interest and amusement to an adult reader than cobwebs and creaking doors, these intrusions really are evidence of a less mature understanding of genre than are conventional details, and their occurrence decreases sharply with age, appearing only rarely in the 11-year-olds' stories. Jason, aged 7, is a splendid example of this stage:

> There was a man called St George he moved in a house where there was a hound in the Grave yard if st George goes into the moor he would die In the morning st George went near the moor a naced lady on a horse she said stop st George said why the lady said if you gose up there you will die because there is a hound up there he is a meat eater he killed one lady and a horse st George went to the ladys house the lady husband was there was the owner of the hound he keeps him in a coffin near some huts the lady and st George went to the hut and there was a grate long cave and the hound was there he had a gun in his arm the hound came in and he shoot the hound and it was dead.

Along with St. George, Lady Godiva, *The Hound of the Baskervilles* and maybe the Minotaur, Jason has included from the story he heard before writing his own, a graveyard, a gun and a stranger. The inclusion of striking details from the model in new stories, whose pattern derives from other stories, is very common at all ages. That is, instead of a conventional ghost story with conventional details, one might get a conventionally shaped ghost story - 'A Night in a Haunted House', for instance – containing a number of images taken from the model they have heard. The story I read them was rather rich in striking images, two of them being a ghostly white rabbit and a bullet which appeared to rebound off it. Large numbers of ghostly rabbits of all colours, other ghostly small animals, and rebounding weapons (stones, swords and knives as well as bullets) turned up in stories which in other respects were quite unlike the original.

The third major possibility is for the children to focus on the proposition in the original – it is important, therefore, to select a story which clearly has one – and to rework it in a different form. In the story of the ghostly rabbit the proposition is that ghosts, whether rabbits or not, are perfectly harmless if left alone, but any violence attempted on them will rebound on the assailant. The minority of children who rework the proposition write by far the most interesting stories. The likelihood of approaching the task in this way increases with age (at least up to twelve, the upper limits of my easily accessible subjects) and is undertaken only by children whose general experience of story is at least average, and probably above average, in range and depth. An interesting feature of these children's stories is that although in re-working the proposition they generally change the pattern of the story (otherwise it would be a retelling, which it rarely is) they usually include some of the striking details. Part of Katie's story gives an example:

> One night the man said to himself 'I don't think it is a supernaturl cat I think it is an ordinary cat. I'm going to get rid of it.' He got a sword off his wall and went out into the garden. The moon was full, so bright you could see a ladybird land on a flower. He saw the cat with its orange eyes, pink tip on its tail and pink paws. He took a swipe at the cat with his sword. He did not hear a single noise from the cat. It was sitting at his feet looking up at him. But he felt the sword go through it. It was a supernaturl cat after all. The man gasped and ran, dropping his sword behind him . . .
>
> Katie, Age 9.

No good, as you can imagine, comes to the man. Apart from the attack on the cat, Katie has included, probably intentionally, the luminous eyes and full moon, and, probably unconsciously, taking a weapon from a wall, from the original. One remarkable feature of stories like Katie's, which transform the original into a new story in this manner, is the sheer speed at which the transformation takes place, mostly, it seems, below the level of consciousness. Another is the way propositions, details and patterns from other stories are combined with the model, not in the conventional manner of cobwebs and haunted houses, but into something far more complex. Eleanor, just eight, seems too young to have got much from *The Owl Service*, even serialised on television. Yet it reappears in the story she wrote next day after hearing the white rabbit story:

> In the countryside where a little cottage has room for four people lives a young child age five and his mother and father because they had a daughter called Lucy who died of bubonic plague. She had had a budgerigar called Juilet. Now after she'd died they did not feed Juilet and Pod the baby used to pull out its feathers. Then there cat Zombe had eaten Juilet. Now the peculiar things started when Pod was playing with his new lego and he heard a flapping of wings he looked up there was nothing there but feathers fell like rain. He screamed like mad and Mrs. bud came in. She ran to her son and hugged him. When she looked up there was nothing there she was hugging a dummy. . .

In the white rabbit story, the rabbit is described as like 'a pretty little child's pet escaped from its hutch'. Eleanor has set herself the question as to why a pretty little pet should be harmful even after it is dead, and unlike the others in her group, has concluded that it *is* harmful, and explains how this could come about. The feathers falling like rain, however, has nothing to do with the white rabbit and everything to do with *The Owl Service*, while 'she was hugging a dummy' shows an understanding of how the owls overwhelmed Alison's personality in that story, which is remarkable for an 8-year-old.

It does seem, from the variety of approaches to writing a story soon after hearing one, that once the possibilities of doing something other than retelling have been grasped an exciting new discovery is made about story, but below the level of consciousness. The discovery is that stories consist of an overall shape or pattern, a proposition, plus any number of images or details, and that any of these elements can be separated from the others and enabled to take on a new and independent life of its own. They can be recombined with patterns, propositions and images from other stories, from personal experience, from other aspects of culture, and this opens up the possibility of an endless generation of new stories in any number of genres. Many of the new stories will be unremarkable, though capable of giving pleasure to a sympathetic audience of classmates and teacher. Many will be rather better than that, and show how young writers' use of story broadens their understanding of themselves and the world. A few, by a happy coincidence of images and exploration of ideas, will be quite outstanding and find their way on to walls and into anthologies.

At the other end of the scale, it must sadly be admitted there are a few children whose experience of story remains so limited that their own stories never move beyond the day-to-day and the here-and-now. For such children, twelve is not 'too old' for listening and retelling, as Nicholas's pleasure in *The Iron Man* shows:

> Crash, bang, boom! The Iron Man was coming from the earth
> Crash bang it was a lot of noise. The iron man was tall, very tall, the Iron Man was 100 metears tall and the Iron Man could not get out because he was tall. At last the Iron Man got out of Hole and you heard crash bang and he was all in pieces. (Nicholas, age 12)

We need to take the stories children write seriously, at all ages and stages. Through writing them, children are learning more about written language, about genre and pattern, proposition and image, about the needs of a reader and about the conventions of written language then we as teachers can teach them by any other means. In turn, we can learn more from the stories children write about their progress as writers than any test can tell us. Stories need to be given their writeful place as the first, and probably the best, writing tutors for children.

Notes

* This chapter is based on research done by the author in the English Department of the University of London Institute of Education during 1982. In that study she considered the relationship between reading and writing by looking at the stories of whole classes of children across the primary age range and mapped out the developmental implications.

1 *Children and their Primary Schools* (the Plowden Report), HMSO, London, 1967; *Primary Education in England A Survey by HM Inspectors*, HMSO, London, 1978.

2 See above.

3 F. Smith, *Writing and the Writer*, Holt Rinehart & Winston, New York, 1982.

4 *5–9: An Illustrative Survey of eighty First Schools*, HMSO, London, 1982.

5 C. and H. Rosen, *The Language of Primary School Children*, Penguin, Harmondsworth, 1973.
6 M. Meek, 'Prologomena for a Study of Children's Literature', University of London Institute of Education unpublished paper, 1982.
7 G. Wells, *Learning Through Interaction*, Cambridge University Press, 1981.

Background reading

A. N. Applebee, *The Child's Concept of Story*, University of Chicago Press, 1978.
G. H. Bower, 'Experiments on Story Understanding and Recall', in *Quarterly Journal of Experimental Psychology*, no. 28, 1976.
B. Hardy, *Tellers and Listeners*, Academic Press, London, 1975.
F. Kermode, *The Sense of an Ending*, Oxford University Press, 1966.

3 What books tell girls: a memoir of early reading

Marion Glastonbury

Some ten years ago, a television producer advertised for listeners' recollections of a radio serial, broadcast on Children's Hour in 1943: the dramatization of John Masefield's *Box of Delights*. 'The response was a sackful of intimate biographies in which the entire labyrinth of career, tastes, friendship, love and marriage was insistently traced back on a thread leading to this single over-whelming radio experience in childhood. All the writers were astonished to discover that it was shared by anyone else.'[1]

Such an experiment, geared as it was to specific recall of a dramatic performance, could not be replicated for books that are permanently available. In them, the energy of art is continuously generated and randomly tapped. So can the long-term effects of reading ever be empirically tested? Even the weight of evidence in the BBC researcher's postbag would probably not convince those sceptics who demand measurable proof and behavioural data before they will concede that literature exerts any influence at all. We take words in by an invisible internal process; we can only report on their assimilation in subjective, anecdotal, impression-istic ways.

Yet the enduring impact of Masefield's story upon the wartime generation of young radio listeners suggests that early impressions, privately remembered, may have a collective significance and determine the direction of many lives. This must be what structuralists mean by the assertion that 'the symbolic order is constitutive for the subject'.[2]

The word is made flesh in what we become.

Autobiographers describe their infant selves discovering literature as their native element, plunging in and being permeated by it, as the sea is in the fish when the fish is in the sea. But the disposition to be drawn to literature, take to it, embrace it, feel at home in it and remain susceptible to its power does not guarantee its

43

congruence with the facts of one's own existence or its compatibility with one's self-esteem. Where there are discrepancies between the worlds of imagination and actuality, the reader feels obscurely at fault, as if the book's authority had reached out to rap her on the knuckles.

Fred Inglis[3] recaptures the unclouded pleasure of learning at home and at Oundle 'to meet with books as both masters and friends', rejoicing in the consistency with which the ideals of boys' adventure stories 'fitted the rugby pitch . . . fitted the Parachute Regiment – they were meant to'. Compare this with the apprenticeship of Robert Roberts and Frank O'Connor who, imitating Bob Cherry's springy stride in the back streets of, respectively, Salford and Cork, belatedly realized that they themselves were the cads, bounders, yahoos and barbarians reviled by their favourite authors.

The luck of the public school reader, repeatedly starring in his own story, and finding in print his own aspirations endorsed on all sides, is seldom attained by working-class children and never, I suggest, by girls. The more eager a girl is to explore what books have to tell her, the more often she will be checked and chastened and filled with self-doubt in the course of literary encounters.

That, at least, was my experience. I was born in 1940 into a family which owed its partial deliverance from manual labour to universal education. Both my grandmothers had been pupil-teachers; both my parents were to train, as mature students, for lifelong employment in schools. Teaching was the only job we knew. From the start, I was recognized as a character in search of an author, forever wanting to be someone else, and pretending to read and write. At the age of three I asked who was the most famous writer ever. 'Shakespeare' they said, and I announced my intention of marrying him. That he was already dead seemed a minor obstacle which could be readily overcome by a really determined bride. (Nor was I alone in believing that girls gained access to literature by marrying into it. In 1973, Margo Galloway, researching *Female Students and their Aspirations* at the University of Edinburgh, asked one girl about what she wanted to achieve in anthropology:

Interviewer: You wouldn't like to go down in history as the woman who unearthed all the important Turkish folktales?
Student: I'd rather be the wife of the man who did it.)

As a toddler, I used to push a book in front of my mother, demanding 'What does that say?' while she went round on her hands and knees polishing the linoleum. Wearying of this, she taught me to read, a risky business in those days for an amateur, since you might do it wrong and incur reproof from indignant professionals later. My grandmothers recommended the Beacon Readers, which have just been reissued with the original illustrations, showing Old Lob the farmer, his faithful collie Mr Dan, and his friend the pig, Master Willy. There must have been a matronly cow – Mrs Cuddy – and there was certainly a Mother Hen, constantly fearful of losing her children. She had four conformist white chicks who all did as they were told – 'Watch me, Mother. I can drink' – and one black-winged rebel who went around saying, 'I am Percy, the Bad Chick.'

Eventually, human females were introduced by means of fables and extended proverbs. Witness the milkmaid who plans to raise poultry and then buy a pretty new dress with the proceeds of the milk she is carrying to market. On the way, however, she trips and loses everything, thus combining the moral: 'Don't count your chickens before they are hatched' with 'It's no use crying over spilt milk', and, at the same time, solidly associating maids with dress, mess, distress and foolishness: 'It was all due to care-less-ness.'

Nursery lore was full of foolish and careless females – Little Bo-Peep, Old Mother Hubbard, Little Miss Muffet, Little Polly Flinders . . . How could one account for the baffling difference in what happened to Jack and Jill after their fall on the hill: *he* bandaged by his mother; *she* whipped 'for causing Jack's disaster'? Sons, I was puzzled to note, usually had more reason to be pleased with themselves than daughters. 'What a good boy am I!' cried Jack Horner as he pulled out the plum, whereas the little girl who had a little curl, right in the middle of her forehead, came to grief:

> When she was good, she was very very good
> But when she was bad she was horrid.

Rhymes lay in wait for girls with a menacing secret or a nasty surprise:

> Needles and pins, needles and pins.
> When a man marries, his trouble begins.

It was not until I had children of my own that I learned the

45

traditional admonition for hungry babies, from neighbours who chanted into the pram, with grim relish and a measure of truth:

Clap hands, clap hands, till Daddy comes home,
For Daddy has money and Mummy has none.

Just after I started school, my father came home from the RAF and my mother polished the linoleum harder than ever. They were Communists who believed theoretically in the equality of the sexes, but the class struggle had top priority, and egalitarian principles did not affect the division of labour within the household. Mothers did the lot, thanking their stars if they weren't widows, glad to have a husband on any terms.

In our uncertain progress towards the emancipation of women, wars customarily entail one step forward and two steps back. Wives and daughters admitted to previously masculine employment relinquish dependence and deploy new skills. They realize their own competence, if they ever doubted it. Then, with demobilization and the return of war-heroes, they retreat into guilty assurances that they know their place, anxious to match the supreme military sacrifice with the domestic abnegation of self. (There's a Victorian instance of this in the career of the best-selling children's author, Charlotte M. Yonge (1823–1901). Her clergyman father had been 'a peninsular and Waterloo soldier . . . the hero of heroes to both my mother and me. His approbation was throughout my life my bliss; his anger my misery.' The Reverend Yonge was prepared to bestow approbation and withhold anger so long as Charlotte worked exclusively for the glory of God. Profits from *The Daisy Chain* went to missionaries in Melanesia and she piously refrained from writing during Lent.)

The debt of the civilian population to the servicemen who had defended them helps to explain the total acceptance of unequal roles that characterized the immediate post-war period. Patriarchal authority was mightily reinforced by our awareness of the risks and privations needed to defeat fascism. In fact, my father had had quite a comfortable war. Stationed in the Shetlands, he had been better fed than we were, and in much less danger from bombs than the inhabitants of outer London. But in our eyes he deserved all the credit for allied victory: he took our butter ration, and every privilege the family had to offer, as his due.

Since I was the eldest, I came in for more interest and attention than could subsequently be spared for the younger children. Admiring the ballads he sang of sad swains rejected by their sweethearts, I hated the likes of Barbara Allen, and deplored the notorious callousness of my sex: 'Young man, I think you're dying . . .'. My father also treated me to readings from Russian folklore, finely translated by Arthur Ransome. A war correspondent who married Trotsky's secretary, Ransome had actually travelled to Russia in the first place because he was attracted by what he had heard about the folktales. He taught himself the language by using the primers issued to infants in school and by chatting to them in the street. The narrator of his anthology *Old Peter's Russian Tales*, published in 1915, is a wise peasant addressing his grandson and granddaughter and ostensibly varying the characters according to his hearers' needs for commendation or rebuke. 'Which is the cross one?' the children inquire. Maroosya must invariably have been the culprit, since 'Long hair, short sense' is Grandfather's watchword, and all his stories castigate demanding daughters or old harridans who nag and oppress their simple kind gentle well-meaning husbands. *The Golden Fish*, familiar in several European versions, shows a covetous wife grasping one magical luxury after another, until the blasphemous desire to become, variously, Tsaritsa, Pope, Ruler of the Sea or of the Sun and Moon, condemns her and her fisherman spouse to destitution. *Winter on the Steppe* provides a peculiarly Russian sanction against greed. A wicked stepmother, wishing to be rid of her husband's child, offers her in marriage to Father Frost who carries her off on his icy sled. Asked 'Are you cold, my pretty?' the long-suffering girl replies 'No, thank you, quite warm', and, as her reward for politeness, gets sent home with furs and jewels. Her envious stepsister seeks the same prize but complains of the cold to Father Frost, and is duly frozen to death.

The theme of punishment is powerfully underlined by phallic symbolism. Fairy children steal an old man's turnips and, in exchange, give him a wooden whistle containing whips that will attack the user. At his wife's touch, they chastise her as she deserves. Inquisitive chatter in marriage is as reprehensible as a sharp tongue or an acquisitive nature. A hunter, escaping from his garrulous wife, rescues a snake from a bonfire in the forest, by allowing it to crawl along the barrel of his outstretched gun. In return, he is granted the gift of understanding animal speech, provided he tells no one. If he divulges the secret, he will die. But his wife's suspicions are aroused, and she questions him so persistently that he resigns himself to the prospect of telling her, dons a shroud, lies down under the icons and prepares himself for death. Then, in a sudden clamour of clucking, the cock drives the hens indoors: '"You see, I am not such a fool as our master here, who does not know how to keep a single wife in order. Why, I have thirty of you and the whole lot hear from me sharp enough if they do not do as I say." As soon as he heard this, the hunter made up his mind to be a fool no longer. He jumped up from the bench and took his whip and gave his wife such a beating that she has never asked him another question to this day.' My father loved these conjugal legends and read them continually, while I pondered their implications as auguries of what lay ahead.

As my parents were staunch atheists, I never went to Sunday school. Indeed, so strong was the commitment to scientific rationalism among socialists at this period that even a taste for fantasy was distrusted as tending to superstition. A bookish dreamer like me was held to be particularly prone to supernatural delusions. The bible remained a closed book for many years. When eventually the Old Testament came to my notice, it coincided with my discovery of Greek and Roman mythology, so I was simultaneously introduced to Eve wrecking the Garden of Eden and Pandora letting sin and sorrow out of her box. Wherever you looked in the creation myths you saw your own kind bringing 'death into the world and all our woe'. No doubt about it: woman's place is in the wrong.

In lieu of Christian indoctrination, I was given an English copy of *Timur and his Comrades*, a Soviet best-seller by Arkady Gaidar, which was first serialized in the newspaper of the Young Pioneers in 1940. Timur is the clear-eyed leader of a gang which secretly performs good deeds to help families who have relatives at the Front. At first their stealthy beneficence is misunderstood, but ultimately they win recognition and gratitude. Moscow's *Literary Gazette* declared in 1941: 'The author has thought up a new game for children, an entertaining and moving game based on our very best feelings. It inculcates in its participants justice, bravery, inventiveness, physical skill and endurance, spiritual sensitivity and resoluteness ¬ all qualities which we want so much to see in our children.' I can't say that it did all that for me. In the Soviet

Union, huge feats of voluntary effort were reported. Teams of Timurites chopped firewood, collected scrap-metal, unloaded coal and peat, cleared snow from railway tracks. I merely did my bit for pensioners in the person of my Gran. But the story impressed upon me the value of collective rather than personal ambition. You were only productive if you were engaged in some form of co-operation and you were only justified in being happy if things were going well for everyone. This was precisely the ethos of mother-hood as I had observed it: an attitude worth promoting in the young wherever the social utility of nurturant altruism is appreciated.

At the age of eleven, I won a scholarship to a boarding school run by distressed gentlefolk. It was a charitable foundation – not unlike Lowood in *Jane Eyre*, we thought – and at every meal we thanked God for our benefactors, aldermen of the city of London, who sometimes visited the school, resplendent in gold watch chains, to cast a lordly eye over the rows of blue pinafores. I spent six years there, and it was like being buried alive. Curiously, nowadays, with rising support among feminists for single-sex education, the long-established girls' schools are defying tradition by appointing headmasters, seeking amalgamation with their masculine counterparts, and, in the case of my alma mater, busily stripping their assets: selling land for development.

Among the founding mothers of education for girls, Miss Buss and Miss Beale are best remembered. And, although we think of them together,

Miss Buss and Miss Beale Cupid's darts do not feel.
How different from us, Miss Beale and Miss Buss.

they had dissimilar goals and contrasting philosophies. As head of the Anglican Cheltenham Ladies' College in the mid-nineteenth century, Dorothea Beale cultivated feminine accomplishments in conservative heiresses, and resisted moves to enter candidates for public examinations. Frances Buss, on the other hand, founded the North London Collegiate for pupils who wanted to earn a living. She insisted on freedom of religion, professional dedication and an exacting academic curriculum. This pedagogic polarity persists in the modern private sector, with fee-paying boarders gracefully 'finished' in accordance with Miss Beale's principles, and day-girls at grammar schools competitively streamed and stretched, as Miss Buss would have wished.

But at my school in the 1950s both objectives were spurned. Our mistresses set their faces equally against the arts of leisure and against academic striving. What they prized was moral fibre, true religion and diligence in darning socks. They trained us for domestic service, ultimately in the privatized nuclear family, and until then in the vocational equivalent: nursing, social work, occupational therapy. Girls with a longing to study medicine must be taught that it was more meritorious to help a doctor than to be one. Lest an individual should aim too high, and get above herself, they took whatever she was good at and persuaded her that it was worthless.

The puritanical conviction that drudgery is divine and anything disagreeable 'good for the soul' echoes through the fictional canon of girls' classics. Spirited heroines must be broken in, humbled and purified by tribulation. Bouncy impetuous tomboys such as Jo March and Katy Carr, Rebecca of Sunnybrook Farm, Anne of Green Gables, and Judy Abbott in *Daddy-long-legs* have the smiles wiped off their faces by some ordeal, illness or accident. On the threshold of womanhood, they either wind up in a wheelchair themselves, or, like Heidi, get to push one. Being female means being vulnerable and catering for vulnerability. Pain is our special province. The rigours of the school regime in a period of national austerity rendered us peculiarly receptive to this doctrine. Maturity was to be reached through martyrdom, and this was ever-present in the literature we read: both what was chosen for us and what we chose ourselves. Irene Payne, in an essay on years spent as a working-class pupil in a grammar school, recalls having to write out in a detention: 'Her voice was ever soft, gentle and low, an excellent thing in woman.' (A prefect I suffered from issued texts to be cross-stitched.) A friend of mine won the Poetry Reciting Competition with Kate's final speech from *The Taming of the Shrew*:

'Fie! fie! unknit that threatening, unkind brow
And dart not scornful glances from those eyes
To wound thy lord, thy king, thy governor . . .

(Beaming glances exchanged by school governors . . .)

. . . A woman moved is like a fountain troubled,
Muddy, ill-seeming, thick, bereft of beauty . . .

I am ashamed that women are so simple
To offer war where they should sue for peace . . .

Nobody I knew was offering war. Meek and biddable as we were,
our nearest approach to mutiny was revelling in Jean Anouilh's
sentimental *Antigone* composed during the Nazi Occupation, in
which the heroine says 'No' and very little else, before dying in a
numb adolescent trance.

We fell for any Muse who glorified our poor tedious threadbare
little lives, who confirmed the cock-eyed system of contraries
whereby the highest aspiration was the lowest self-abasement, and
who promised that self-denial would somehow gratify our sensual
and emotional yearnings. Gerard Manley Hopkins wrote the
theme-tunes for this anorexic ideal. In *Heaven-Haven: a nun takes
the veil* and *The Habit of Perfection*, he celebrates the negative
gratification of every sense: the music of silence; the illumination
of blindness; the eloquence of being dumb; the feast of Poverty:

'Palate the hutch of tasty lust,
Desire not to be rinsed with wine.
The can must be so sweet, the crust
So fresh that come in fasts divine!'

I didn't want to be a nun, but abstinence and emptiness and
inhibition had generally been my portion, so it was good to hear
that at least one poet thought I was getting the best of the bargain.
Hopkins' message of repression and renunciation fitted the strange
course women were supposed to follow: entering by withdrawing;
gaining control by giving it up; getting ahead by taking a back seat;
enrapturing the flesh by mortifying it, and altogether winning by
losing.

A journalist considering the outlook for last year's school
leavers was told by a teacher: 'Something happens to girls at
puberty . . . a mysterious despair.'[4] But there is no mystery about
the foreshortened future, the progressive decline, the losing battle
against wrinkles and decay that are held out to them. At puberty,
the end is already in sight. Once ripe, you begin to rot. Ask any
golden treasury of lyric verse . . . Youth alone makes you briefly
valuable, and thereafter there are no parts for women but figures
of fun and images of monotonous duty. To her sixteen-year-olds,
Polly Toynbee put the question: 'How do you see yourselves in ten

years' time?' Had she said 'Twenty or thirty years', I think the prospect would have appeared too appalling to contemplate, calling forth the response: 'We might as well be dead.'

When the teenage fiancée of John Ruskin asked whether he would always love her as he did then, he replied that it was up to her – a husband's constancy always depended on the wife's conduct – though it was hard, he confessed, to envisage her at forty. As we now know, Ruskin never fancied mature women at all. He fell in love with Rose la Touche when she was nine and he was forty, and proceeded, literally, to plague the life out of her.

I went to Somerville College in 1958 to read Modern English Literature, a course in which Latin and Old English were still compulsory. Although the syllabus had been newly extended to include T. S. Eliot, our Senior Tutor declared that she had never read James Joyce and never would. She was an Austen scholar and an aristocrat who wincingly begged us not to fidget in tutorials. (Long before our time, Jane Austen had been regularly recommended as a model of discipline and restraint for unruly females such as Charlotte Brontë, who told G. H. Lewes in 1848 that Jane was too elegant, fastidious and confined for her taste: 'a carefully fenced, highly cultivated garden with neat borders and delicate flowers.')

In Oxford's carefully fenced and highly cultivated parterre of English Literature we were not encouraged to relate what we read to what little we knew of life. History was irrelevant to the persual of timeless masterpieces. Biographical circumstances scarcely entered my head until, in the post-graduate Dip.Ed year, a philosophy lecturer disparaged the child-centred precepts of *Emile*, on the grounds that Rousseau had dumped his own four children at the Foundling Hospital. Could preaching then be challenged by reference to practice? Was progressive thought invalidated by rumours that the thinker was a heartless swine? Such doubts had never assailed me in the realms of aesthetic gold. We absorbed the best that had been thought and said, conversing with great minds, simultaneously present, as it were, in the eternal salon of civilisation. Attention was focused exclusively on texts. If you scrutinized them closely enough, they would yield up their glories. This habit of detailed analysis, ignoring the material conditions in which works were produced, was inimical to broad views, sweeping statements and political perspective. It was a training for miniaturists, for connoisseurs of Jane Austen's little piece of carved ivory – and it left us more at ease with quotations than ideas. One consequence of so much early peering and poring is that I now review fiction as meticulously (some would say nit-pickingly) as if I were to be summoned to cite chapter and verse at the Day of Judgement.

F. R. Leavis defined his discipline as 'Interrogative'. The critic's function was to invite fellow readers to agree 'This is so, is it not?' Given this acquiescence in a shared interpretation of particular works, we could do without an abstract systematic exposition of the criteria on which his judgements were based. Eschewing theory, Leavis urged us to cherish the *healthy, vital, actual, living* literature he held dear. Of course, the prerequisite for consensus about what constitutes literary health, vitality, actuality, etc. is a unified and stable climate of opinion, a common set of premises, embodied for Leavis in the vanished preindustrial community of the past, where wheelwrights and organic sensibility flourished. Fortunately, the virtue of this lost arcadia was concentrated in the integrated psyche of D. H. Lawrence. Anyone who wanted 'an instinct for life', 'clarity of being' or 'true relatedness' need look no further. As it turned out, 'the intuitional faculty', 'the complex need of the whole being' was at bottom 'phallic consciousness, which is the basic consciousness and the thing we mean in the best sense by common sense'.

Seeking wholeness in the 1960s, readers of Lawrence were assured 'The novel can help you: to be alive, to be man alive, to be whole man alive: that is the point.' Indeed it was. For a woman, there remained queer obedience, blind surrender, the extinction of her female will. Like Lady Chatterley, we had a choice: 'Her tormented modern-woman's brain still had no rest. . . . If she gave herself to the man, it was real. But if she kept herself for herself, it was nothing . . . at last she could bear the burden of herself no more. She was to be had for the taking.' The redundant self could simply be excised with a knife, as the Woman who Rode Away was glad to find: 'The quivering nervous consciousness of the highly bred white woman was to be destroyed again.' She welcomed 'the exquisite sense of bleeding out into the higher beauty and harmony of things. She did not mind. She wanted it.'

I tried. I really tried with my tormented modern-woman's brain to espouse all this. For want of a better guide I even noted that

Lawrentian spokesmen – Mellors, Aaron, Don Cipriano – disliked women who moved in bed. Female friction must be suppressed if we were to pursue what Professor William Walsh called D. H. Lawrence's 'route towards spiritual health' and attain a remedy for 'the wounded nature of man in contemporary society'.

English graduates were happy to learn that their subject was the chief of the humanities and that their trained sensibilities could resolve conflict and contribute to the restoration of fragmented souls in a divided world. Equipped with the insights of Lawrence, 'a diagnostician of incredible skill', some of us offered liberal studies to day-release students in Techs, while others carried the crusade into the classroom. David Holbrook led the way in tapping the sources of creativity in working-class kids, eliciting 'the rhythms of sincerity for which one must strive.' One example is worth quoting at length from 'The Point of Making Things Up'.[5] Holbrook calls this 'the wisdom of a small boy about marriage.'

> *Should a Wife Obey?* Yes because the husband goes out to work and earns all the money. On Monday most wives do the washing and the man comes home to dinner she still hanging out the washing and there's no dinner waiting for him he's got to fry himself some bacon and eggs for dinner and no man likes that and he gives her half of his wages and hardly gets a square meal once a week. On tuesday most wives go to Cambridge to buy a new hat or skirt while when he comes home he finds a note saying back 20 to 2 – dinner in the overn, custard under grill. They only do housework and they have all the afternoon off because they have finished by dinner time.

Any teacher, says Holbrook modestly, can stimulate work like this, once he 'has a sense of what to encourage . . . for it is the voice of the heart in which all men are equal.'

Extraordinary as it now seems, novices like myself turned to Holbrook and other disciples of Leavis, since theirs was the only pedagogy that allowed art a social context or permitted any consideration of the working class – whose place in Eng. Lit. had been previously represented, as Orwell pointed out, by a large hole. Yet this belated and minimal concession to political realities brought with it a Lawrentian heritage of bitterly irrational misogyny, which those of us who needed mentors were too awed to question.

In this recapitulation of the making of an English teacher, I have surveyed my pilgrimage as a crushed bookworm with the benefit of hindsight. When I was young, these authors represented truth as I knew it. They were the limit of my intellectual horizon. I could not see beyond them. Trusting them implicitly, it never occurred to me that they were partial or partisan or could speak from self-interest. But middle age is a time for questioning motives and tracing ideas to their human source. Lenin asked 'Who? Whom?' Quarrelling children are wiser than they know when they shout: 'Look who's talking! What do you take me for?'

I don't suppose anyone would seriously maintain that Wordsworth was referring literally to the male gender when he described the poet as 'a man speaking to men'. But still the assumption prevails unconsciously, blunting awareness and obscuring vision in men of letters. The novelist John Fowles remarks that he never describes women in detail because the reader prefers to fill them in himself. The philosopher Georges Bataille distinguishes humanity from beasts by 'the universal taboo on contact with menstrual blood'. The critic Geoffrey Grigson reviews the *Penguin Book of Women Poets* as 'a jellyfish . . . worth stamping on'. Such men preside over the feast of literature at which I have been avidly present for four decades. I now feel entitled to bite the hands that fed me – for their own good.

Notes

1 An article by P. Plummer in *The Times Educational Supplement*, 24 July 1981.
2 J. Lacan, 'Seminar on "The Purloined Letter"', in *Yale French Studies*, no. 48, 1972.
3 F. Inglis, *The Promise of Happiness*, Cambridge University Press, 1981.
4 An article by Polly Toynbee in the *Guardian*, 8 June 1981.
5 In B. Jackson and D. Thompson, (eds), *English in Education*, Chatto & Windus, London, 1962.

4 Diverse melodies. A first-year class in a secondary school

Tony Burgess

This first-year humanities lesson was one where pupils made a choice between reading or writing, as activities; and among books provided mostly by the teacher, as a class library. The class includes pupils of various linguistic (and cultural) repertoires. Among the black London pupils, mostly of West Indian origin, no two may be described as identical in presence of Caribbean features in their classroom speech or in use made of London Jamaican vernacular. These pupils make up about half the class. As central as speech to defining their classroom identities, at this point in time, are hierarchies conferred by special knowledge, open to some through older brothers. *They* know the school and local youth culture more surely. Through them, a dub/soul distinction in music and dress is beginning to be constructed as an important differential. The white pupils' speech is also finely differentiated: on a continuum between a full London and a speech rather closer to Standard. A little knot is growing 'hard' in style, while others still carry the feel of junior school ways. There are three bilingual pupils, one of them, David, from Burma, whose experience will, later, concern us. It is an all-boys school. My notes are selected from observations made at the time.[1]

11.15 a.m.	Teacher begins lesson by initiating a general class discussion on reading in primary school. Books enjoyed are recalled and, also, systems for encouraging reading. Possibilities are stressed for recording details of good books in their individual journals and for suggesting purchases.
11.32	Transition to class activity. 'Choice is a really good piece of work for parents' evening or reading.' Teacher brings out and empties on to front desks the book box. A wide selection.
11.35	Choosing, clustering . . .

56

11.42   . . . most are reading (some settle immediately), seated in the following plan:

Johnny   Andrew (*Football Annual*) Edward/Paul
(*Boy who was Afraid*   Chris   Michael/Daniel
Moped story)   (*Goalkeeper's*   (*Talking Blues* –
                Revenge)   Anthology)

     David/Martin/Rickie/Derek/Peter
     (*Myths*) (*Talking Blues*)

Simon   (Book selection)   (Teacher's desk)
(*Don Quixote*)

11.42   . . . teacher circulating.

11.47   Teacher reads, very quietly, one verse from a *Talking Blues* ballad to Martin/Rickie/Derek/Peter. He does the same to Edward/Paul.

11.50   Daniel tries to make Edward read in patois, declining to do so himself. Eventually Daniel withdraws and wanders.

11.51   Martin and others are reading out from *Talking Blues*, drumming on the desk. Edward/Paul join them and a reading develops.

11.59   The reading of *Talking Blues* has subsided. Martin and Rickie are reading Anansi stories. David has read throughout the lesson in a book of Greek myths.

12.02   Johnny, who has read continuously, out loud ('hearing reading' fashion), throughout the lesson, completes *The Boy who was Afraid* and goes straight on to a moped story which he reads in the same fashion.

12.03   Edward/Paul have returned to their original places and are writing a poem about Jamaica. 'How do you spell pretty?' Paul asks.

12.05   Period continues. I leave.[2]

If the multi-cultural setting poses new and special demands, these are, perhaps, for a new kind of listening to pupils, whose experience is likely to be different from the teacher's, and whose accommodations to diversity in British society are likely to differ, to take, in some measure, individual paths, and to be embedded in different personal histories. Individual accommodations to diversity within a multi-cultural setting are complexly oriented and derived: they may reflect, especially at secondary-school age, strategies towards school and towards the achievement of a classroom identity as well as attitudes, directly, towards language and literature. Pupils' cultivation of language uses and of linguistic and cultural awareness has to be seen developmentally, over a longer period of time than that implied by lessons or sequences of lessons or even a school year. The teaching of literature takes place within more general processes of classroom construction. It is necessary to keep in mind, as this teacher is doing, both differentiation and longer-term possibilities, which are presently below the horizon.[3]

Martin, in this lesson, for example, is at the centre of a group which developed a reading of a patois ballad. Though one of the quietest boys in the class and certainly not one of the most literate, the fact is that he is acknowledged by all to be closest to Jamaican origins and, at this stage, to be the most experienced speaker of the most authentic patois. The others gather round his confidence and experience. None in this group wholly appreciates, yet, the peer-group and within-school significance of London Jamaican. They are simply interested by a Jamaican ballad and especially in the possibilities of speech and rhythm in a mini-performance. The olden timers are wiser and more wary about classroom strategies: Johnny and Daniel do not use patois in the classroom and keep their distance from the options provided. Separate in this lesson, they are, also, united by both having brothers who have been through the school and by knowing the black culture of older pupils, in which they are already anticipating their role. Daniel, his eye on leadership and control, flirts with organising those less experienced than himself before moving on to something else. Johnny is serious about doing well academically in school. He, therefore, uses this lesson to drill himself in reading, selecting from the material on offer two short stories with the appearance of 'real readers'. As a final example of differentiated strategy, there is David. He sits with Martin and Rickie and others because they are his friends from football. He spends his time, however, not on their ballads or Anansi stories, but on mythology, a special interest, as he later revealed, arising from his interest in Burmese art.

Such pupil perspectives are not necessarily consistent, nor static, nor permanent. They evolve and develop, as part of an evolving classroom culture, in which pupils, as in any classroom, both contribute and derive interests. Later on in the term the group round Martin composed and recorded, with drum accompaniment, their own ballads, work which in itself represents no more than a moment within developing competence and awareness, just as the reading from *Talking Blues* is a moment here. In due course, the story of Mr Spenser and his battle with Bulldog was read; and it so happened that the most sustained patois dialogue in the sequels written by the class was composed by one of the white London boys who is also a good speaker of London Jamaican. West Indian stories are read in this classroom, not just out of abstract recognition of diversity, but because there is no reason to limit the sources of good stories. Thus there is no surprise that the most charged moment in the class's history, that term, came, not from West Indian material, but from the telling, by a student teacher, as it happened, of the story of Prometheus.

The catalogue is intended to evoke both the development of different interests over time and the contribution of underlying classroom processes. This brings me to a crucial intersection, exemplified in this lesson, on which I want to concentrate. I am interested in ways in which the activities of literature are constructed from within deepening and elaborating classroom discourses.

In this lesson, there were two poems begun in draft; several poems read; a reading of a poem prepared and performed; novels selected, flipped through, exchanged and sometimes continuously read; practice at reading gained; new reading and new literatures explored and old books, known at primary school by some, revisited. There is a conception of literature behind such activity for which I should want to argue. What can be done in making sense of the world, by writers and readers, is put at the centre of classroom experience. It seems to me right to seek to get beyond, as this teacher is doing, our inherited abstraction of literature from its own and from other forms of cultural making. Also, those restricted, selective and specialist traditions of literary work which have dominated schooling are being, here, importantly qualified. Out of the book box there tumbled a wide selection: stories from many different cultures, myths, poems, novels, readers, school texts, books contributed by pupils, working-class and minority autobiographies, community publications, and so on. However, the argument for a socially and historically developed view of literature must be referred to those who have done the work of historical and cultural analysis.[4] I want to concentrate on a further point. Accepting and trusting this conception of literature as activity, I am interested, in this classroom, in processes which help ways of working, within this conception, to be realised and which give them specific form.

When this teacher reads aloud a verse from a *Talking Blues* ballad, the move has several implications. It is signalled that reading aloud is an appropriate activity in relation to literature and appropriate to the expectations of this classroom. Because the poem is written in patois, however, further considerations are added. Intended, but implicit, is the understanding that a poem in patois is literature and further, that patois may also be read aloud, appropriately, in this classroom. This understanding is demonstrated rather than merely stated; and the manner in which it is demonstrated contains yet further signals. Because the understanding is made available, in this lesson, to small groups, in a relatively private moment with the teacher, pupils are left free to decide themselves the use to which this understanding is to be put and how publicly it is to be made available. Also, the brevity of the time spent by the teacher on this and the fact of the teacher's reading patois have an additional implication. The classroom has been shown to be a place where patois is understood, but the pupils' expertise in this, rather than the teacher's, has been recognised. Finally, in making this move, especially towards Martin rather than others, the teacher is recognising and partly helping to confer a different source of expertise, either from himself or from other more apparently successful pupils in the class. This represents, it may be noted, about a couple of minutes, teaching. The impact of this tiny exchange is supported, however, both by the consultative and choosing frame established for the lesson overall and by other such moments, earlier, which, in this lesson, begin to collect and gather. The achievements in this lesson need, therefore, to be complexly attributed and perceived. What happens is supported by what has been. And as interesting as this little moment and its aftermath is an underlying convergence of activity, expectancy, assumptions, expertise and dialogue which is being constructed.

In referring to this classroom process as one of the construction of discourse, I am making a very wide set of assumptions. By discourse I have in mind a concept which cuts across accepted divisions between spoken and written language, between language and context and social relations, and between form and content. I am not using discourse to refer, then, just to the verbal level of actual utterance. I am meaning more than merely stretches of utterance and more than the internal, systematic organisation which such stretches of utterance may display. Because my use of this term has a bearing on thinking about language outside as well as inside the classroom, it is necessary to explain this more fully. Discourse is offered here as a category which, above all, preserves the perception that behaviour in language *is* behaviour. In using language, something is done. Language reflects intentions, motives, purposes, interests, actions. Intentionalities of this sort, however, do not simply happen. Even in their individual origins, they are socially constructed and, as they become regularised, are socially maintained. I am seeking, then, to include within the notion of discourse these further assumptions, as well as that of behaviour. Discourse is also offered here as a category which preserves the perception that behaviour in language is social and historical as well as just linguistic.

It is useful to consider this through relatively public examples before returning specifically to the classroom. Behind literary or scientific uses of language, for example, there exist traditions of specific and historical social practice. These practices have been 'made'. As they are maintained and 're-made' in the conduct of discourse, they exhibit both specific sets of interests and 'content' and assumptions about social relations within which they are institutionalised. Connections between language and this social reality are often displaced, theoretically. Language is abstracted and projected beyond society as an autonomous 'system', for example. Or speaking and reading and writing are thought of as 'individual abilities' rather than as shared social practices through which individuality is realised. Or else 'society' is separately polarised and seen only as supplying 'contexts' for particular 'uses of language'. Here, however, I am using the term 'discourse' to insist that uses of language are (inseparably) historical, social and cultural practices.

The Russian psychologist Vygotsky rightly draws attention to the fact that, in development, language is first social and socially experienced and then 'internalised' and put to the child's own use.[5] His work represents an extraordinarily adept formulation of the links between individual experience and social history. Social practices and language have this double face. Social practices are something into which individuals are socialised. Social practices, in turn, provide the means by which individual selves are produced. This double-sided nature of experience will seem a paradox only where, conceptually, the 'Individual' and 'Society' are forced apart, rather than people being seen as active, social individuals. In participating in discourse, individuals both contribute within (and to the maintenance of) social practice and acquire, through practice, the conditions of their own individualisation. I am labouring the point partly in order to avoid the misunderstandings about an historical emphasis on social activity which issue from separating the notions of individual and society. Also, I want to make my way towards the developmental and educational claim that through discourse individual subjectivity, the self, is constituted. In their contribution to a recent set of papers, *Children Thinking through Language*, Cathy Urwin and Valerie Walkerdine have carried conceptions of discourse directly into the context of thought about education and about language development. Discourse and discursive practices, they argue, 'constitute' the child as a subject and as a learner. Their argument draws on a critique, mounted by post-structuralist thinkers such as Derrida and Kristeva, on the rational, autonomous and fully conscious subject, assumed (rather than argued) in structuralist linguistics. The anti-rationalist and anti-idealist stance of their thought seeks to give weight to the psycho-analytic perception that much mental life is unconscious, inconsistent and fragmented. Personal and human identity does not flower independently of social experience but is, rather, produced by and within it. This, they add, is in ways of which the individual is never fully aware. Discourse is identified as the means by which the human subject is created.[6]

Both Urwin and Walkerdine understand by discourse a practice in language which includes social relations and which is, further, historically specific. Citing the post-structuralist philosopher Foucault, Walkerdine exemplifies this by considering the example of a couple discussing child-rearing. Behind and within such a discussion there will be available a range of historically developed discourses – moral, psychological, medical, informal – concerned with child-rearing. These may be both written and spoken. In the discussion the couple proposed as an example will not merely draw on these discourses. They may be described as constituted by these discourses in their roles as caring and knowledgeable parents. In a critique of assumptions prevalent in developmental psychology, both Urwin and Walkerdine argue more generally against the conception of the autonomous, unitary, conscious self. Instead, the self may be regarded as essentially fragmentary. In place of idealist separation and autonomy, Urwin and Walkerdine offer the only partially conscious sum of different constitutions through discourse.

Whether or not the full force of this critical argument is to be accepted, the emphasis on the constitutive nature of discourse adds importantly to my earlier stress on social practice and social relations. By this emphasis, as Urwin and Walkerdine well appreciate, the route is opened into an educational perception about language. Many enterprises, educationally, may be conceptualised as turning on ways in which pupils are constituted as participants in different kinds of practices through discourse. Indeed, striking in both writers is the subtlety and usefulness of empirical work in which these general ideas have been explored and applied. Walkerdine, in this respect, develops a bold and challenging argument that some issues in mathematics, which have been thought of in terms of abstraction or disembedding, may be reformulated as questions of discourse. In one telling classroom example, she shows how a teacher intuitively eases children's transition between types of discourse associated with classroom mathematics: from the 'as if' (metaphorical) assumptions on which concrete mathematical problems are usually formulated into what she terms the 'metonymic' axis of formal mathematical reasoning. Following Walkerdine's lead, I want now to return to literature in the multi-cultural classroom and to the story of this first-year class.

Discourses are constructed in classrooms, just as, in very much wider social terms, public discourses are constructed historically. Classroom discourses, then, do not just happen. They are not to be reduced always to modes of teaching, even though many researched examples may have been constructed round the teacher's power. This point, slightly to one side of Walkerdine's emphasis, is a necessary step towards approaching directions developed in this classroom. Classrooms, it might be argued from the account which I have given of discourse, ought directly to reproduce the available public modes connected with curriculum subjects. Alternatively, it might be argued that classrooms should be constituted as critique. Such a debate about values is at the heart of teaching literature, as it is at the heart of all teaching. Neither of these baldly characterised arguments is of much force, however, simply as intention.

Towards the end of the term, there was read the story of Sharlo's strange bargain with the Devil.[7] It was read with a dozen or so of the West Indian boys in a separate classroom. Not a policy of separation, it perhaps has to be said, just an opportunity taken for some time spent on them on their own. There had been an earlier single period used like this, a fortnight before, in which the Dub/Soul distinction, dress and West Indianness had been discussed. 'Sharlo's Strange Bargain' tells the story of a Faust-like pact made with the Devil in return for a constantly filled calabash. In a familiar pattern, the teacher read the story, with pauses for comments and responses. Patois dialogue is interspersed with narrative in Standard written English. Here is the way in which an early moment of patois dialogue was treated.

Teacher (reading): This always made him laugh and as he laughed his eyes would close and his many chins would tremble and his belly would shake like that of a pig when it runs, but all he would say is . . .
. . . And I can't say this next one so somebody'll have to help me . . .
Pupil: What . . .
Teacher: How do you say that . . . how would you say . . .
Antony (softly): Shut mout' no catch fly
Rickie (correcting and adjusting): Shut your mout'
Teacher: No, not Shut your mout' . . . Shut . . .
Antony (more confidently): Shut mout' no catch fly
Teacher: What's it mean?
Henry: When you open your mouth like that, they think you're catching flies
Edward: Yeah it goes . . .
Pupil (repeating to himself): Shut mout'
Teacher: What . . . what is that all it means . . . what . . . just
Henry (new suggestion): Telling him to close his mouth or he'll catch a fly
Paul: Or is it don't be too nosey?
Teacher: Yeah, something like that probably . . . yeah

When the teacher cedes expertise in the manner of saying a patois phrase, here, it is a genuine cession, not because he would have been unable to say it himself. It is made genuine, partly, in ways which have nothing directly to do with patois, by the teacher's becoming one with the children in their difficulties in reading, just as the tone of his reading has earlier sought to reflect their relish and humour in the story. The tone of this cannot be caught by a mere transcript. A similar point is to be made about the questions about 'What it means'. These questions may be initiated by the teacher, but his questioning, again partly signalled by tone, seeks *not* to go beyond what similarly might be asked by a pupil. This imaginative attempt on the teacher's part to see his own lesson as it might be seen through the eyes of a reflecting, judging pupil is more explicitly signalled in the response through which the answer to his question is received ('Yeah, something like that probably . . . yeah'). The reader, here, may have to take on trust this matter of tone, but it needs to be unambiguously recorded.

Crucially, what is ceded in this exchange is how and by whom the gap between West Indian culture and a London classroom is to be filled – as much as working out a specific patois saying. The point is important enough to my argument to be made exactly. The authenticity of text and of patois syntax is preserved decisively by the teacher. So also is the existence of the two systems, patois and English Standard, together with the possibility of translation between them. Left with the class, however (an all London/West Indian group), is their possession of the cultural and linguistic experience. Also left with them is choice and the right to individual difference in making this experience available. Thus, it is assumed that 'somebody'll have to help me' and that somebody will. The formulation of this choice offers a space to be filled on a basis of complementary expertise and mutual support between pupils and teacher. What may be noted is not merely that these discourse assumptions are the same as those in the invitation to a reading from *Talking Blues*. In several ways, the discourse has itself grown, and its centres of interest become more explicit. The lesson is thus an important step in developing a discourse shared between the teacher and the black pupils in the class about literature, about West Indian culture and West Indianness, and about central issues in linguistic and cultural diversity.

For the last part of this lesson, after the story had been read and discussed, the group were left on their own by the teacher with the story and with a tape recorder. Their task was to tell the story, as a group, in their own words, on to the tape. The telling continues, uninterruptedly, for twenty minutes and was still unfinished at the close of the lesson. I can only, here, make the essential descriptive comments and cannot reproduce its flavour. Because these are London/West Indian children, it would be wrong to foresee a flood of idiom and patois released. The narrative is anyway written in Standard English and this format is wisely preserved. Before any telling, the first matter is the fair apportioning of the task, with each pupil allowed the recounting of a moment in the text – enough but not too much to permit boredom or the text being pre-empted by an individual. There is, however, a flexible tolerance for longer turns seized by tellers who generate greater interest and relish. Relish is the appropriate word to describe what each teller seeks; and the tape is marked by moments of delight interspersed with passages of inward concentration as names and incidents are recalled. Patois, dialogue exchanges, Sharlo's fat belly, whistled sound effects for Sharlo's fife, the sinister appearance of the devil, are all enjoyed in equal measure. I shall have to ask the reader to take on trust, again, both that it is a fine piece of tape to listen to and that an important piece of work is accomplished. Set within the growing discourse assumptions which I have sought to illustrate, the activity of telling re-presents and re-makes the story. It is possible for the story to be re-made because, having originated with the teacher, it has been handed over.

Literature has had such redoubtable claims made on its behalf that it seems reasonable to stress more modest virtues. Story, as here, may be as significant for what it quietly enables and teaches as for any profounder education of emotion. It is with a style of humour and the voice of a storyteller that the boys chiefly make contact here. Unsurprisingly, the humour which they take from the story is not unlike their own. There are sharp phrases and swift rejoinders to be enjoyed. There is a succulent culture of food, including bellies and fat which wobbles, favourite dishes, a fantasy of as much as may be eaten and more. And there are people who make and break promises, who act with still amiable jealousy, self-protectiveness and self-interest, but who are caught out by their own tricks at last. The claims to be made for this are not insignificant, but neither are they excessively grand. A voice is being offered them which may join, somewhere, with voices which they are seeking to develop for themselves. There are things being learned about life and the world and also about West Indianness. Possibilities such as these enter this classroom not only because they are contained in story. They are kindled as possibilities because interests and curiosity and an appetite for exploration are brought by the pupils – processes not very different from those underlying the writer's own interest in his story. Literature, as many have noted, would not make contact with readers' lives if it were not foreshadowed, quite ordinarily, in living. Those fore-shadowings are multiple, however: gossip, stories heard and told, the inward narrative of mind, actings out – speaking and writing as well as reading, processes and practices as well as products.[8]

Therefore, I have stressed in my comments here the multiple activities of literature; but also the classroom discourse with which these intersect. The point is not simply that stories may better enter the classroom where pupils have engaged in making story themselves. I have tried to suggest more precisely the discourse which the story of Sharlo enters in this classroom. This is a discourse, ultimately, about identity in a multi-cultural society. When the story of Sharlo is read, therefore, there exists a sufficient history of expectations for pupils to be able to move directly into the story and to make it their own. Correspondingly, the experience of the story and of their time in making something from it has its own contribution to make: to pupils' sense of themselves, to their expectations about literature and to the consolidation and development of cultural identities. In calling discourse this gathering and developing set of expectations realised through language, I am referring to the behaviours and practices as well as to the social relations which are inextricably involved.

On offer, above all, in this classroom is the space for different sorts of expertise to be proposed and accepted. That is a construction of discourse assumptions which is as fundamentally critical of current social arrangements as it is simple. What evolves is mutually constructed. A description of this process needs to attach weight both to the ways in which pupils are constituted as learners and to the manner in which they, in turn, act on and order much of the content of the classroom culture. This invitation to the proposal of different sorts of expertise catches at an important, general idea, both in education and in the teaching of literature. A story told by David, the reader of myths in the earlier lesson, allows the point to be made more exactly.

> The Burmese king had a white elephant. They used to say that, sir, and they got the tusk of it, it's about the size of this room, sir . . . a white tusk, sir . . . and they had . . . er . . . at the top right sir, the king put 24 carat gold around the thing, sir, around the tusk, and he kept that elephant as his own treasure, and they say sir he used to fly, and in the museum they had a big tusk, I saw it for my own eyes, sir, and he had gold around it . . .

Manifestly, in diverse settings forms of collaborative work become possible, to which wide understandings about language, literature and culture can be contributed by pupils. The point, though, is not that positive response to diversity means allowing for the telling of Burmese stories. In the multi-cultural setting, rather, when stories are told, there will be diverse melodies.

Notes

1 This categorisation of the pupils' language reflects that developed within a continuing and long-standing investigation into 'Language in Inner-City Schools'. This collaborative enterprise is based within the English Department of the University of London Institute of Education and shared between some eight hundred participants. See H. Rosen and T. Burgess, *Languages and Dialects of London Schoolchildren*, Ward Lock, London, 1981, for a more formal presentation of the categories.
2 *Talking Blues* is an anthology of West Indian poetry, published by (and available from) Centerprise, Kingsland High Road, London, E.5. Other books being read include Armstrong Sperry, *The Boy who was Afraid*, Heinemann Educational, London, 1942; B. Naughton, *The Goalkeeper's Revenge and Other Stories*, Puffin Books, Harmondsworth, 1977.
3 On pupil strategies, see P. Woods, *Pupil Strategies*, Croom Helm, London, 1980. Pupil strategies have traditionally been defined round the central axis of conformity/non-conformity with school culture. Hammersley in Woods (op. cit.) argues for more subtle differentiation. The need for differentiation is even greater where accommodations are also to linguistic and cultural diversity.
4 The argument for a 'socially and historically developed view of literature' is a wide-ranging one. I have in mind, especially, Raymond

Williams's account of literature as a practice which forms part of cultural production and his use of the concept of 'the selective tradition' as a term of analysis (R. Williams, *Marxism and Literature*, Oxford University Press, 1977). There is now a considerable body of argument which supports and extends Williams's general stance, while advancing more specific concerns. For cultural analysis, generally, see the volumes from the Centre for Contemporary Cultural Studies, University of Birmingham, published by Hutchinson. On working-class writing and modes of literary production, see D. Morley and K. Worpole (eds), *The Republic of Letters*, Comedia Publishing Group, 1982. For a critical history of the development of English Studies, see B. Doyle, 'The Hidden History of English Studies', in P. Widdowson (ed), *Re-reading English*, Methuen, London, 1982. Clearly, a socially and historically developed view needs also to include considerations of gender and ethnicity as well as those of class, though I would want to argue for not isolating these separate strands. On considerations deriving from a multi-cultural society, see A. James and R. Jeffcoate (eds), *The School in the Multicultural Society*, Harper & Row, New York, 1981.

5 See L. Vygotsky, *Thought and Language*, MIT Press, 1962. Also, and especially for Vygotsky's more general stance as a psychologist, *Mind in Society*, Harvard University Press, 1979.

6 On discourse, see C. Urwin, 'The contribution of non-visual communication systems to language and knowing oneself' and V. Walkerdine, 'From context to text: a psychosemiotic approach to abstract thought', in M. Beveridge (ed.), *Children Thinking through Language*, Arnold, London, 1982. The approach taken there and in my own account here is rather differently oriented from some current linguistic approaches. For a perspective which stresses the linguistic system, rather than social relations and social practices, see J. Sinclair and M. Coulthard, *Towards an Analysis of Classroom Discourse*, Cambridge University Press, 1975.

7 R. Prince, '*Sharlo's Strange Bargain*' in *The Sun's Eye, West Indian Writing for Young Readers*', Longman, London, 1968. Grace Hallsworth, *Listen to this Story. Tales from the West Indies*, Methuen, London, 1977.

8 This argument for literature's 'more modest claims', together with its assumptions about the traffic between reader and writer, rests on James Britton's account of 'the spectator role'. In this role, Britton argues, there is an essential continuity between informally going over experience (as in gossip) and more developed works of art. See J. N. Britton, *Language and Learning*, Penguin, Harmondsworth, 1971, and his more recent *Prospects and Retrospects*, ed. Gordon Pradl, Heinemann, London, 1983. See also articles by Britton and by D. W. Harding in M. Meek, A. Warlow and G. Barton (eds), *The Cool Web*, Bodley Head, London, 1977.

These ideas were developed in collaboration with John Hardcastle, whom I would like to thank.

5 The language of literature

Richard Exton

Much teaching of literature in schools suffers from a double handicap. On the one hand, it exists within an educational framework which is rigidly hierarchical in countless interlocking ways. On the other hand, it operates within that English tradition which penetrates all aspects of cultural life in this country: namely, a firm separation of creation from criticism, of practice from theory. I would like to explore the consequences of this double handicap and the implications of that inheritance, before offering some modest proposals which may point to avenues of escape. It is not only teachers and teaching which suffer, but also the children who are being educated into the 'naturalness' of the situation in which they find themselves. We owe it to these children to find ways of teaching literature which break out of the narrowing confines of the hierarchies, be they institutional or conceptual, and which free them from the culturally imposed separation of theory and practice.

The English education system is a complex amalgam of often contradictory assumptions, and English as a subject has a strange existence within it. In the earliest stages, 'English' is learning to read, and then to write. The verbs tend to be intransitive, though the question of subject-matter *is* raised from time to time. Then 'English' becomes comprehension, stories, poems and projects. Stories and poems are read (or listened to) and stories and poems are written: there is not much connection between the two. At the other end of the system, 'English' becomes English literature and, to a lesser extent, English language. Here, literature is read and written *about* or language is studied and written *about*. Never are stories and poems written. In between these two extremes, lies the secondary school, which contains, in miniature, the features of the whole system. In the lower school, stories and poems are written and read, but rarely studied; in the middle school 'creative writing'

70

and 'study' take place but are rigidly separated. The examination system confirms/imposes/reflects the conceptual and cultural assumptions built into the total educational system, which in itself contains a giant contradiction: 'creativity' is celebrated, valorised, championed, while 'criticism' is at the pinnacle of the educational hierarchy. And, as if our culture is aware of this contradiction, an intellectual sleight-of-hand comes into play. Only sensitive people can be great artists; criticism is about developed sensitivity; therefore, all parts of the education system can unite in a flowering of sensitivity, and somehow theory and all related problems disappear completely.

What follows is an account of two approaches to literature in the second year of secondary education. The approaches challenge the implicit hierarchies and are firmly rooted in theory, while remaining eminently practical. One 'studies' literature – a short story by Graham Greene – yet is language-based and involves 'creative writing'; the other studies a poem, 'teaches' the idea of simile and metaphor and yet demands that poetry be written. Both lessons challenge the tyranny of taste – that other unwritten hierarchy inscribed in Eng. Lit. – and assume that literature teaching is to do with developing understanding and conceptual skills in *all* our pupils, and concerned with exploring the complex relationship between the formal qualities of a text and the producers and consumers of those texts. More than anything the methods used are designed to give children confidence and recognise their creative power when they read and negotiate with poems, stories and novels.

The starting point for teaching *I Spy*, a short story by Graham Greene, was to demonstrate to the class, a 'lower band' second-year form in a mixed comprehensive in Hackney, that language is a rule-governed system and that every pupil present was a highly skilled manipulator of those rules. I began by asking them to 'read my mind', that is, to predict what word I was about to speak. They had no trouble completing the phrases 'bread and . . .', 'apples and . . .', 'cat and . . .', though I cheated by accepting 'jam' when I had 'butter' in mind. As the game developed with 'the old man crossed the . . .' I was able to show that the answer had to be a particular kind of word – in this case a noun – and once this was accepted I complicated matters with 'the woman put on her hat and . . .' in this case 'left the room'. In other words, it was possible to operate a range of rules, and only knowledge of context would permit a 'correct' mind-reading.

The next stage was to assert that just as language could be seen to be rule-governed, so could literature. And just as the pupils had proved themselves skilful in using their knowledge of the rules of language to read my mind, now I wanted them to demonstrate their knowledge of literature by completing a short story whose first half I would give to them. The class worked in pairs, examining the text closely for clues and trying to identify the rules that were in operation in the story. Although not everyone in the class spotted all the features of the story which permitted accurate predictions, the sharing of different possible endings – all accepted if they developed plausibly from features in the first half – allowed rich discussion to take place about the nature of narrative and literary conventions. Not all the points made were articulated in the terms I am presenting them here, but there was no doubt that learning was taking place and that the class were beginning to think about *how* a narrative worked rather than what it meant or how they felt about it. They were all doing this, whatever their 'ability', and without being intimidated by feelings that they lacked sensitivity or were 'not good at literature'. Indeed, this seems to me to be a crucial strength in work of the kind which derives from a structuralist or post-structuralist tradition.

Many of the issues raised by the children were related to what Roland Barthes calls the cultural or reference code. For example, the crucial fact that the story is set in war-time is indicated by passing references in the text to searchlights and to blackouts. Not all the children recognised, or registered, these references, and consequently their predictions existed within totally different frameworks. Similarly, those children who failed to recognise the signifying system in the 'strangers'' clothes, invented a whole range of possibilities which were logical, but within different narrative frameworks.

The crucial role of cultural reference embodied within the language of a text was clearly revealed; but equally important was a recognition of the notion of genre. The children were able to offer satisfactory endings to the story because they recognised elements in the first part which they had seen in other stories or films. And when, after talking from notes about the ending of the story, I asked them to write, as a continuous narrative, their version, they revealed themselves to be highly skilled manipulators of generic conventions, using totally appropriate language and registers. They also demonstrated that they had a good understanding of what Barthes calls the hermeneutic code – that code which carries a narrative forward through a series of enigmas and resolutions until the final resolution which ends the story. They clearly identified a series of potential enigmas in the first part of the story for which they offered a variety of resolutions in their versions.

What I would like to stress in this is the way that the 'study' of a text was combined with 'creative' activity and was firmly rooted in a theoretical framework. The class did further work once they had been provided with the complete text. Drawing upon the idea of all narrative being the movement from one state of equilibrium through a disruption to another modified state of equilibrium – a concept deriving from the French structuralist, Todorov – I asked the pupils, again in pairs, so that ideas and hunches could be tested and shared, to note down a list of facts from the beginning and ending of the story which remained unchanged, and another list of things that had changed. What was revealed was most illuminating. As well as making accessible to thirty 'less-able' 13-year-olds the central theme of the boy's feelings towards his father, the exercise also drew attention to the way that the mother in the story is totally marginalised: she is asleep in bed throughout! A whole range of issues could have been pursued with the class at this point, but the one I chose to concentrate on was the construction of the characters of father and son, once more turning to Barthes, but this time using his notion of the semic code – the narrative code which operates as the organising principle for character. The class were asked to list similarities and differences between Charlie and his father, and through this exercise they developed deeper insights into the story, its language, form and structure. They noted what is made obvious in the story, the tugging at the collar and the use of proverbs, but they also explored more fully that other explicit similarity, the 'doing things in the dark which frightened (them)'. They were able to speculate most fruitfully upon the title of the story in relation to all this. It seems clear that structuralist and post-structuralist approaches to narrative can work well in the second form as well as in the postgraduate seminar.

Approaches deriving from the same tradition have been equally valuable in the teaching of poetry. Poetry presents a problem for many English teachers. They feel that it is somehow 'special', yet may fall victim to the contradiction I mentioned earlier in relation to the whole school system. Of all the 'creative' activities, writing poetry is felt to be the most 'creative', and there are teachers who are quite happy to correct spellings and make critical interventions into children's writing of narratives, who say they 'won't mark poetry'. But poetry criticism is a semi-scientific activity, post-I. A. Richards, and therefore demands rigour. However, Leavis asserts that it is response we are after. So what is the poor English teacher to do? Very often the answer is to forget poetry altogether for large stretches of the school year and then guiltily to bring it out as something special, without providing ways of understanding how poetry works.

The lesson I am going to describe uses an approach[1] that was developed in order to find a non-threatening way of reading and developing understanding of poetry in the English classroom. It is appropriate at all levels and abilities in the comprehensive school, but it does assume that in junior school and in the first years of secondary school children will have been given plenty of opportunities to browse through poetry anthologies, to copy out favourite poems, to make their own mini-anthologies and to experiment themselves with writing poetry of all kinds. In particular it assumes that they may have had the chance to explore, through reading and writing, the formal elements of poetry: rhyme, rhythm, typography, 'sound' poems, 'shape' poems, and so forth. It seems to me to be vital to develop in teaching an understanding of what is specific to poetry. I would not argue, as the Russian formalist critics have done, that poetry is about nothing but itself, but most of my approaches derive from work they developed, and I do think it crucial to understand precisely *how* and therefore *what* a text says, and how we make those meanings, before moving on to make statements about 'life' outside the poem.

The lesson was taught to a mixed-ability second-year class in a girls' comprehensive school in Hackney, in response to a request from a teacher who wished to explore new ways of teaching poetry and who also wished the class to learn about simile and metaphor. The poem I chose to use was 'The Locust'.[2] The lesson took the form of a series of steps. Although in this case the teacher took the traditional position at the blackboard with chalk and duster conducting a 'whole-class' lesson, the aim was to provide the class with a methodology which they could operate in small groups on other poems.

Step one was to instruct the pupils that they must not for the rest of the lesson think about meaning, about what the poem is 'about'. Nor would I ask them about what they 'felt', what their 'response' was, arguing that 'feeling' was a complicated matter and would take a lot of thinking about, and in any event was private to them. I also explained that this first step was the most difficult one – after this things would become easier – but only if they didn't think too hard! All of this was designed to take away any idea of threat from the lesson and to make it absolutely clear that every single person in the class was going to be able to take part.

Step two, though not particularly appropriate in this case, was to give the class the title of the poem and invite them to speculate in as free a way as possible on what a poem with this title could be about. This did not contradict Step one because they did not yet have the poem. The value of the exercise is to set up a framework where free association can take place, and frequently the metaphorical implications of poems become clear before the poem itself is seen.

Step three was to read the poem itself, with the class following in their own copies, and to invite them to read it through a few times themselves.

Step four became easier as the basic idea was established, namely, that the class would call out, and I would write haphazardly on the board, any word or phrase which – for whatever reason – drew attention to itself. It might do so because it was unusual, because it rhymed, was repeated, was a contrast, was an echo, was on a line of its own, or for any other reason. Very soon the blackboard was filled with words. In some senses what we had on the board was the poem, but jumbled up. And at that point we moved on to *Step five*, which was simply to list on the board as many of the linguistic features of the poem as we could.

What was interesting at this stage was how observant the class were. They noted very quickly that the poem was structured around the basic device of the question followed by answers; that the pronoun 'it' was constantly repeated; that there were very few verbs apart from 'is'; that the whole poem exists in the present tense. They also said that it had lots of description but noted that there were very few adjectives. It was through this last point that the class were able to explore the functioning of simile and metaphor and to lay the basis for their follow-up lesson, which was to write – in groups – their own poem, using the same structure and form as the poem we were studying: creativity and criticism were brought together and were seen to be mutually supportive and illuminating. The following poems are examples of what the class produced:

> What is a human being?
> It's a machine made to do things
> Its brain, a snake coiled up together
> Its head, the figure point of the body
> Its hair, as long as the grass
> Its skin, as smooth as silk.
> The eyes, the image of a camera
> The nose, the air it breathes.
> Its mouth, made to talk
> Its feet, made to walk
> The body, the main production of life.
> Life and death is it.
>
> (Marian, Androulla, Barbara)
>
> What is a Person?
> The hair, strands of thread
> The fingers, bendable sticks
> Finger nails like see-through glass
> The eyes, glowing torches reflecting the world
> The feet, a blind person's stick guiding them through
> the path of life
> The teeth, the human knife and fork
> The tongue, the taster of food
> The brain, the ruler of the body
> The heart, a steady beat of a drum
> The voice, a telephone
> The nose, like a human oxygen tank and also a sniffer
> The toes, a shorter form of fingers
> The skin, the clothing of the body.
> A person is neither man or woman: just a person.
>
> (Sharon, Corita)

Step six was to return to the blackboard with the jumbled poem on it and to suggest ways that the words could be grouped. Different classes could suggest different groupings, or 'boxes', as I called them. What this class suggested included the following: a *sharp* box – which contained 'knife', 'saw', 'scissors' and 'razor'; a *life* box, which contained 'grain', 'corn', 'eggs', 'rain', 'sun' and 'plant' and a *death* box, containing 'knife', 'clothing for the dead' and 'Desolation'.

Step seven was to look for any patterns that were beginning to take shape. Clearly the dominant one which presented itself was the life/death opposition, and when we moved on to *Step eight*, which is to read the poem again and to try out a few hunches about what the poem might possibly be about the class drew attention to the way that Life and Death are inextricably bound up within the figure of the locust and what it is.

Step nine is a series of questions which shifts the work from the 'creative structuralism' of the previous steps and looks at the poem's relation to a particular social and historical formation. To begin with the class were asked who was 'speaking' the poem. Was it the poet or someone or something the poet has invented to speak through? And next, who is the poem 'spoken' to? Is it to a particular person, or to the poet him- or herself, or to the public in general? What is the speaker's attitude to that audience?

The class decided that the poet was speaking in her or his own person but as a member of a community that had direct experience of the locust. They had problems with the other questions and indeed we were under pressure of time, though those questions have proved invaluable in working on poetry further up the school. The final stage is to consider the poem's shape and form and organisation in relation to all the thinking and talking and exploring that has gone on so far, and certainly by the end of this process the question of meaning, which was banished in *Step one*, has taken care of itself. What is most important, as a teacher of English Literature, is not that a class understand the 'meaning' of a particular poem, but that they can read *any* poem, have insight into how it works and how its meanings are produced, and also have a model for their own writing.

The two lessons I have described are examples of a range of approaches to literature which are based in particular theoretical perspectives but are 'practical' and possible in inner-city mixed-ability classrooms. They do not aim to develop sensitivity but, rather, to contribute to a developing understanding of the nature and function of prose and poetry. They attempt to build on knowledge pupils, of any ability, already have and to combat some of the mystifying rhetoric which often surrounds poetry and Eng. Lit. They also start from a position which argues that it is important for pupils to have access to our assumptions about English as a subject: it is not good enough for a pupil to define what goes on in English lessons as 'reading books and writing stories'. We must begin to break down the anti-intellectual, anti-theoretical tradition which informs much of British cultural life, so that pupils have the tools to analyse the world around them, the literature they read, the films and television they watch, and to make their own decisions.

Notes

1 *HOW TO READ A POEM – a guide in ten easy steps*

If possible, follow this guide with one or two friends. If you do, talk about all the possibilities before you write anything down.

STEP 1 Forget about what the poem may or may not mean, or what it may be about.

STEP 2 Look at the title and jot down about half a dozen things that it suggests to you. Give literal meanings as well as associations.

STEP 3 Read the poem once quickly and then three times very slowly. Try to hear the poem aloud in your head.

STEP 4 Make a list of all those things which force their attention on you or which catch your interest for one reason or another. You might jot down unusual/odd/striking words

or striking rhymes

or striking rhythms

or repetitions

or patterns

or contrasts

or echoes etc. etc.

STEP 5 Look at and list any features of the language used in the poem, e.g. No capital letters

No full stops at line-ends

Presence/absence of adverbs/adjectives

All verbs active/passive

Tense – all past until last line, etc.

STEP 6 Try to find groups of words (thematic boxes) e.g.

(a) All similes make reference to animals/death/plants, etc.

(b) All the first words of lines are conjunctions, etc.

N.B. Don't worry if your groups of words seem silly or improbable.

STEP 7 Look at your lists, notes and groups. Do you see any pattern taking shape? Try out a few.

STEP 8 Read the poem again and then try out a few hunches about what the poem may mean.

STEP 9 Answer the following questions

(a) Who is 'speaking' the poem?
     Is it the poet or has s/he invented someone or something to speak through?

(b) Who is the poem 'spoken' to?
     Is it to a particular person
     or to the poet him/herself
     or to the public in general?

(c) What is the speaker's attitude to that audience?
     Is it angry, sincere, jokey, teasing?

(d) What is the poet's attitude to his/her audience?

(e) Why is the poem organised in the way it is?

(f) What is the effect of all the things you have noted at Steps 2, 4, 5 and 6?

STEP 10 Now, if you wish to, or *have to* (because of an exam) you can write a critical appreciation of that poem.

NOW Read the poem again. Good, isn't it?

2 The Locust

What is a locust?
Its head, a grain of corn; its neck, the hinge of a knife;
Its horns, a bit of thread; its chest is smooth and burnished;
Its body is like a knife-handle;
Its hock, a saw; its spittle, ink;
Its underwings, clothing for the dead.
On the ground – it is laying eggs;
In flight – it is like the clouds.
Approaching the ground, it is rain glittering in the sun;
Lighting on a plant, it becomes a pair of scissors;
Walking, it becomes a razor;
Desolation walks with it.

(Translated from a Madagascan language by A. Marre
and Willard R. Trask, Traditional)

6   Reading literature with a slow learner

Judith Graham

We have yet to regard literature as the best reading scheme we have and to use it to confirm our children as readers.

(Margaret Spencer)

A good author is a very efficient teacher.   (Roger Gurney)

Trevor, aged twelve, is reading to me in a small withdrawal classroom at Clissold Park School, Hackney. I think he's made some progress since he arrived a year ago at the school, scarcely able to read and write his own name. The book I've given him is called *George and the Bus*,[1] a book by Andy Fenner written for 'new adult readers'. It's new text for him and I've told him very little about the book before he starts reading. Here is an extract from the tape which was recording throughout the lesson; it is the last four minutes before he emphatically rejects the book.

Trevor	*Me*
'So by Tuesday the . . . rush (1) was . . . (2) easing off a bit. (3) So it was Tuesday and George could go on the bus to go to work.' (4)	(1) Good. (2) 'easing'. (3) Good.
	(4) Good. Now you were really trying then. That was coming out really well. It's hard work reading Trevor. You've got to put a lot of effort into it. It's not going to be easy until you've got over the hump. That was lovely though. Everything correct except that word 'easing' which I gave you. On you go.
(Trevor sits in silence.)	
'As I said George was 57. He didn't believe . . . (5) he'd been working at the same job for 25 years now. (6) It was as if . . . nobody in his life . . .	(5) 'he'd been' (6) Good

80

that was . . . for as long as he could remember . . . do you know now (7) how that feels.' (8)

(7) 'Do you know *how*'
(8) Yes. 'It was as if nothing in his life had changed for as long as he could remember.' Do you know how that feels?

(Question ignored.)
On the bus that morning he . . . sat . . .' dunno (9) 'he thought of work, he thought of the . . .' dunno (10) 'din of the factory' (yawns) 'the long hours . . .' (11) 'long wait for the dinner break and the end of the day. (12)
The thought of the silent faces of the men as they sat round the table at dinner. (13)
The bus went slowly on. It came slowly to a hut . . . (14) halt, hut at the corner of the street. (15) came slowly to a . . .' – dunno Miss (16)

(9) 'thought'.
(10) 'din of the factory'.
(11) 'wait'.
(12) Good.
(13) Yes, good.
(14) 'halt'.
(15) Just read that again.
(16) I've just told you that word Trevor. You must try and remember.

Can't remember (17)

(17) Well try and remember, 'bus came slowly to a . . .'

Dunno (18)
'Halt . . . (19) at each stop. Then it went slowly on one, once more. (20)
George looked at the face round him (21)
Then all sat . . . seemed (22) moany The some . . . (23) the same till, except . . . (24) tired and lazy' (25)

(18) 'halt'
(19) 'at each'.
(20) Good.
(21) Good.
(22) Good.
(23) 'Then all seemed the same'.
(24) 'tired'.
(25) 'empty'. All the faces were looking worn out and with no expression.

(interrupts) 'The bus came to George stop' (26)
(Trevor mutters angrily.)

(26) Good. Well there was some very good reading there Trevor. Very good. Come on, no, we . . . go on with this. You must push yourself much harder.

It's rubbish. (27)

(27) It's not rubbish Trevor you're reading it very well.

Can't I read another book? Any book. Except this one here. (28)

(28) All right then. You go and choose any book then.

You choose it. (29)	(29) No, you choose it. I want to see what you would choose.
You choose a book for me except this one here. Any book, any book at all. (30)	(30) No you choose it Trevor and then I won't be responsible. You won't throw it back in my face.
I won't throw it back, I won't throw it back. I can't choose a book now, Miss. You choose it. (31)	(31) You're doing very well with this book.
It's rubbish (32)	(32) Don't you want to find out
no (33)	what happens (33) when he
no.	gets off the bus?
(long pause)	
Any book except that one there (34)	(34) We'll come back to this another day.
(incredulous) Another day?	

Now two obvious questions need to be asked about this reading lesson.

(a) Why do I react so positively to Trevor's reading? (Notice I commend him at least ten times and my tone throughout is encouraging until I turn sulky on his rejection of the book.)

(b) Why does Trevor give up?

To answer the first question you need to remember that when I first met Trevor he could read nothing. For the best part of a year I had read to him and we had shared well-known texts. Now I was pushing him on to unseen and unknown text and the miracle for me was that he was able to read many words correctly (approximately nine out of ten in this extract). I was also encouraged that there was some evidence of successful semantic grouping and prediction indicated by intonation and speed (e.g. in 'he'd been working / at the same job / for 25 years now') and also by one self-correction (e.g. 'The bus went slowly on c $\genfrac{}{}{0pt}{}{once}{one}$ more').[2]

Now of course these are encouraging signs in any beginning reader, and I don't think I was wrong to feel excited by this progress. But the mistake I made was to assume that these surface achievements added up to a meaningful reading experience for Trevor.

And that is, of course, the answer to the second question.

Despite my praise and despite any competence he was showing on the decoding level, Trevor must have known that very little of this story was reaching him. His firm opinion is that this book is not worth reading. Now we could say that in actual fact one error every ten words counts as reading at 'frustration' level and that he rejects the text because he does not understand it. I would, however, especially in the light of the rest of this particular lesson, like to argue that he understands the text quite well enough to know it holds nothing for him.

It is worth pausing to conjecture what 'it's rubbish' means to Trevor in relation to this book. There seem to me to be one or two clues in his miscues. His need to make the bus arrive at a 'hut at the corner of the street' (15) and his insertion of the word 'till' followed by another insertion of 'except' (24) both suggest to me that he has a real hunger for 'complication' in this story, which is not being met. He wants something to happen, and a middle-aged man's spiritual adventure does not qualify. George's glum contemplation of his routine day (9) mystifies Trevor and reduces him to yawns and passivity. This rejection of a depressed adult's thoughts or stream of consciousness was to appear a year later when I gave Trevor some of the Spirals books to read (*A Game of Life and Death* and *The Dream*).[3] By then I was much less personally affected by Trevor's rejection of books and pushed him to define *why* they were 'boring'. He argues that the 'I' of the story has no right to our interest if he just presents us with his bitterness or depression. Why should we care about such a person if no history or context is given? Unlike many teenagers, Trevor was not captivated by the horror genre which the 'Spirals' series relied on and was merely irritated by the repetition in the texts ('Why does it have to say everything twice?') and offended by the invitation to spend time with at best inadequate, at worst immoral characters. I am aware that both the Spirals series and *George and the Bus* are intended for much older readers and that the mistake was all mine in giving Trevor such books, which may well have important things to say to more contemplative or introverted readers. Nevertheless, it is possible that poor readers of any age value themselves according to the spirit of the characters they read about (which might explain the popularity of the valiant heroes and noble heroines of myth, legend and fairy story) and certainly Trevor had no wish to be associated with George. Notice how when I turn a rhetorical question of the text on Trevor, 'Do you know how that feels?' Trevor has nothing to say.

It also seems of great significance that this text, for the most part, stimulates very little tangential comment from me and indeed is used quite clearly as a vehicle for somewhat questionable pedagogic drives on my part. Thus I specifically tell Trevor effort will not go unrewarded (4) and that forgetting is a cardinal sin (16). It is not surprising that such a text is to be avoided if it can never create a teacher-proof secondary world. Readers of this chapter may like to know that we never did 'come back to this another day'. So at least Trevor and the book were spared further ill-assorted encounters.

By a happy coincidence the lesson so far described progressed to a reading of a very different sort, which helped me to feel more relaxed about myself as teacher and more trusting of Trevor and of the power of literature to do its work, however 'poor' the reader.

Remember we left the room with Trevor adamant that any book would be an improvement on the earlier one and with me totally confusing Trevor's rejection of the book with his rejection of me and the reading lesson and almost on the point of abdicating responsibility for what might happen next. Some of my disappointment (and my determination to retrieve my authority) is audible at the start of this section, but gradually the power of the story works on me too, and a full half hour later we close the book on a real reading experience. The book has taught Trevor what reading can be like and what it might be for and has coaxed me into being a better teacher. Here are the first four minutes of *Sir Gawain and the Loathly Damsel.*[4]

Trevor	*Me*
	Do you know the story of King Arthur and the Knights of the Round Table?
No.	
	You don't know any of those stories?
No.	
	Well, long, long ago in England there was meant to be a king called King Arthur . . . who lived in a place called Camelot and he had several knights who served
Yes.	

'Long, long ago there lived a
king called Arthur who was . . .'
Miss? (1)
'ruler of all . . .' Miss? (2)

'Britain (3)
He had many . . .' (4)

'powerful' (5)

'B' (6)
'b' (7)

'brother (8)
brave knights but perhaps the
bravest and the one that Arthur
loved best was his . . . (9)
nephew Sir . . . (10) Gawain' (pause
to look at glorious picture on
next page).
'It happened one day when Arthur
and his knights were having a
feast at . . . (11) Carlisle
that into the feast (12) hall round
. . . (13) rode a . . . (14)
sorrowing

long (15)
gipsy, lady on a white
h . . .' (16)
What's a palfrey? (17)
(We look it up in the dictionary; Trevor whistling happily under his
breath.)
'My Lord Arthur,' she . . .(18)
cried, 'Help me I before, pray (19)
beg of you. My name is
Alia. No (20)

him and went out on errands and
adventures and the bravest of his
knights and the one he loved best
was called Sir Gawain and this is a
story about Sir Gawain and an
adventure he had. Right?

(1) 'ruler'.
(2) I just told you . . . 'ruler of all
. . .?' Which country do you live
in?
(3) That's right.
(4) What did I tell you? Who
served him? Do you remember?
I'll tell you that (pointing) word.
That's 'knights'. Look (pointing
to picture) there's one of his
knights. He had many . . .?
(5) What letter does it begin with
Trevor?
(6) Good.
(7) And that has a what sound? –
br. . .
(8) 'Brave'.

(9) 'nephew'.
(10) 'Gawain.'

(11) 'Carlisle'.
(12) Good
(13) 'rode'.
(14) Now that's difficult 'sorrowing'

(15) Who is she? A sorrowing?

(16)'palfrey'.
(17) a sort of horse.

(18) 'cried'.
(19) 'beg'.

(20) It's just the same as that
(pointing to earlier text).

85

Lady (21) My husband has been crossed . . . (22) captured by the Black Kings, Knights of Tard . . . (23)	(21) yes. 'Lady Moldron'. (22) 'captured'. (23) 'Tarn Wathelyne'. That's difficult.
This evil king, no, knight, has . . . (24) boasted that not ever . . . (25) not even King Arthur himself dares to do before . . . (26) battle with him I beg that you fight up, take up his challenge.'	(24) 'boasted'. (25) 'not even'. (26) 'battle'. Good. How did you know that was 'challenge'?
Dunno. I just knew.	

The two questions to put now are

(a) Why am I much less encouraging with this text? (Two reproofs, one attempt to pin him to phonics, only three commendations.)

(b) Why does Trevor keep going? (He finished it during the lesson and it became one of his favourite books.)

Now, allowing for subconscious punishing of Trevor for the abandoning of *George and the Bus*, what I suggest guides my muted response to Trevor's efforts with this book is my deeply held conviction that this text is too hard for him. By any readability measures it would be impossible for someone of Trevor's experience. (We must also not discount the widespread but little acknowledged need for teachers whose pupils persist in choosing unsuitably 'difficult' books to withhold their best help and thereby validate their original misgivings.)

Now the assumptions I was making about the difficulty of the text were all based on the surface structure – the complicated proper names (Tarn Wathelyne), the archaic phrases and inversions (e.g. 'It happened one day . . . that into the feast hall rode'), the literary vocabulary (palfrey, sorrowing), the sheer number of words with rich associations (ruler, knights, nephew, challenge), not to mention phonic snares. It is not only pupils who grow to believe that all they can read are short simple sentences with no embedded clauses, preferably one sentence to one line, controlled vocabulary (i.e. short and phonically soluble) and everything said twice.

So was I justified in thinking this story too hard for him? By chance the two extracts quoted are the same length as well as occupying us for approximately four minutes apiece. If asked, I would have said that I gave Trevor far more help with the second text than the earlier one but, in fact, on analysis, the help is still of the order of one word in ten. So where does this illusion come from? My belief is that because I was giving more help with central, 'charged' words (knights, nephew, captured, boasted) compared with less pivotal words in *George and the Bus* (he'd been, now, wait, halt, same), it *feels* as if I'm giving not only more but also more *fundamental* help than on 'easier' text. This misapprehension, of course, blinds me to the child's mastery of the framing around those pivotal words (which often make no concessions to the poor reader). But most important, and what I only subconsciously knew at the time, is that my supplying of a word like 'nephew' or 'sorrowing' is actually *not* critical. In some obscure way the reader knows the type of word needed, both on a syntactic level and on an emotional level, because the text is rich enough to teach him what to expect. The teacher is one of many resources the reader might use, often the most immediate, but not actually indispensable. But in the *George and the Bus* passage there is not the redundancy, the emotive power of the language to enable the reader to read independently.

This is made much clearer as Trevor's reading of *Sir Gawain and the Loathly Damsel* continues. He makes increasing use of self-monitoring (as in (20) and (24)). His substitutions (as in 'pray' for 'beg', 'gipsy' for 'lady', 'powerful'[5] for 'brave') show total understanding of the story. He feels it is quite permissible not to know a word in a text as rich as this ('what is a palfrey?') because learning to read and reading to learn at such moments are fruitfully fused. His 'memory' for words given once is no longer under attack. Indeed, he never 'forgets' words once given. Why should he? He can read them.

So what this boils down to is that the text itself is teaching the reader and that only rich text can do that job. Does this mean the teacher is redundant? Patently not; and some of the ways in which I can help Trevor to use the text to learn from are apparent in this lesson. I *can* provide the book. I *can* give him an idea of the sort of story to expect before he begins. I can learn to give information when it is asked for and not accompany it with raps on the knuckles about memory and effort. I can accept semantically, syntactically sound substitutions, I can draw attention to successful reading strategies.

Not in evidence here but obviously a role the teacher can perform is in encouraging the reader to predict what might be going to happen so that personal response and investment is seen as relevant and valuable. Later in this taped lesson I relax and share the reading with Trevor, and together we cackle and gasp, sneer and wail; and undoubtedly our enacting of the story makes Trevor's reading more important to him. When the book is finished, we talk about the situations and characters very much as if they were real and certainly as if they matter to us.

In explaining my niggardliness of response to Trevor's reading when he begins *Sir Gawain and the Loathly Damsel*, and tracing its disappearance to the fact of Trevor's commitment and our joint yielding to the power of the story, I have mostly answered my second question 'Why does Trevor not give up?' In the sense outlined above, my feedback is not essential to his entry into this secondary world, and indeed conventional praise may well be distracting. Trevor knows, with this text, when he is getting it right from the unfolding story itself. He must also be immensely satisfied as he hears those ancient phrases of story-telling ('Long, long ago . . .' 'It happened one day . . . that into the feasting hall . . . rode a . . .') rolling off his tongue. Obviously there is much more to be said about the power of myth and legend, but it is clear that it speaks to poor readers as much as to all of us. 'Wanting to know what happens next' is a powerful reason for going on reading and it is an ambition worth having in a story such as this. And finally and most importantly, as I suggested before, Trevor's sense of his own worth is reflected and formed by what he is given to read. This story puts him on stilts.

Generalisations are difficult. After all, I have examined only eight minutes of a single reading lesson. But I think it would be safe to say that Trevor's behaviour with books both here and on many occasions, and indeed the behaviour of other poor readers, confirms what we all suspect: that the author's structuring, message and language are all-important. We can't expect people to learn to read on texts written by nobody for anybody; a bond with the author must be formed. We need to inspect our contribution as teachers in the reading lesson and ensure that preconceptions about what makes difficult text are justified; in my experience the help we need to give with a real book is quantitatively no more than on a 'reader' and qualitatively less demoralising (there is no stigma attached to not knowing 'palfrey') and more lastingly significant. A good text makes us into better teachers. We have no difficulty in responding and thus giving positive models to our pupils, and a good text can teach all the conventions of print that will prepare the child for the widest possible range of reading. A diet of poor texts equips the readers only for more of the same and teaches the dangerous lesson that books only provide challenges on a luke-warm, decoding level and never have powerful reverberations. Let's let the message be powerful, let the decoding be worth the struggle. We need to get clear in our heads that complex text does not have to be difficult to read and that simplified text is often anything but simple to make sense of and frequently a waste of time.

Notes

1 Andy Fenner, *George and the Bus*, Centerprise, London, 1975.
2 This way of marking a reader's miscues in order to understand what strategies are in operation comes from the work of the Goodmans. See, for instance, K. S. Goodman and Y. M. Goodman: 'Learning about Psycholinguistic Processes by Analysing Oral Reading', *Harvard Educational Review*, vol. 47, no. 3, 1977. The mark c)$_{\text{one}}^{\text{once}}$ indicates that this reader corrected his first reading 'one' to 'once'.
3 Spirals: *A Game of Life and Death* and *The Dream*, Hutchinson, London, 1975.
4 *Sir Gawain and the Loathly Damsel*, retold and illustrated by Joanna Troughton, Puffin, Harmondsworth, 1972.
5 Later, when I had been mellowed by the power of the story, I was able to see a substitution such as 'powerful' for 'brave' as the promising sign it actually was.

7 Cook a poem – a poetry tasting

Heather Kay

'What shall I call it?' Advertisers and organisers always want titles, so you have to think up something to keep them happy and to help them sell their wares. Sometimes the title comes afterwards, as a summary of your ideas, sometimes it provides a framework that stimulates you to explore new ways of looking at familiar territory.

I chose this title for a poetry workshop afternoon with a group of mixed, mostly West Indian, 11–12-year-olds. I wanted the word 'cook' to throw out reverberations of everyday activity – concocting something together – and also of eating, because poetry happens in the mouth. Like food, it needs to be tasted, chewed over, rolled around the tongue and relished. I like the way Seamus Heaney[1] describes his reaction to Hopkins's 'consonantal lines that rang and ricocheted between the teeth and tongue.'

I had not met these children before so I needed to find some common background experience to draw on, like cooking, and an activity that would evoke some immediate universal response. I started with basic rhythm. A reggae record was playing as they entered the room. This covered any moments of anxiety about the unknown encounter, channelled any physical tensions into rhythmic bodily movements and gave time for both parties to size each other up. It also gave rise to some introductory chat on common ground:

'My brother's got that record!'
'Have you heard the latest one?'
'What's this got to do with poetry?'

Here was a wonderful cue for playing a record of Linton Kwesi Johnson [2] (or John Cooper Clarke, Paul Weller or many others). In this case Kwesi Johnson was familiar and very acceptable to the children, and after they had listened to 'Sonny's Letter' they agreed that the poem seemed to emerge from the rhythm and ride on it and that this was therefore a basic ingredient.

90

Ingredients

We talked about these in relation to cookery and divided up a card index of recipes among small groups in order to have a quick look at the variety of ingredients that were asked for. We compared these with some of the constituents of a poem in addition to rhythm – words, rhymes, sounds, pictures, feelings, images etc.

William Stafford[3] says that the writer's certain way of dealing with language and experience is 'simply to be willing to start with local, insignificant ideas or phrases and to have faith in them'. So, we should be able to make a poem by putting together some everyday instructions.

Method

Turning to the recipe cards again we extracted as many *activities* as we could find and wrote them down so that we could repeat them over music, like rapping. Rapping started in Harlem and is essentially urban. The word is used in the sense of rapping out orders – it is sharp, rapid, rhyming speech chanted over funky music, a bit like 'calling' for square dancing or bingo.

We experimented by chanting the words over a recording of 'Cultural Rock'[4] and we found it exhilarating. Verbal patterns began to emerge, so we put together the group collections and eventually came up with this:

Wash and trim
Peel
Stir
Rub through the fingers
Mash.

Chop finely
Sauté gently
Separate the whites and
Beat.

Weigh
Sieve
Add a little water
Put it in the oven at Regulo 3.

Initially the speaking was unison incantation, but later we experimented with different words and phrases repeated, alternated or superimposed – two verses spoken simultaneously, for instance – so that counterpoint rhythms could be orchestrated. We also tried increasing or reducing the number of voices and counterbalancing tenor and bass, whispered and spoken sounds. In order to have more flexible control over the rhythm we abandoned the tape-recorder and used a couple of drums for the ground bass or ostinato. Hands, feet, heads and shoulders inevitably responded to this primitive stimulus. It was easy to join in, in the way that playground chants are catchy and inviting. There are many ritual chants and spells that could be employed together in this way, harking back to nursery rhymes and dancing songs and anticipating such poems as 'Dry Bones' and 'Kubla Khan'.

I stuck with the recipe cards for subject matter because the material was to hand, I wanted to keep the pace going and because this followed my 'theme'. I have to confess though that the last reason is spurious – it is easy to get carried away by one's own gimmicks. The lurking danger in the use of themes is the temptation to include inferior material for its sometimes tenuous link with the subject rather than for its intrinsic quality. However, for this particular exercise the words can be plucked from any source: school rules, nicknames, flowers or vegetables, the atlas – or groups of alliterative, sensuous or evocative sounds. Everyone has their own examples of words that they roll around the tongue and savour, like the pleasure of fingering a smooth pebble in the pocket. Often the articulation of the word is a sheer kinaesthetic or musical pleasure, especially in childhood, before the meanings have become attached. Try 'monosodium glutamate', 'mangrove swamp', 'soporific', 'translucent', 'Piccadilly Line' or 'Tolpuddle Martyrs'.

W. J. Turner,[5] in his poem 'Romance', captured this feeling of being possessed by the magic incantation of a word:

> When I was but thirteen or so
> I went into a golden land,
> Chimborazo, Cotopaxi
> Took me by the hand . . .
>
> I walked in a great golden dream
> To and fro from school –

Shining Popocatapetl
   The dusty streets did rule.

More recently Edward Brathwaite[6] started a poem 'Calypso' by
stringing the names of native islands together:

The stone had skidded arc'd and bloomed into islands:
Cuba and San Domingo
Jamaica and Puerto Rico
Grenada, Guadaloupe, Bonaire.

Brathwaite talks about 'the need to break out of the prison of the
pentameter, especially if you have the rhythms of the Caribbean in
your blood.' Certainly the calypso is a good rhythm to start with.

I think it is important to make time in the classroom for
sustaining and developing this verbal relish, by rubbing together
words and rhythms, stirring them about and tasting them, making
daring and exotic concoctions. If you are used to doing this the
odds are you could take Joyce and Beckett in your stride later on.
But you must be able to flex your voice on the stuff, it is not
enough to read it and write it and listen to it. Adrian Mitchell[7] says
'my poems should ideally be spoken aloud – or sung' and most
poets would agree with him. You need the chance and encouragement to declaim it, intone it, sing it, mutter it – maybe even *learn*
it, so that you can possess it for all time and any time. I know
learning by heart produces bad vibes; echoes of punishment lines
or the horror of mindless parrot-like repetition. I think this is a
great pity. We soak up so much in childhood, so easily, that it
seems an opportunity wasted if don't take advantage of this to store
in the memory some literary treasure that can be carried around
for a lifetime. Poems are so self-contained and portable, learning
them doesn't have to be a mechanical chore. If you are rehearsing
a play you soon pick up everyone else's lines as you work over a
scene. It can be the same with a poem. If, for instance, you
experiment with a group interpretation – sorting out lines for
different speakers, trying it out for sound, stretching the range of
your voice unselfconsciously because there is safety in numbers –
you suddenly find that you have the whole poem in your head,
there it is, it's yours!

Heather Kay

Leave to cook

There comes a time when the dish you have prepared needs to go in the oven and be left alone for a while. This is important for a poem too. If you are writing one you certainly need to leave it to prove and then perhaps have another go at kneading it into shape later on. The same goes for reading, excavating the meaning for too long can be as disastrous for a poem as overbeating is for a cake. Let it alone for a bit and then you can experience the particular joy of recognition when you meet it again. This way understanding has a chance to *dawn*.

So at this point in the lesson we turned aside to sample something more delicate. We had a look at 'The White Mouse' to see if we could sort out the recipe for a different kind of poem.

```
my
    eye
is a wink!
   a whisk
   my
      frisk –
            y
          tail;
       my
           pink
feet
     spread
under
      my
few
     ounces
i
  sit
upright
   and hold
my feed
    be
        tween
              my
        fingers.
```

```
my drink
     i muzzle
inqu-
     is - it?
          ive
i am
  and twitchy.
i sleep and
          wake
to my
     own
  small rhythms.
i stare
     blink
and am
     gone.     Twink!
```
                    (Gerard Benson)

I read the poem aloud without the title and then handed out
copies, still with no title, and the children read it to each other in
pairs. I noticed how they responded quite physically as they
identified with the small creature. They hunched over their
fingers, twitched their noses and picked up the way the words
articulate neatly in the front of the mouth. They decided it must be
a mouse because

'It's small and twitchy.'
'It jumps down the page.'
'It looks like a long tail.'
'You have to say it in a nibbly voice.'

We talked about the shape of it on the page, the way the poet had
spaced out and broken up the words to make sure that when we
read it we could reproduce the mouse-like quality that he was
after. Whatever it is we want to capture in a poem we have to
scrutinize it very minutely, pick out the exact sound and shape and
size and flavour – weigh out the ingredients carefully, as we do in a
recipe.

We decided to have a go ourselves and spent some time working
in groups trying to extract the essence of a different animal, as far
removed from a mouse as possible – cow, elephant, giraffe, etc.

We tried to feel the way they moved, how they fed, what they felt like to touch – physical and verbal explorations. We tried to capture a communal pig on the blackboard before the time began to run out,

> I roll in mud
>> Mucky, soggy.
> My snout is shiny slippery
> I slobber my swill, I slurp
>> Grunt, snore, hoying!

Finally, for a good laugh, we listened to 'The Loch Ness Monster's Song' by Edwin Morgan[8] and everyone left the room hissing and spluttering and conversing in pre-historic underwater noises. Just as well it was the end of the day!

To sum up. Poetry belongs with music as much as it does with books. Young people making their own music and songs today are greatly influenced by the West Indian and Asian poets, many of whom have emerged through the musical rather than the literary scene. Rapping, which I mentioned earlier, and which has been described as 'graffiti for the ears', may not be welcome in the classroom, but it is worth considering the elements that make it appealing. It is rhythmic, rhyming and fast and can unlease a flow of anger and humour, energy and frustration.

> Don't push me because I'm close to the edge.
> I'm trying not to lose my head.

sings Grandmaster Flash.[9] The driving rhythm helps to create the same kind of crisis, or 'inner stress', as Ted Hughes[10] calls it, that is needed to germinate a poem. Maybe we can cash in on this.

Poets today see themselves as performers, with a microphone in the hand as much as a pen, so we must make sure that children experience poetry as something that is released from the page, a physical experience. It is something to be shared aloud, to be held in the memory and repeated as well as to be left alone. Above all, poetry is to be relished and enjoyed – good enough to eat.

Shakespeare on the menu

For me it goes without saying that much of all this applies to dramatic literature, especially Shakespeare. I suspect, however, that there are still children whose experience of a Shakespeare play is a sedentary occupation and, except for the good readers, a silent one.

How can you capture the nervous tension of that exchange between Macbeth and Lady Macbeth after Duncan's murder if you are reading at the back of your partner's head two rows in front? At the very least it demands a face to face confrontation; as soon as you do this the staccato dialogue reveals the nervous starts and stops and jerky movements that are implicit in the lines. Since he was writing for actors, Shakespeare's timing always included the moves. It can be an exciting exploration to uncover the clues in the text by rehearsing different ways of pacing the lines or placing the actors in different spatial relationships. Macbeth's dazed reiterations and long vowels 'Sleep that knits up the ravelled sleeve of care' . . . 'balm of hurt minds' reinforce the 'brainsickly' reaction that begins to set in and almost paralyse his limbs. While Lady Macbeth's pent-up nervous energy bursts forth in hard-edged consonants and taut sudden movements: 'Go get some water' . . . 'Give me the daggers.' As you discover how to say the lines the meaning comes alive:

> No; this my hand will rather
> The multitudinous seas incarnadine,
> Making the green – one red.

looks unapproachable on the page, but roll your voice around the syllables and the speech rhythm will dictate the meaning even before the intellect has sorted out the emphases; and what satisfaction there is in sounding these words aloud!

I am convinced that it really pays off if you can spend time on exploring at least one scene in physical detail, discovering what happens to the speed, volume and timing of the lines in action. Even Macbeth's very first line in the play –

> So foul and fair a day I have not seen

is coloured by his experience of the battlefield he has just left and cannot be delivered as if he has just come in from a visit to the supermarket.

And how do you start on the witches? What are they – outcast, deformed old women, gypsies born and bred, are they hallucinating through imbibing their own potions? And where are they – spread around lurking in the gorse bushes, or conniving in some threatening huddle in a crevice of the rocks? All this affects the way the lines are spoken. And if the witches can't work up the frenzy of their spell-casting with books in hand throw them away and let others speak the lines for them.

Once a part of the text has been brought to life like this it is easier to lift the rest of it off the page in a straight reading. But if it starts to sound like audible print again break it up with another spell of activity.

Suit the action to the word, the word to the action.

Notes

1 Seamus Heaney in *Worlds*, ed. Geoffrey Summerfield, Penguin, Harmondsworth, 1974.
2 Linton Kwesi Johnson, 'Forces of Victory' (Island Records); see also Paul Weller, late of The Jam, now a punk poet.
3 William Stafford in *Worlds*, as above.
4 'Cultural Rock', from 'Dub Out Her Blouse and Skirt' (vol. 1, Revolutionary Sounds).
5 W. J. Turner, 'Romance', in *Come Hither*, ed. Walter de la Mare, Constable, London, 1923.
6 Edward Brathwaite, 'Calypso', in *Penguin Poets 1969*, Harmondsworth. Quote from BBC broadcast 1982.
7 Adrian Mitchell in *Worlds*, as above.
8 Edwin Morgan, 'The Loch Ness Monster's Song', from *Twelve Songs*, Castlelaw Press, recorded by Barrow Poets on 'Magic Egg', Argo ZSW511.
9 Grandmaster Flash and the Furious Five, 'The Message' (Sugar Hill Records SHLD 1001).
10 Ted Hughes, *Poetry in the Making*, Faber & Faber, London, 1967.

8 Poetry in the first three years of secondary school

Paul Ashton and David Marigold

Teaching poetry is more of a high-risk activity than teaching any other aspect of English. After one lesson you can end up retrieving crumpled copies of 'Glory be to God for dappled things' from behind the radiator, and thinking murderous thoughts; after another, you can find yourself marvelling at the originality, intelligence and awareness that the same group of pupils has shown, and deciding to deal with poetry much more often in the future. We have probably all shared the despair of that one-time teacher, D. H. Lawrence –

> Why should we beat our heads against the wall
> Of each other? I shall sit and wait for the bell

– whose context is the effort of making unwilling children write. Yet the optimism of another poet and teacher, Kenneth Koch, is equally widely-shared: 'The educational advantages of a creative intellectual and emotional activity which children enjoy are clear. Writing poetry makes children feel happy, capable and creative. It makes them feel more open to understanding and appreciating . . .'[1] Some of the risk lies in differences between the teacher's and the pupils' response to high-art objects, and some of it lies in the teacher's intentions for the poetry activity, be it reading, writing, or both. But there is a third and important source of difficulty in the state of the art itself. It's axiomatic that teachers who want to encourage the pleasure and appreciation of poetry must read and enjoy poetry themselves, and feel enthusiastic about it, but enthusiasm is not enough; when pupils come to write poems, conflicts arise about the fundamentals of making poetry that are also shared by adult poets.

When somebody asked Robert Frost why he didn't write free verse when he was at Harvard, he said, 'I don't like playing tennis with the net down'. In his metaphor is embodied the idea that writing poetry is principally a formal activity whose self-imposed

99

constraints give the activity its value by marking it off from ordinary uses of language. But in reading Robert Graves on the writing of poems, we get what seems to be a contradictory view: 'Poetry can't be planned or discovered. It forces itself on you. It comes like the tense headache before a thunderstorm, which is followed by an uncontrollable violence of feeling, and the air is ionised.' The priority in Graves's metaphor is on a feeling so unforced, so far from deliberate, that it's like a natural phenomenon which is bigger than the poet. Can this mean that writing poetry is like playing tennis in a thunderstorm, with a headache? (The problem is compounded when one reads the two poets' work, and realises that Robert Graves's poetry is at least as consciously and deliberately organised as Robert Frost's.) At a different level, the significance of the whole activity is called into question by Linton Kwesi Johnson: 'Poetry is basically entertainment; it's no substitute for political speech'. If this is the case, and we should like our pupils to have the kind of language that gets things done in the world, we shan't give poetry a very high priority in our teaching. But, paradoxically, Linton Kwesi Johnson is immensely popular as a poet, and constantly communicates political ideas in his poetry. As if this weren't enough, the best of contemporary poetry in this country and in the USA can be formidably difficult to understand and enjoy, and it's not easy to put these modern practices into one's teaching in the fruitful way that colleagues in art and music departments seem able to do in their respective fields.

So teachers who set out to think about the place of poetry in a lower-school secondary curriculum may find themselves lost in a thicket of contending priorities and apparently polar oppositions like these:

– the expression of feeling/the crafting of a made thing;
– formality/sincerity;
– pleasure/the pains of developing a skill;
– traditional forms/the forms of modern poetry;
– the usual privateness of poetry-writing/the communality of the classroom;
– the unpredictable nature of response/the demands of the timetable;

– relevance/irrelevance to pupils' lives;
– the heritage of admired poetry/the pupils' own language and culture;
– the largely mono-cultural references of English poetry/the multi-cultural classroom
– traditional critical approaches/contemporary critical strategies.

Perhaps the common case, then, that a first-year class bristling with enthusiastic readers and writers of poetry leads to a fifth-year class with only one or two, if that, is as much due to the predicament of the teacher as to the development of the pupils. We can add to these problems the fact that creativity – the making of it yourself – is credited at O and A Level in Art and Music, but not in English as far as poetry is concerned; and you can get through English exams without reading much of it either. If an aspect of English is seen as marginal to certification, only the commitment of the teachers will sustain it as a priority in the lower and middle school, and the commitment can be expensive in time and energy. The radical alternative, of offering poetry only to an extra-curricular interest-group, or as an option, is unacceptable for a number of good reasons. We all feel that opportunities for reading and writing poetry *must* be available to all pupils – and that all are capable of making full use of those opportunities. That, for now, is *why* we do it.

There wouldn't be time to write – or, perhaps, read – the volume that would explain this curious optimism we share. This chapter proposes merely to look at some different kinds of current practice, and then to group together some of the elements that might usefully form part of a poetry curriculum in Years 1–3. By 'poetry' in this context we mean reading it, talking about it and writing it, as interconnected activities. Although there will be lessons where the emphasis is placed on one of these three, bringing into play the others will always be a possibility. There is no need at all to introduce into the lower school curriculum the sharp distinction between 'critical' and 'creative' work that characterises the exam-oriented upper-school curriculum.

For many teachers, the experience of poetry teaching has been of lessons something like these:

Paul Ashton and David Marigold

Lesson type 1

Aim: understanding and appreciation.
Method: comprehension questions for written answers.
Material: 'The Golden Boy' by Ted Hughes.
Result: class treated it as a prose comprehension; invented answers without really attending to the poem; the questions seemed to get in the way of them encountering the poem whole. Rather tedious session going over it with the class.

Lesson type 2

Aim: to stimulate free writing on a topic.
Method: read and discuss poem; encourage personal anecdotes.
Material: 'House Fear' by Robert Frost.
Result: good discussion and writing, but poem was of minimal use; didn't really need a text for this work.

Lesson type 3

Aim: to explore the theme 'Childhood'.
Method: reading, talking, writing, research etc., involving choice of work.
Materials: stories, poems, pictures, film, books from library, newspaper extracts, etc.
Result: theme went well, good wall-display; only a few worked on the poems, perhaps because the content was marginal to their interests – or too difficult?

Lesson type 4

Aim: understanding and appreciation of ballad form.
Method: read poem, class discussion.
Material: 'Ballad of the Bread Man' by Charles Causley.
Result: the pupils liked the poem, but the discussion went awry, with teacher doing most of the talking.

Lesson type 5

Aim: to write poems about Autumn.
Method: working from direct experience to describe colours, smells, sounds, etc.
Materials: a walk in the park.
Result: a lovely walk; some good poems written by a few; the rest happier with prose description. A lot couldn't get started, and some insisted on feeble rhyming.

No one would want to denigrate the intentions behind these approaches, and much good poetry reading and writing has come from them. However, the total experience offered to children is, in general, rather narrow, and the common feeling is that by the third year we don't seem to have generated the kind of enthusiasm we had hoped for. Discussion of poems tapers off, comprehension exercises based on poems are for keeping things quiet, pupils do less poetry writing for themselves, and we begin to leave poems out of theme work when it becomes obvious that Blake's 'London' isn't as easy to incorporate as the GLC Tourist Guide. Poetry remains a big issue in the syllabus document but less of it is done.

So we need some variations, for ourselves as much as the pupils, to freshen and extend the approaches described above. Our aims for these alternatives, though, are still the familiar mixture:

– to encourage children to experiment with language and form;
– to read widely in poetry, and without inhibitions;
– to encourage speculation and sharing of both the delights and
  difficulties of poems;
– to provide insights into those features which make poetry
  different from prose;
– to offer a variety of structures which support children in
  expressing their own thoughts in poetic form.

The use of anthologies gives children the opportunity to read a wide variety of poems which please them. However, we will find it difficult to allow this to happen unless good collections are readily available in the class library or in a separate poetry book-box. There is not space here to list and annotate the twenty-odd anthologies which we think useful to make available in this way, but our list would start with:

The New Dragon Book of Verse, ed. Harrison and Stuart-Clarke;
Poems, ed. Harrison and Stuart-Clarke;
Junior Voices Books 1–4, ed. Summerfield;
Voices Books 1–3, ed. Summerfield;
Dragonsteeth and *Tapestry*, ed. Williams;
Ways of Talking, ed. Jackson;
Caribbean Anthology, ed. Cocking and Goody.

Between them these books provide a mixture of classic and contemporary poetry with the variety which is essential to anthology and theme work. But even with such anthologies to hand, it's important to search further in order to bring to pupils' attention poetry which is not, to put it broadly, mostly written in England by white male poets of mature years and considerable education, if we want to give priority to a fresh and wide-ranging reading experience. So we'll be looking as well for collections of poems:

– by poets like Mike Rosen with an ear for the humorous/the
  quirky/the domestic;
– by young people (as in ILEA's *Hey Mr. Butterfly* and *City Lines*
  and in James Berry's *Bluefoot Traveller*);
– by women (still difficult to come by with reference to this age-
  group, but there is the *Penguin Book of Women Poets* and *A
  Book of Women Poets* to select from);
– by writers in English from the Asian sub-continent (*Indian
  Poetry Today* is a large collection to select from);
– by writers in those languages other than English represented in
  the classroom;
– by poets in the oral folk tradition (perhaps using records such as
  The Iron Muse and *Ye Mariners All*) and by contemporary
  working-class poets published by community writers' workshops.

The *Voices* anthologies have as a particular strength a willingness to take poetry from modern 'unpoetic' sources and *Ways of Talking* enlarges one aspect of this concern by sticking close to the way we, and particularly young people, speak. From a practical viewpoint, poetry should be the easiest part of the mixed-sex, multi-ethnic urban curriculum to resource since poetry, in the widest sense, is a more natural and accessible form of expression than longer prose-works.

We take it for granted that poets don't write in a vacuum, but that each has an anthology in his/her head of favourite lines or images or whole forms culled from past reading. Consider what has happened here – is it conscious or unconscious reference?

Where the Bee Sucks
Where the bee sucks, there suck I:
In a cowslip's bell I lie;
There I couch when owls do cry.   (Shakespeare)

Clock a Clay   250 years
In the cowslip pips I lie,
Hidden from the buzzing fly,
While green grass beneath me lies . . .   (John Clare)

These personal anthologies, often compiled from childhood, form reference points for poets' work, no matter how invisible the influence of the past has become in their own production. It would be useful for children, too, to develop this hearing device. In other words, poets plunder both past and present for ideas, themes and models; aware of what has been said and how, not to copy but to press into service for their own concerns, and what we do with anthologies in the classroom mirrors this process.

One of the most satisfactory kinds of poetry lesson, and one worth making a regular occasion, is that where the teacher simply distributes copies of a good anthology (or several anthologies) to the class, who then browse, choose favourites, read them aloud to the class, or dramatize a reading of them in some way, or tape them, or copy them out for wall display. Various devices are possible here to provide excuses for reading and rereading; but the emphasis is on pleasure and talking about poems you like, as an essential first step towards appreciation. This regular, relaxed meeting with poems seems to us to be an essential preliminary to reducing the difficulty, and appreciating the conventions, of poetic language (especially metaphor and other figurative devices).

Most poetry anthologies are arranged by themes, and a common practice is to read with a class a number of poems on a theme from an anthology, and then to invite pupils to decide the one they like best or to write their own on the same theme. The problems here are that the themes in anthologies are often very large and vague (e.g. 'Creatures', 'The Five Senses') – and that poems are

105

sometimes conscripted into a theme merely because of some reference in the poem, while the poem itself may point in a quite different direction. If the thematically arranged poems are linked with the other thematic material that the class is studying, pupils may get the impression that poems exist only for their overt content, and that what makes a poem a poem is the least important aspect of it. Furthermore, inferior or very difficult poems may have been included to make up the numbers on a particular theme. Nevertheless, the idea of putting poems with similar concerns alongside one another is obviously a useful one. If the selection and grouping of poems is carefully done, so that the focus for comparison is narrower and sharper than it often is in anthologies, this way of presenting poems can put understanding and response into a higher gear than looking at individual poems, for it invites pupils to notice (stimulated perhaps by the simple question, 'what's different?') contrasting forms and patterns, differences in 'voice' and variations in the use of images and other devices; the starting-points for explaining preferences are here too.

It is a pleasant department meeting that gathers teachers together just to go through anthologies to make these smaller groupings, which can later be expanded by including poems written by pupils using them. There's an example here from a series put together by one ILEA department. (We've printed four poems here from a small collection called 'Machines'.)

Machines

Steam Shovel
The dinosaurs are not all dead.
I saw one raise its iron head
To watch me walking down the road
Beyond our house today.
Its jaws were dripping with a load
Of earth and grass that it had cropped.
It must have heard me where I stopped,
Snorted white steam my way,
And stretched its long neck out to see,
And chewed, and grinned quite amiably.
(Charles Malam)

The Chant of the Awakening Bulldozers
We are the bulldozers, bulldozers, bulldozers,
We carve out airports and harbours and tunnels.
We are the builders, creators, destroyers,
We are the bulldozers,
LET US BE FREE!
Puny men ride on us, think that they guide us,
But WE are the strength, not they, not they.
Our blades tear MOUNTAINS down,
Our blades tear CITIES down,
We are the bulldozers,
NOW SET US FREE!
Giant ones, giant ones! Swiftly awaken!
There is power in our treads and strength in our blades!

We are the bulldozers,
Slowly evolving,
Men think they own us
BUT THAT CANNOT BE!
(Patricia Hubbell)

Song: The Railway Train
You see the smoke at Kapunda
The steam puffs regularly,
Showing quickly, it looks like frost,
It runs like running water,
It blows like a spouting whale.
(Traditional Australian Aboriginal poem, trans. George Taplin)

Carbreakers
There's a graveyard in our street
But it's not for putting people in;
The bodies that they bury here
Are made of steel and paint and tin.

The people come and leave their wrecks
For crunching in the giant jaws
Of a great hungry car machine,
That lives on bonnets, wheels and doors.

When I pass by the yard at night,
I sometimes think I hear a sound
Of ghostly horns that moan and whine,
Upon that metal graveyard mound.
(Marian Lines)

Having a poet in school seems to be one of the most productive ways of stimulating an interest in poetry. The visiting, or in-residence, poet is not a teacher, and can enjoy a relationship with the pupils that has little or no authority or routine aspects. Any full-time practitioner of an art seems to hold a special fascination for pupils, and often the practitioner manages a very good kind of teaching without ever assuming a 'teacherly' stance.[2] Poets who have had regular contacts with schools have often provided helpful insights into the teaching of poetry generally. For example, in the days before certain *idées fixes* about the preservation of culture seemed to swamp all his writing, David Holbrook, while not primarily a poet, and without spending a very long time with children, was able, by his firmly-held and well-developed theories of the relationship between poems and pupils' emotional needs, to influence a generation of English teachers.

Many teachers have more recently been influenced by Kenneth Koch's two books *Wishes, Lies and Dreams* and *Rose, Where Did You Get that Red?*[3] Koch is a New York poet who spent time on a visiting basis in P.S.61[4] in Manhattan and found himself captivated by the responses of pupils to the poems he took in, and by their own writing. The first book (subtitled 'Teaching Children to Write Poetry') has chapters on some twenty different stimuli he used, with his own records and examples of the pupils' poems. The second (subtitled 'Teaching Great Poetry to Children') begins with a section called 'Ten Lessons', in which he describes lessons on poems by Blake, Herrick, Donne, Shakespeare, Whitman, Stevens, William Carlos Williams, Lorca, Ashberry and Rimbaud with pupils aged from 8 to 14, and which contain many examples of poems written after the readings and discussion. The rest of the book is mainly an anthology of poems by classic writers with suggestions for classroom approaches. Although Koch's work has not been widely publicized in the UK, it seems to us to offer some of the most exciting approaches we have come across to poetry-work with children. Koch's intention is to give quite young children access to some of the great poems in the tradition – ones which adult readers feel are the pinnacle of the art. Since most of these poems contain difficulties which appear to put them outside the reach of young readers he decided to work on the texts in such a way that the children were asked to consider only those features which were accessible to them, and to use those features to support themselves in trying out their own versions. Rather than try to summarize, this, for instance, is how he approached Blake's 'The Tyger'. He prints the poem in full, and then continues:

> The idea of talking to an animal appeals to children a great deal. The whole air of mystery and magic about 'The Tyger' is very interesting to them too. The main question the poet asks is a question they often think about: How did something get the way it is? They ask this question about animals, about apples, about the sky and clouds, and about themselves. Blake has an excited idea of how the tiger got to be the way it is: that a Superpowered Being gathered materials from ocean, earth, and sky, and then pounded and twisted them all together until He had made a tiger. Blake stresses the amazingness and scariness of this Being: He has wings and can fly, can hold fire in his hand, and can control the terrible force of the tiger . . .
>
> The poetry idea I gave the children was 'Write a poem in which you are talking to a beautiful and mysterious creature and you can ask it anything you want – anything. You have the power to do this because you can speak its secret language.' Children asked me if the creature could answer. I said yes. That would make the situation of the conversation more believable for them. I was also asked if a different creature could be questioned in every line, and I said yes to that too. Some children might be more inspired if they could rove over the whole realm of creatures instead of being obliged to stay with one. I told the children they needn't use rhyme, even though Blake's poem did. It was usual for poems to rhyme when 'The Tyger' was written, but most poems written now don't rhyme. Blake wrote a lot of non-rhyming poems too. I suggested as a form for their poems a series of questions, like those Blake asks the tiger. If they wished, they could also repeat certain words the way Blake does.

And here are two responses to the idea from the twenty he supplies:

Dog, where did you get that bark?
Dragon, where do you get that flame?
Kitten, where did you get that meow?
Rose, where did you get that red?
Bird, where did you get those wings?

Snake, snake, hiding in the thick bush forest.
Sometimes surrounding the trunk of a tree like rope or string.
What kind of head do you have?
Because I see only a funny thing on your front end.
What kind of teeth do you have . . . you can't laugh and you
   can't sing.
What kind of movement do you have?
Because I see no foot, no claws, no legs.

Koch's sequence is: a powerful poem (one that adult readers of poetry enjoy and wish to communicate) is presented to children; it becomes accessible because it is not analysed in full (though questions are often raised by the class and are discussed) and because the written response to the poem is simple enough for children of all abilities to attempt, while the structure of the original poem helps to support the children in what they wish to say. Other examples Koch uses are: A Mad Wish (using a sonnet by Dante); An Invitation (using a Shakespeare song); A List of Everything Happening In The World At This Moment (from a Whitman poem).

There are many poems like 'The Tyger' that have a structure, or arrangement, that is clearly apparent to pupils: they can see how the poet has organized the poem, and can use the same organization in a poem of their own. The traditional formal arrangements (the ones many teachers ask children to use) are metrical (ballad-form, iambic pentameter, etc.) and stanzaic (ballad, sonnet, etc.), and involve very complex manipulations that are usually easier to appreciate than they are to reproduce. What we learn from Koch is that there are vastly more ways of organizing a poem than these, many of them structures that are quite familiar patterns of speech. His techniques are transferable to a much wider range of poems than he uses. Examples abound in anthologies, particularly in those which contain more modern poetry. The provision of a simple structure can have a liberating effect on pupils who 'can't write poems', and they can often vary the structure or produce structures of their own. Of course, slickly-written formula writing is as dull as unorganized expression; clearly it's important to try to keep a balance between the formal and the expressive dimensions.

Closer to home, two recently published books by Sandy Brownjohn (a teacher in an ILEA primary school) provide some lively and original ideas for structure – support techniques for poetry writing (*Does It Have to Rhyme?* and *What Rhymes With Secret?*) and Mike Rosen's book *I See A Voice* is a serious attempt to encourage pupils to look at the craft of poetry and stimulate thoughts about what to say. However, effective suggestions of this sort can be put together simply by using the poems in anthologies published for schools like the two teacher-made examples here. (Obviously the idea of providing suggested structures doesn't apply only where a poem is the stimulus for writing; it can apply also where photographs, films, etc. or first-hand experience offer starting-points.)

Example one

DAYS WHEN

NATURE
We have neither Summer nor Winter
Neither Autumn nor Spring.

We have instead the days
When gold sun shines on the lush green canefields –
Magnificently.

The days when the rain beats like bullets on the roofs
And there is no sound but the swish of water in the gullies
And trees struggling in the high Jamaica winds.

Also there are the days when the leaves fade from off guango
    trees
And the reaped canefields lie bare and fallow in the sun.

But best of all there are the days when the mango and the
logwood blossom.

When the bushes are full of the sound of bees and the scent of
honey,
When the tall grass sways and shivers to the slightest breath of
air,
When the buttercups have paved the earth with yellow stars
And beauty comes suddenly and the rains have gone.
(H. D. Carberry)

The place described in this poem doesn't have seasons of the
sort Britain has. The poet uses the words 'days when . . .' to
break up his description of the weather in the place he is
describing, and wherever you live, even in the city, you can do
the same. For example:

'In Winter we have *days when* the greeny-grey fog blots out
the sign over Marl's butcher's shop,
and there are *days when* the drains are blocked with leaves so
the cars go through the water up to their hubcaps . . .'

You could write about one season, or about all four, and you
might want to have a line starting, like the poet's – 'But *best of
all* there are the *days when* . . .'
(Or you could have lines starting, 'But the worst of all are the
days when . . .') You may prefer to write about a place you
know other than London.

Example two

COME ALIVE!

RAINTREE
The hope of the river
is never to be frozen
the aim of the trees
is the top of the sky
the wish of the wind
is to be somewhere else
the fear of the rain
is how it will die
(Jean Meyer)

112

In this poem, the poet gives human feelings to river, trees, sky, wind and rain. She imagines them having human feelings, having *person*alities. This idea is called *Person*ification.

Using non-human things (like a car or a stone or clouds, for example) write a short poem using the pattern of 'Raintree'. The pattern is:

> The hope of . . .
> is . . .
> The aim of . . .
> is . . .
> The wish of . . .
> is . . .
> The fear of . . .
> is . . .

When you have filled the pattern with your own ideas, you can extend it yourself, with words like love, dream, anger, worry. (Then make up a title for it that gets your readers thinking . . .)

Read through one of the poetry books with a partner. See if you can find a poem which uses *Personification* to make a non-human thing speak, think or feel.

Most of the continuous writing that pupils do in school is the written equivalent of convergent thinking. It's done with a concern for accuracy, it seeks to approach teacher-set norms, and it's done as part of clearly defined tasks. What is true for continuous writing holds even more strongly for the smaller, more discrete, kinds of writing like notes, answers to questions and exercises of various kinds. It seems important, therefore, that a poetry curriculum should include opportunities to use words in a way that is, on the face of it, non-productive, but is experimental, playful, funny, even daring. This kind of activity has clear connections with poetic uses of language, and without it pupils may come to regard poems as merely another category of teacher-provided school text, and miss the qualities that actually make poetic manipulations of words unique. Such games will stress the flexibility of language and its odd habit of falling into patterns of meaning, sound and rhythm. Pupils can knock words into shapes, invent them, mutilate them, extend them, redraw them, destroy them. The logic of sentences can be subverted, producing nonsense that has its own lunatic sense, double-entendres, jokes, puns and images that arise as the

Word Bans

What if one day the government abolished the words
    'four'
    'for'
and 'fore'
and said from now on everyone must say 'five'.
What would people say?
    What for? becomes What five?
    Forget becomes Fiveget.
    Forefinger becomes Fivefinger.

KNIFE AND   ?

Think of some more.
Invent some other changes.
e.g. In space you cannot stand or lie – you float.
    Ban 'sit', 'stand' and 'lie'.
    Write 'float'.

    Let sleeping dogs float
    Do you underfloat?
    Float up when I come into the room

semantic function of the words pulls against their syntactic role. Cut-ups of prose, found-poems, word-association and word-substitution games can reveal the ambiguity and constant potential for surprise that words have, and the fun that comes along the way is not wholly different from the pleasure we have in reading rhymed and metrically-arranged patterns in the work of serious poets. Provided that the status of the activity is kept firmly experimental, there seems no reason why such games[5] shouldn't lead into work with rhythms, metres, rhymes, similes, alliteration and even those figures of speech whose names are so hard to remember.

It's instructive for teachers, while walking round the British

Museum, to encounter the displays of authors' and musicians' manuscripts. Our eyes have become so attuned to highly-finished artefacts that the messy, scrawly, blotted pages of Beethoven's or James Joyce's early drafts can come as something of a shock. But the message is clear: if we want pupils to engage seriously with writing poems, there's going to be mess, there are going to be dead ends – in other words, there's going to be re-drafting. If Joyce found it difficult, it's unlikely that a member of 3B will be able, after forty minutes or one homework, to produce a neatly-written and completed poem *that is the best s/he is capable of*. Yet re-drafting poses such problems of organization of time, organization of the classroom and of teacher-intervention, that it's much easier to justify than implement throughout out practice in English.

Perhaps the most powerful reasons for making re-drafting an expected element in poetry-writing classes are:

- that often the pupils are under too much pressure in ordinary school work to be able to re-draft, and certainly examination technique encourages the hit-and-run method of composition (which is itself part of a tradition of rhetoric rather than a tradition of creative writing – an interesting digression that isn't really relevant here but has managed to survive the re-drafting of this chapter);
- that a sharpened awareness of *how* a thing is being said leads to a consideration, or re-consideration, of *what* is being said, and in poetry the *how* and the *what* are at their closest conjunction in the whole field of writing;
- that the satisfaction of improving your writing (by adding, changing, juggling, deleting) probably comes more readily when you work on poetry because – to put it crudely – there's less stuff to mess about with and minor changes can make major differences to how a poem sounds.

What follows is a list of eight very modest ideas for making the re-drafting process a possibility for younger pupils that won't weigh them down too much, together with a printed version of Blake's first draft of 'The Tyger'. As a visionary poem, and one that was originally published with a beautiful illustration as an integral part of the conception, it has such an inspired, spontaneous, almost inevitable quality that one might have thought it owed little to deliberate reworking.

Paul Ashton and David Marigold

1 Drafting a poem together on the blackboard with the class contributing alternatives.

2 Looking at examples of adult writers' drafts (poets'/teachers') to show: (a) that there is nothing to be ashamed of in reworking; and (b) what re-drafting actually involves and what difference it makes.

3 Providing an audience other than the teacher for the writing, to give the drafting a particular intention.

4 Distinguishing between proof-reading (improving spelling, punctuation and handwriting) and re-drafting for meaning and style.

5 Providing copies of a thesaurus[6] to help pupils find alternative words.

6 Intervening tactfully during the writing, rather than always reserving remarks until it's finished.

7 Having pupils exchange work in progress with friends in the class for comments and suggestions.

8 Making priorities in drafting, and being prepared to sacrifice one good quality in the writing for the sake of another, if a pupil has little confidence. Drafting might involve *at any one time* only one of such points as layout, logic, 'voice', rhythm, imagery, etc.

```
Tyger Tyger burning bright
In the forests of the night
What immortal hand or eye
~~Dare Could~~ frame thy fearful symmetry
        ~~Burnt in~~
        ~~In what~~ distant deeps or skies        Burnt in distant deeps or skies
~~The cruel Burnt the~~ fire of thine eyes        The cruel fire of thine eyes
        On what wings dare he aspire              Could heart descend or wings aspire
        What the hand dare sieze the fire         What the hand dare seize the fire


                                                    dare he ~~smile laugh~~
        And what shoulder & what art              And ~~did he laugh~~ his work to see
        Could twist the sinews of thy heart
        And when thy heart began to beat
        What dread hand & what dread feet


        ~~Could fetch it from the furnace deep~~
        ~~And in thy horrid ribs dare sleep~~
        ~~In the well of sanguine woe~~
        ~~In what clay & in what mould~~
        ~~Were thy eyes of fury rolld~~
        Where              where                                ankle
        ~~What~~ the hammer ~~what~~ the chain    What the ~~shoulder~~ what the knee
        In what furnace was thy brain             Dare
                              dread grasp         ~~Did~~ he who made the lamb make thee
        What the anvil what ~~arm arm grasp clasp~~   When the stars threw down their spears
        Dare ~~Could~~ its deadly terrors ~~clasp grasp~~ clasp   And waterd heaven with their tears[7]
```

Tyger tyger burning bright
In the forests of the night
What immortal hand & eye
    frame
Dare form thy fearful symmetry

It follows that if we require pupils to take this amount of trouble with their writing, we have a responsibility to preserve, display or publish the work, so that it's taken seriously at all stages. School and Class magazines, wall-displays and poetry performances are a feature of many departments' work.

In an article by Pat Chambers[8] called 'Writing Full Circle' he describes the effects of using poems written by pupils as objects of serious study and appreciation by other pupils in the same class. It seems also a valuable idea to ask a pupil who has written a poem to write an account of how it came to be or explain difficult passages in it. Here's an example by a 13-year-old from *City Lines*.

Who is That Woman?

Who is that woman?
Don't know.
Well, I heard she lives
down the street. And
she just moved in, she
looks kind of friendly,
but I don't know. Somehow
her face seems quite natural,
but I don't know.
She smiles, if you smile,
she smiles at the sun,
and runs up and down
the street, energetically.
She is so sympathetic,
asking no questions,
demanding nothing of us.
But I don't know.
I heard she comes from Cyprus,
and does not speak our language.
She wanders sadly home,
looks back,
but there is no-one to be seen.

117

She listens,
trying to catch a few words.
Silently, silently
the door shuts.
I don't know.
(Sonia Vigo)

How I came to write this poem was from a childhood memory I used to have. I remembered the woman very clearly; she lived in my village in Spain. I thought she was lonely, and at times I felt sorry for her. Rumours went round the village she was mad, and that she came from another planet. Of course that was nonsense and childish. But the men in my village really believed this, and the women as well. The children used to tease her a lot. But she tried to make friends with them. I remember that woman so well, that she will always stay in my mind as a special woman. She could cope with loneliness, and she could understand what was happening. But she was not mad, she was just unhappy, because I think she was not loved by anyone.

Assuming that pupils are given a variety of opportunities, like those described above, to read and work on poems and to work on the writing on their own, what further support can we provide in order to encourage close study of individual poems? The ancient method of setting half-a-dozen uninspiring questions on a poem to which pupils, after perfunctory preparation, provide solo written answers, has long been recognized as the best way to kill poetry stone dead. In our view, writing *about* poems, in the first three years at least, ought to be, like the Greater-Crested Grebe, extremely rare. We should expect what writing there is to be homely, casual and exploratory rather than formal, polished and expository. And even this kind of writing is only likely to be effective if it follows a chance to talk about the poem or poems at some length and in some detail.

While some teachers are able to achieve considerable and consistent success in getting pupils talking about a poem simply by handing it over and saying 'go', this strategy clearly doesn't work for every class on every occasion. Many teachers are now making use of a range of game-like devices to 'scaffold' a shared reading and discussion of a poem by pupils in pairs or small groups. The intention behind these activities is to encourage pupils to hang around the poem together and try out their understandings and misunderstandings of it. Some of these activities (those involving 'deletions' of various kinds; 'sequencing'; 'pupil question-setting'; 'boundary-marking') have been found particularly successful as ways of encouraging pupils to think and talk about how poems work.

Here is an example of the device of mixing into a poem a chunk (or chunks) from something else. The pupils are asked in pairs or in a small group, to identify the alien chunk and be prepared to explain their decision.

THE PROJECTIONIST'S NIGHTMARE

This is the projectionist's nightmare:
A bird finds its way into the cinema,
finds the beam, flies down it,
smashes into a screen depicting a garden,
a sunset and two people being nice to each other.
The wrinkled sea beneath him crawls;
He watches from his mountain walls,
And like a thunderbolt he falls.
Real blood, real intestines, slither down
the likeness of a tree.
'This is no good,' screams the audience,
'This is not what we came to see.'
(Brian Patten)

(The alien chunk here is three lines from Tennyson's 'The Eagle'.) The bit inserted into the poem could be difficult or easy to spot; in either case the task for the children is to articulate what the differences are, so that they may suddenly find themselves discussing line-length, tone and vocabulary, as well as the context of the poem.

It is extremely hard to generalize about 'progress' over three years in an area where even the tentative framing of norms begs so many questions. Essentially we feel that the same *kinds* of activity – wide reading, choosing and 'displaying' poems, more focused reading, playing with words, writing and working on your own poems and having them attended to in some way – need to recur in a cyclical pattern, but that poems presented by the teacher will become more adult in content and more complex in organization over the same period. How a department actually assembles its programme so as to incorporate the full range of poetry activities will depend on the form of curricular organization it prefers:

– special 'free-standing' poetry lessons (once a fortnight?);
– poetry given a special place within a number of topics or themes in each year;
– special poetry-only units (given a 2–3 week space?) in each year.

The common word here is 'special'; as the experience of many departments is that the amount of poetry that pupils read and write tends to diminish under other curriculum pressures unless special attention is given to keeping it firmly established. The same experience, though, shows that the rewards for this effort can be enormous, both in terms of individual pupils' development and for the creative life of an English department. There is a kind of truth in Keats's stern dictum, that 'if poetry comes not as naturally as the leaves to a tree, it had better not come at all', and Cole Porter expressed a different kind of truth when he wisecracked that the only inspiration he needed was a phone call from his producer. Somewhere between the two, as usual, the lesson starts.

Notes

1 K. Koch, *Wishes, Lies and Dreams*, Vintage Books, New York, 1971.
2 The best way to get hold of a poet is through the 'Writers in Schools' scheme, which is now administered through regional art associations. G.L.A.A., which covers the London area, is at 25, Tavistock Place, London, WC1.
3 K. Koch, *Rose, Where Did You Get That Red?*, Vintage Books, New York, 1973.
4 A public school in New York.
5 The example here is taken from *Playing with Words*, published by and available from the ILEA English Centre, Sutherland Street, London, SW1.
6 For instance, J. Green, *The Word Hunter's Companion. A First Thesaurus*, Basil Blackwell, Oxford, 1977.
7 Taken from the pages of Blake's notebook, printed in this form in B. Phythian (ed.), *Considering Poetry*, Hodder & Stoughton, London, 1970.
8 In *The English Magazine*, no. 9, Spring 1982.

Anthologies

The New Dragon Book of Verse, ed. Harrison and Stuart-Clarke, Oxford University Press.
Poems, ed. Harrison and Stuart-Clarke, Oxford University Press.
Junior Voices, Books 1–4, ed. Summerfield, Penguin, Harmondsworth.
New Ships, ed. Wilson, Oxford University Press.
Voices, Books 1–3, ed. Summerfield, Penguin, Harmondsworth.
Dragonsteeth and *Tapestry*, ed. Williams, Edward Arnold, London.
Ways of Talking, ed. Jackson, Ward Lock, London.
Caribbean Anthology, ed. Cocking and Goody (ILEA Learning Materials Service, Highbury Station Rd, London, N1; pack of anthologies, with cassette tapes and Teachers' Book).
Hey Mr Butterfly, ed. Aston (ILEA LMS, address as above).
City Lines, ed. Ashton *et al.*, ILEA English Centre.
Bluefoot Traveller, ed. Berry, Harrap, London.
Penguin Book of Women Poets, ed. Cosman, Keefe and Weaver, Penguin, Harmondsworth.
A Book of Women Poets, ed. Barnstone and Barnstone, Schocken Books, New York.
Indian Poetry Today, Indian Council for Cultural Relations, New Delhi (available from Soma Books, 38, Kennington Lane, London, SE11).
The Iron Muse, Topic Records (27, Nassington Road, London, NW3).
Ye Mariners All, Argo (115, Fulham Road, London, SW3).
Wishes, Lies and Dreams, Koch, Vintage Books (available from Chelsea House Publishers, 133, Christopher Street, New York, N.Y. 10014).
Rose, Where Did You Get That Red?, Koch, Vintage Books (available from Random House Inc. 201, E 50th Street, New York, N.Y. 10022).
Does It Have to Rhyme? and *What Rhymes with Secret?*, Brownjohn, Hodder & Stoughton.
I See a Voice, ed. Rosen, Hutchinson/Thames TV.
Playing with Words, ILEA English Centre.
The Rattle Bag, ed. Heaney and Hughes, Faber & Faber.

9 Literature in the fourth and fifth years of the secondary school

Maureen Worsdale

Many secondary school English teachers would subscribe to the view that if they are to enable their pupils to use language effectively they will be wise to identify the abilities children and adolescents already have, and to work from there.

In reading literature, however, we have perhaps been less aware of the extent and importance of the knowledge the children themselves bring to the task, both as readers of literature and as writers of essays. If we can find ways of identifying this knowledge, we may become able to give our pupils greater confidence in their own abilities, and also to be more specific in our suggestions for improvement and development.

Two methods of analysis that I have found helpful concern the level of generalization reached in essays, and the range of knowledge and experience that have informed reading.

In considering levels of generalization, I have adopted the model developed by James Britton.[1] This sees the least generalized writing as a form of record. In writing at this level about literature, pupils reproduce almost the exact words of the text, and are unable to distance themselves from it; they offer a chronological, often first-person, account, a running commentary on the text.

At the next stage, the 'report', pupils are able to describe the text in their own words, but without distinguishing between significant and less significant events within the narrative.

At the level of 'generalized narrative', there is some apprehension of the relative importance of events. The pupils do not directly indicate this awareness, but imply it in their retelling of the story. Although still bound by particular incidents in the narrative, and by the order in which they occur, pupils nevertheless seem able to detect patterns of repetition and to express them in generalized form.

A further level is the 'analogic, low level of generalization', in

122

which loosely general statements are made, and the principle of organization has become classificatory, rather than chronological. Parts of the structure of the work are perceived, but are not related in such a way as to show perception of the structure as a whole.

Most fourth and fifth year pupils do not pass beyond this stage to reach the 'analogic' level proper although more could and should do so. Here generalizations are hierarchically or logically related, the writer can distinguish the most significant events from others, and can generalize about structure, theme, characterization, and so forth.

The further levels in Britton's model, concerned with 'speculative' and 'theoretical' writing, would usually not be achieved by members of this age group, and I shall therefore not consider them here.

The importance of reaching the analogic level lies in the intellectual freedom it affords the pupil; freedom to express concepts through other concepts without being unduly tied to the concrete example, and perception of the over-all structure of a text, which allows more complete understanding of the work through seeing it as a totality.

This model is useful in helping teachers to chart the changes of level of abstraction in pupils' work and to recognize and encourage movement to higher levels, and between levels, from generalization to the concrete instance.

In trying to identify the kinds of knowledge children bring to their reading, I have made use of Roland Barthes's account of the 'codes' embodied in works of literature.[2] According to his account, narratives are constructed by readers in the light of their knowledge of the codes employed. The kinds of knowledge and experience people bring to their reading are, he suggests:

(a) discernment of character: the means we use to 'read' the characters of those around us, and also to understand characters in novels;
(b) insight into outcomes of action: how things usually turn out. This knowledge derives from experience and also from reading and hearing narrative;
(c) expectation of being mistaken, of things being more complicated than they seem: awareness and enjoyment of being mystified and the satisfaction which comes from solving problems;

123

(d) knowledge of symbols, gained from our experience that one thing can represent another. This may derive from many sources, including literature;
(e) knowledge of societies and cultures, especially our own; everyday and 'common' knowledge, specialist and esoteric knowledge.

These are the codes, or forms of knowledge and experience, through which we re-create the text in our minds; they derive as much from our ways of coping with ordinary experience as from reading and there can surely be few adolescents whose grasp of them is not extensive. Although teachers should acknowledge the extent of this grasp, nevertheless it can be developed and refined.

Readers of long experience, whose knowledge of the codes and conventions of reading is highly developed, will be able to discern what a particular writer requires of the reader. They will know that they are expected to look for deeper significance in the text than the surface pattern of events. For example, in 'Through the Tunnel' by Doris Lessing,[3] we are expected to construct a picture of the boy Jerry's problems which cause him to risk his life in an adventure neither witnessed by, nor recounted to, anyone. We do this by constructing the characters of the fatherless boy and his mother and abstracting from their actions and interaction their feelings of guilt, responsibility and inadequacy towards each other and the effect of these feelings on Jerry's relationships with his fellows. The piece can be 'understood' purely as an adventure story, but, in order to make full sense of the boy's actions, which as experienced readers we assume is possible, we must be aware of the relative significance of events, indications of character and situation, and must generalize from these to a fuller picture of the past and present lives of both characters. At the same time, we can generalize about the possible future effect of his secret achievement on the boy's image of himself.

What does the less experienced reader make of these demands? Kay wrote this piece at the start of her fourth year, on 'Through the Tunnel', one of her favourite stories.

> *Why was Jerry willing to risk his life or permanent injury just to swim through the tunnel?*
> 1 Jerry decideds that he must risk his life or permanent injury to swim through the tunnel.

2 Jerry as an only boy without a father is very guitly about leaving his mother on her own and feels obliged to stay with her when ever she goes somewhere.

3 When Jerry sees this hidden cove or bay he wants to go there. He asks his mother and she says he may go but she is very worride about him but she says to herself, 'Of course he's old enough to be safe without me.' and carries on down to the main beach.

4 Jerry at first is guilty at leaving her and keeps watching her till she is safly on the beach. Then he starts down the cliff to the bay.

5 The first thing he does is swim out to the open sea to see if his mother is safe. She is so he swims back to the bay.

6 Jerry now sees some french boys above him but unlike other boys he keeps his distance. It is not until the boys smile and wave at him does he go over, but when he gets there instead of being friendly towards them he gives a pleading smile.

7 The french boys tried to ignor him but Jerry is happy to be with them.

8 The boys began to dive and Jerry dived too and feels he is accepted.

9 The boys swim through a tunnel and Jerry can not and when the boys returned Jerry tries to attract attention in an unnatural way.

10 The boys run off leaving Jerry on his own. Jerry is upset about this, for it had probably happened before, and he crie's.

11 When he gets home he demands some goggles and his mother gives in very easily.

12 With the goggles he could tunnel, now he must train his breathing.

13 For days he tried and he got nose bleeds and his mother got fussy but his aim was to swim through the tunnel to prove to himself that he could protect his mother and to gain confidence in himself.

Despite its brevity, untidiness, shaky spelling and illogical paragraphing, the use of language and sentence structure suggests that the poor third-year English report she received derived from underachievement rather than lack of ability. My first task was to estimate what she is able to bring to her reading.

It is clear that she possesses insight into character and the ability to sum up a person's motives (a). Paragraph two, for example, neatly sums up Jerry's attitude towards his mother. This summary of character is extended in paragraphs four and five where she is able to support her generalization that he feels guilty by identifying several manifestations of the guilt. Again in his dealings with the foreign boys the version of the character which she presents acts with consistent awkwardness. The speculation that he has probably been deserted before reveals an ability to extend character reading beyond the confines of the story, as is also shown in paragraph two where Kay suggests that Jerry feels obliged to stay with his mother 'whenever she goes somewhere'. Paragraph three shows some insight into the character of the over-anxious mother, trying to reassure herself.

Insight into outcomes of action and ability to grasp plot (b) are evident where she suggests that this is probably not the first time Jerry has been rejected by other boys, and in her economical references in the first three paragraphs to the relevant facts about Jerry which contribute to his state of mind: being an only child, fatherless and guilt-ridden. She also reveals ability to grasp the plot in selecting events to go into her generalized narrative, and these are, in the main, the significant or key points in the story.

Her understanding of how a one-parent child might feel, and her apprehension of Jerry's anguished sense of responsibility towards his mother, reveal Kay's knowledge of her own society and its culture (e). The difficulties of the single parent, torn between providing proper parental care and being over-protective in her dual role, are also grasped although Kay has not been able to generalize about these feelings and, in paragraph three, quotes the mother's own words instead. Knowledge of present-day culture is also shown in paragraph six when she points out that Jerry, in keeping his distance from the foreign boys, is acting unlike other boys, and that his pleading smile is a mistake; but she fails to connect explicitly this mistake with the boys' ignoring and leaving him, and with Jerry's acting in an 'unnatural way'.

Moving on to the generalization level of the essay: paragraphs eleven, twelve and the first half of thirteen are merely at the level of the report; purely narrative and also rather muddled. She is trying to express the difficulties that Jerry encounters, in order to give weight to her theory about the boy's motives, but she cannot escape from a chronological account of what he had to do or differentiate trivial from more important detail.

However, the generalization level of the essay as a whole is 'generalized narrative' in that there is some apprehension of the relative importance of events, but it is implied rather than stated. In her first sentence, for example, Kay does not merely re-state the essay question. The emphasis is on 'must', and this is a far stronger word than the 'willing' of the essay title, suggesting that Jerry is impelled from within. The implication is that she will tell us why he 'must' in the rest of the essay. Instead, the chronological sequence of the story is followed and reasons are not explicitly put forward until the end. Yet really she is throughout implicitly answering the demands of the essay question and giving reasons for the boy's actions. She just omits to make the kind of general statement early on in the essay which would have made her intention clear and given added relevance to the rest. The meeting with the local boys, in paragraphs six to nine, is at the same generalized narrative level; the incident is obviously recognized as important, as a key event in the story, from which further events derive, but Kay is unable to generalize sufficiently to pinpoint its importance. She is able only to narrate what occurs.

Nevertheless, she is able to rise above generalized narrative in places: for example in paragraphs eight and nine, where the speculation is offered that Jerry feels 'accepted', that his behaviour was 'unnatural', and again in paragraph ten when she suggests that he has probably been deserted before. She sometimes reaches the analogic (low) level of generalization, as when she connects Jerry's being an only child and fatherless to the boy's guilt about leaving his mother alone, and the obligation he feels to accompany her. All this is achieved in one short sentence. The end of the essay, where she sums up the reasons for Jerry's endeavour, also reaches this higher level. An ability also to move up and down the levels from generalization to concrete instance is displayed in paragraphs four and five. Here Kay again makes the generalization that Jerry's obsessive behaviour derives from 'guilt', and the concrete examples of how symptoms of this guilt are manifested in his behaviour: the recounting of the things he had to do 'at first' are illustrations to back the generalization.

However, Kay's powers of generalization do need developing to give her greater intellectual freedom. Without the higher levels of generality the pupil is a prisoner of the concrete example, of the necessity to express concepts through themselves and not through other concepts. It is not enough just to show Kay that comments on a text are better prefaced with an abstraction to show where they are leading and where they fit in with her concept of the structure of the text as a whole. She needs to be more aware of the generalization level in her essay and of the usefulness of generalization in real situations.

One way of helping her might be to place her in a small group for discussion work on literature, where corporate generalization often emerges. This process can be seen below when a member of a group places a construction on a character or incident. Other members demand to know exactly what is meant and then later this same construction is tried in a different context by other members of the group. The character of Baines in *The Basement Room*[4] is being discussed by a group of fourth years:

Paul: He always wanted someone, Baines, with a . . . er . . . well . . . he was three different people: one with Mrs Baines . . . with Philip and with that Emmy, he was different with each of them.
Peter: What do you mean by that?

There follows a teasing out of just what Paul does mean and he is forced to cite examples; then, later, when the group has passed on to Mrs Baines:

Peter: I think if you go back to the part where Mr Baines has three different personalities. . . . I think she has too, don't you think? Because one minute she'd be giving orders and . . .

Peter benefited from listening to the different slants that other minds can give on a problem. If Baines can be three different people then perhaps Mrs Baines can be too. Peter tries out this construction on a new situation to see if it fits; he adapts the generalization to another set of data. He is using these fresh generalizations to develop and extend his own thinking, and, of course, exploring ideas orally is a means of sorting them out before committing them to paper. Kay needs to develop the ability to move with ease up and down the various levels of generalization: to move from the analogic to the concrete instance and back again, which group work should help her to achieve. In this way she can, by moving up the levels, gain control over material through achieving an over-view, and by moving down through the levels become more involved with it, through exploring its particularity.

The higher levels of generalization require the ability to discern the structure of a text through differentiating the key points of story, character or atmosphere from less important detail. The key points are the growth points, out of which further action or development emerges within the text. Kay does recognize what is important; she perceives more in a text than she is able to convey adequately in words. She needs to be shown the advantage of scribbling down ideas in rough prior to writing so that she can see beforehand what she wants to say.

Her sense of story-line and character are quite well developed, as is the social and cultural knowledge she is able to bring to stories. Obviously, more experience of reading would increase her knowledge of possible outcomes, awareness of symbols and so on. Gaps between the knowledge and experience the pupils can bring to a text, and the kind of knowledge and experience the text demands, in order for readers to be able to recreate it for themselves, can, again, often be bridged by the small group. Set the task of formulating questions about the text, for the teacher to answer, members of the group discover they know more than they had realized.

There is an interdependence between our ability to generalize and our knowledge of the codes. It is only through an act of generalization, involving searching out information, instances of behaviour and action and abstracting from these that we come to a knowledge of character, plot and theme. It is also an act of abstraction to recognize and understand elements of our own and others' culture in stories. In the same way it is only through our knowledge of character, plot, theme and culture that our discernment of the key points in a story comes and therefore our ability to perceive structure and to reach higher levels of generalization. Progress in reaching the higher levels of general- ization, achieving fluidity between these levels and development of the codes of reading happen in parallel.

Going over written work with the pupil and pointing out her existing ability to generalize, and the knowledge she is able to bring to the text, will help most of all and can have a liberating effect. Through making explicit an activity which appears to be natural the pupil gains in self-awareness. Also, becoming aware of what readers do to a text and what they bring to it makes it easier for the pupil to see how and why some texts are difficult, and why increased reading experience can help.

What Kay already perceives, knows and understands needs to be acknowledged. She needs to be shown how relevant the skills she already possesses are to reading, to talking and to writing about what she reads.

Notes

1 J. N. Britton, T. Burgess, A. McLeod and H. Rosen, *The Development of Writing Abilities 11–16*, Macmillan, London, 1975.
2 Roland Barthes in S/Z refers to this knowledge or skill as the codes of literature, which he groups under the headings of semic, proairetic, hermeneutic, symbolic and referential or cultural codes.
3 Doris Lessing, 'Through the Tunnel', in *Short Stories of Our Time* (ed. D. Barnes), Harrap, London, 1963.
4 Graham Greene, 'The Basement Room', in *Modern English Short Stories*, ed. D. Hudson, Oxford University Press, 1972.

10   Comics and magazines for schoolchildren

Paul Hoggart

Problems and approaches

The whole field of popular literature, specifically the kind that is produced primarily for financial gain, remains a blind-spot within academic study. There are three academic areas that might reasonably have been expected to address such texts: literary studies, education and sociology-based disciplines such as cultural and media studies, but although all have produced a certain amount of work in the field, it has generally been regarded as marginal within each discipline. There is little continuity and less debate, and the total bibliography of a field such as the one I am concerned with here would disgrace a minor poet and a comparable genre in film alike.

Particularly odd has been the reluctance of Marxist literary critics to take on the literature that the proletariat themselves read. Brushing awkwardly against the issue, Eagleton,[1] in my opinion, evades it by 'sleight of logic'. Williams in *Politics and Letters*[2] describes how he came to question the canon in the early 1970s but has not, to my knowledge, done much work on popular literature. This doubt about the canon, moreover, was a little delayed considering that a certain amount of work on spy and detective fiction was done at the Centre for Contemporary Cultural Studies in Birmingham (scarcely mentioned in *Politics and Letters*) in the mid-1960s. Recent thinking, one suspects, has been a response to theoretical pressure from outside literary studies.

The immediate practical consequence of this silence within English Studies and, indeed, on most English PGCE courses, is that English teachers have little, if any, formal knowledge of working-class reading habits, either historically or as they impinge on the lives of the children they teach.

Marxist approaches to popular literature, new and older, share

131

with Leavisite commentaries a model of the relationship between text and reader inherited from the numerous evangelical commentaries on 'licentious' and 'seditious' publications of the nineteenth century. Because the spiritual/moral/ideological meanings are likely to deprave/enervate/mystify they constitute a form of disease against which the potential victim must be inoculated through some form of education.

The natural complement to this view is the long-standing tradition within British cultural analysis that has sought to isolate the 'authentic' from the 'mass' elements in working-class culture. Early work in cultural studies, by Hoggart,[3] for instance, and Hall and Whannel,[4] represented an important development over the kind of polarity asserted by F. R. Leavis and Denys Thompson,[5] which separated a disappearing folkloric (good) culture from a ravening industrial (bad) culture, by locating the battles between the expressive and the phoney *within* industrialized culture itself. I would wish to push this boundary back a bit further by arguing that there is evidence of conflict between these poles within the most commercial and formulaic cultural products and that it is one source of their success. There is, generally speaking, a reluctance to face the possibility that brazenly commercial culture might, to some extent, be central to people's lives, particularly to the lives of the working classes at whom most of it is directed. This is a particular fault of certain recent sociological commentaries, which, in properly resisting the 'negativity' of 'mass-culture' theory, whether Leavisite or Frankfurt School Marxist, misleadingly claim that bourgeois-controlled commercial culture is not important.

The desire to resurrect and to generate 'authentic' forms of working-class writing has led to some extremely interesting and valuable work, and I do not wish to detract from this in any way. The work of Centerprise in Hackney and projects such as those described by Parkinson[6] and Worpole[7] represent a fruitful blending of British 'culturalism' and Althusserian Marxism, particularly as developed in the work of Freire,[8] from which the more vituperative academic gladiators might learn much. There is, however, a danger in too readily separating the elements of cultural experience. I hope to show here that the success of popular literature resides at least *in part*, in the way it incorporates 'authentic' elements of working-class experience, in its ability to 'swallow' the oppositional and the co-operative.

Most approaches to popular literature presuppose almost total passivity on the part of the consumer. There are two levels at which this needs to be questioned. First, readers do, to a certain extent, exercise control over content by choosing *not* to buy. The history of the medium is littered with the corpses of *failed* attempts to impose constructions of reality. This is a crude and arbitrary form of selection of material; far subtler is the intervention of the writers and graphic artists, who are to be distinguished from the publishers. Many share the background and preoccupations of their readers, as Baxendale[9] makes abundantly clear, and build them into their material. To be successful, publishers are obliged to *negotiate* meanings with the readership, and we remain largely ignorant as to how this occurs. It is necessary to look much more carefully at the extent to which, for example, ideologies for children that might best suit 'bourgeois hegemony' actually have been internalized within texts. How far are they a site of competitive wrestling over meaning, what Corrigan and Willis[10] refer to as 'battles around the sign'?

The second area in which we need to question the passivity of the reader is in the process of reading itself. The question of differential reading is one that has, at last, begun to open out within literary studies: traditional assumptions that any text offered only one 'correct' reading are, I think, responsible for many teachers' disdain for comics. For middle-class children, reading the *Beano* is associated with a 'phase', the pleasure intensified by parental disapproval, and it is highly unlikely that they identify with the contents of the comic in the same way as the working-class child, for whom it was really written.

Reading in general has a distinctive power in that it is both a communal and a private activity. Comics and magazines offer intense forms of group identification; they locate the reader, sometimes with a ruthless rigidity, within a complex pattern of attitudes and responses. But, because the offer is made privately, the child is free to 'read' the text, to accept or reject its formulations, without *immediate* reference to the expectations of peer group, family or teachers. Almost any schoolchild will tell you, if asked, that they know their comics and magazines are 'silly'. This is not entirely because they think that's what you want to hear, for they are brutally honest or disarmingly ingenuous on many other matters; it is because many children are aware at some level of the limitations and absurdities of what they are being offered. As well as experiencing the pleasure of being personally addressed, the reader has the pleasure, even if it is illusory, of ideological 'window-shopping'.

Much of the work that has been done on children's reading has been characterized by what Corrigan and Willis have called 'the massive confusion of role performance with role internalization'. We need to discover in what ways children actually do 'consume' texts, how far when performing their role as readers they internalize the meanings on offer, and, where they don't, how selections are made. As Angela McRobbie makes clear in her searching analysis of *Jackie*,[11] texts only have the power to *suggest* meanings. We need to know more about when and how they are accepted.

One of the most interesting aspects of the work deriving from 'discourse theory' is that it seeks to explain the organization of emotions *in conjunction with* the organization of political and social consciousness. It is a speciality of all fiction (and most children's commercial literature consists largely of fiction) that it continually offers ways of combining social attitudes with feelings. The discourses of *Bunty* or *Superman* can be employed to 'construct' the perception of a murder, a divorce case or an election campaign in the popular press. Comics are an early stage of a process upon whose success the popular press feeds.

It is one of my purposes here to demonstrate ways in which the comics and magazines that children read in such abundance set the agenda for the popular press, which children read alongside their periodicals anyway. In many respects, the tabloid dailies and the popular Sunday papers are compendia of the bottom shelf at the newsagent's (and sometimes the top one).

John Richmond of the ILEA English Centre did a survey with 87 girls at Vauxhall Manor Girls' Comprehensive school in South London, drawing his samples from the first three years. His findings are reported in 'What do 87 Girls Read?'[12] I used his survey on a comparable group of boys at Hackney Downs Boys' Comprehensive, a school in North London with a similar class and racial balance. Both schools are predominantly working class and have a substantial minority of black (mainly West Indian) students. The sample is, of course, too small to be representative, but it has served as a basis for selecting texts for analysis. The discussion is based on periodicals published at the time the boys' survey was conducted in May 1979.[13] As a final observation, I have just marked over 800 essays submitted by candidates for English Language O level, Mode Three. The influence of this type of literature, particularly on girls' writing, is constantly apparent. Doubtless any English teacher would confirm this.

The market in children's magazines is almost entirely in the hands of two publishers: D. C. Thomson of Dundee, and IPC. The American groups, Marvel and DC, are the only significant exceptions.

Type	IPC	(Day)	D. C. Thomson	(Day)	Marvel/DC
Funny	*Whizzer*	(Mon)	*Dandy*	(Tue)	
	Cheeky	(Mon)	*Beano*	(Thu)	
	Jackpot	**(Thu)**			
Girls'	*Pink*	(Mon)	*Bunty*	(Tue)	
	Oh Boy!	(Thu)	*Mandy*	(Thu)	
	My Guy	(Sat)	*Jackie*	(Thu)	
	Fab 208				
Boys'	*Roy of the Rovers*	(Mon)	*Victor*	(Mon)	*Spiderman*
	Tiger and Scorcher	(Mon)	*Warlord*	(Thu)	*Hulk*
	Shoot	(Mon)			*Superman*
					Batman

All the D. C. Thomson publications listed here are of some antiquity. The IPC funny comic and girls' comic ranges, however, are relatively new. The survey showed clearly that children read comics and magazines in large quantities, alongside newspapers. Both boys and girls read large numbers of funny comics and newspapers, but the sexes diverge, reading other publications aimed specifically at both groups. A clear pattern emerges which is, perhaps, best set out diagrammatically. I have included pornography because, although the Hackney Downs boys may have been too young (or shy) to list it, it is widely read by older boys and can be seen to hold a certain equivalence to girls' magazines in defining sex roles. Solid lines represent continuities of content, dotted lines continuities in the organization of representations of reality.

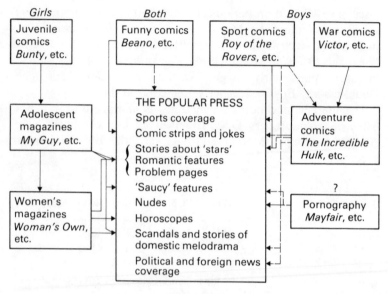

Fig. 10.1

From comics and magazines to newspapers: continuities in 'preferred meanings'

I have borrowed this phrase from Hall,[14] because in the absence of detailed research on the ways children actually *do* read these publications we have to settle for what appear to be the dominant meanings they offer. Like the interpretations offered in the early chapters of Barthes's *Mythologies*, this is not so very far removed from the traditional practices of literary criticism. I have isolated five main types of comic and magazine and shall attempt to suggest ways in which they anticipate the popular press.

(i) *Funny comics*

These comics have a peculiar potency, the more so for being common to the experience of children of most social strata and both sexes. Yet they are more or less exclusively about working-class life (Lord Snooty apart). There are two major themes, which represent different ends of the same continuum. At one end there is an often dignified nostalgia for an age unknown to the readers (if it ever existed in any sense, anyway). At the other is an aggressive, disruptive anti-authoritarian populism. Most stories are united in being about *marginal* characters who lack both responsibilities and power: there are children, animals, grandparents and vagrants, all locked in combat with the agencies of social control: teachers, parents and police.

Orwell noted with amusement the dated nature of many boys' weeklies when he wrote his famous essay. The very titles – *Beano*, *Dandy*, *Whizzer*, *Cor* – suggest that datedness is a continuing feature of comics. It not only pervades the language, and the serial stories ('Black Bob' in *Dandy*, 'Mystery Boy' in *Cheeky*) but it is built into the graphics of the comedy. The Bash Street Kids seem to attend a 1950s Secondary Modern school, as does Little Plum, despite living on an Indian Reservation (both in the *Beano*). Desperate Dan, we are told, lives in Texas, but with its small terraced housing and Victorian street lamps, it looks more like Salford in the 1930s. Presumably these strips originally drew on the experience of their creators, like Leo Baxendale, but they seem to have a force independent of anything that might be taken for reality. They posit a humble working-class version of a golden age and, presumably, lay a kind of sediment in the reader's mind. Nostalgia for an innocent past is, of course, a recurring, if minor, preoccupation of popular newspapers, particularly in the letters columns. The habit is suggested to children in these comics at a stage when they can hardly have anything to be nostalgic about.

At the other end of the scale are the characters who are in a state of permanent struggle with authority. The ideology of Dennis the Menace, The Bash Street Kids and Minnie the Minx is a close parallel with the attitudes of disruptive schoolboys described by Paul Willis[15] and Paul Corrigan, the title of whose book, *Schooling the Smash Street Kids*,[16] deliberately echoes the *Beano* story. Dennis is one of Willis's 'lads', constantly demonstrating the intrinsic worthlessness of the 'softies', Willis's 'lobes'. Much of the struggle centres around attitudes to education and, in both Minnie the Minx and The Bash Street Kids, liberal progressivism is specifically attacked in a way which corresponds directly with the findings of research projects on working-class children's perceptions of 'progressive' education techniques. Most of these stories end in corporal punishment (although not in the IPC publications) and there is a powerful, recurring model of just and inevitable retribution. A clear continuity here is the cartoon strip 'Wack' in the *Sun* about an amiable, skiving young workman. More importantly, the attitudes towards education are present in a degenerate form. Where the ritual resistance to the school as an agent of social control that appears in the *Beano* has vanished, there remains a diffuse anti-intellectualism and hostility to anything that could be considered 'progressive' or 'radical'. Finally, there is an undoubted continuity in the responses that are offered to issues of crime and punishment. Coverage of crime in the newspapers often shares the comics' fascination with illegal acts and preoccupation with the personality of the criminal. Ronald Biggs has the same sort of 'charm' as Dennis the Menace. What the papers cannot supply, however, is the ritual retribution. The law often fails to administer a good slippering over Dad's knee, and this raises the question as to whether public attitudes to punishment, often alarmingly reactionary, are in any way affected by the frustration of an ingrained pattern of retribution which the comics reflect so strongly.

The IPC comics are far more interested in television and constantly refer to it in a way which anticipates the preoccupation with 'personalities' that characterizes women's magazines and popular papers alike.

(ii) *Sport comics*

The survey suggested that although many boys read these regularly, interest wanes along with interest in the funny comics. Perhaps a phase has passed. The overriding concern is with football, and the comics are intensely preoccupied with the cultural values of the game. Several commentators have defined aspects of this and what they mean, both in the history of the game and within the lives of supporters. *Roy of the Rovers*, *Shoot* and the others are entirely concerned with the traditional, pre-aggro forms of support, and where there is opposition it is between the selfless, team-centred ethos of the 'traditional' player and the flash materialism of the 'star'. This is, of course, a constant preoccupation of the press and corresponds to a duality within working-class life, in which the co-operation of the shop-floor and the culture of unions, friendly societies and other working-class institutions are challenged by the external pressure, particularly of advertising, to express the self through consumption. The story of Mervyn Wallace's crisis in *Roy of the Rovers* relates to general controversies within football such as the bedevilment of the careers of George Best and various subsequent *enfants terribles*. These comics appear to give boys a grounding in the discourse of traditional support before they make their excursions into aggro support, if they are going to do so. Like the diffuse nostalgia already noted, it lays a bedrock of emotional/ ideological referents for future use. The foundations of middle age are firmly laid before the 'rebellion' of adolescence. The role of the manager is central here. Roy is the model of the perfect NCO or shop-steward, and his struggles serve as models for all problems surrounding the relationship of individuals and groups. Jock Wallace, manager of Leicester City, presents the issues in a distilled form in *Football*:

> During the war I was part of an eight man unit. Sometimes we had only a handful of rice a day to stay alive, but we managed. Above all we depended on one another. No one in that team could afford to let anyone else down. And that's the kind of attitude I demand from my players. It's all for one and one for all.[17]

Wallace's words indicate another aspect of the sports comics which anticipates the popular newspapers, and that is the way in which language is used to *refine* and *restrict* events within the sport. *Roy of the Rovers* specializes in ludicrous matches in which Melchester storm back from 8–0 down to win in the last second of injury time. The events in a game are heightened and dramatized, but in a very stylized way typified by the stilted comments of the crowd. By the time we reach the match reports in the back pages of the tabloids the accounts of matches are composed entirely from a limited and predictable vocabulary of possibilities ('the ball crashed home from twenty yards', '. . . sent the goalkeeper the wrong way', 'silenced his critics with a dream goal'). This tendency towards the stereotyping and conventional dramatization of events, as well as of people, is extended into the discourse of the next category of comics, adventure comics, but it also penetrates the language in which the press report 'straight' news.

Paul Hoggart

(iii) *Adventure comics*

There are two main kinds of adventure comic: the British war comics, like *Victor* and *Warlord*, and the American superhero comics. War comics did not figure prominently in the Hackney Downs survey, only one boy reading those small square pamphlets with titles like 'Suicide Commando'. Again the tension between older more traditional formulations and newer more aggressive ones is apparent. The face of a captain on the cover of *Victor* – 'This is not going to be easy, chaps' – comes from an old British B-film, whereas a snarling renegade in *Warlord* evokes the American horror-comic. Superhero comics form by far the largest single segment of boys' adventure comics and seem to hold a central position in the development of boys' reading habits. They are equivalent to the phase when girls are reading *My Guy* and *Oh Boy!*, but they are utterly abstracted from reality, where the girls' magazines are locked in a constricting view of it.

These comics are primarily concerned with fantasies of power and the ability to redress wrong by physical force. The villains usually pose a threat to *public* rather than private life, but although we now identify with the forces of law and order, whereas in Dennis the Menace we were invited to identify with anarchic aggression, the model of crime and punishment remains the same. The situation is resolved through violent, ritualized retribution.

These comics also have a long pedigree and are the sanitized descendants of the ghoulish horror comics decribed in Wertham.[18] A mere selection of illustrations from these earlier products was enough to have Wertham's book placed on the restricted list at the British Library. Since the 1960s the market has been defined by the struggle for circulation between the two giant companies: DC (*Superman*, *Batman*, etc.) and Marvel (*Spiderman*, *The Hulk*, etc.). Perry and Aldridge[19] have described this process, noting the elements of deliberate exaggeration, the excitingly lively graphics, the 'liberal philosophizing' and the 'Homeric ring' introduced by Marvel. Although DC comics remain distressingly stilted (and the Star Trek cult suggests this may in itself hold some appeal), they have been forced to adapt, raising the standard of graphics and heightening both the topicality and the element of existential angst in their comics.

The Hulk is probably the most extreme example of the Marvel hero. He is, in fact, an anti-hero and belongs to a tradition which can be seen as a metaphor of the struggle between the ego and the id. Like the werewolves of medieval folk tales, he cannot control his transformations. Inspiring fear, like Frankenstein's monster, he cannot communicate his sensitivity. Like King Kong and Moby Dick he arouses fascination and aggression and is blindly persecuted. Hence, Hulk hates men in uniform.

There is no obvious correspondence for this streak in comics within the popular press, but *The Hulk*, with its ambiguous attitude to the morality of law and order, is exceptional anyway. The angst suffered by nearly all other Marvel heroes – they all have some kind of Achilles heel and periodically writhe in self-doubt – relates to a more general mythology of the star system, which is reflected in the endless features in the papers describing the struggles of the famous and the torments that accompany success.

Superhero comics provide the press with both a vocabulary ('wham', 'bam', etc.) and a model for perceiving conflict within society. 'SLAMMED! THE "WINE AND DINE" MINISTERS – Rap for Labour "high livers"' says the *Sun*, and it is thereby intimated that some Tory Superman has taken up arms against the morally weak and criminal-minded. The crucial point is, however, that over and over again the issues and problems of public life are presented in a form that evokes the discourse of boys' comics. In this respect newspapers propagate the division of emotional and ideological labour between the sexes found in both boys' and girls' comics, but more of that later. The point is that unlike the comics, the newspapers are rarely in a position to supply the ending that the discourse demands. The resolution is perpetually denied. There are, occasionally, exceptions, like the SAS storming of the Iranian Embassy, in which supermen in futuristic uniforms did actually 'zap' a group of 'sinister terrorist fanatics', and the reaction in the popular press was orgasmic. Generally, however, the indefinite suspension of the 'right' ending induces a sense of disillusion and impotent dissatisfaction. It abets a characteristic fatalism, whereby a ritualistic or retributive solution is offered if solicited – 'I think they should sack the lot of them' – but generally it is felt that these things are best left to Superman. Impotent anger is reflected in the reporting of issues of public morality, such as the release of a notorious murderer on parole, in such newspapers as the *Sun*.

Finally, it is worth noting the arrival on the market of a large range of super-heroines. Like the television series, 'Charlie's Angels', they are obdurately sexist, for all their active heroines. Red Sonja is a *Playboy* centrefold in a chain-mail bikini. Ms Marvel drools over her repulsively 'smooth' boyfriend with all the abject doting of the girls in *My Guy*. The *Sun*'s cartoon strip 'Axa' is a direct derivative of the *Red Sonja* style of science fiction comic.

(iv) *Pre-adolescent girls' comics*

The staple ingredients of this range of comics, the most successful of which are *Bunty* and *Mandy*, are stories of happy bands of chums and social melodrama. The most striking and alarming feature of the comics I examined was that the happy bands of chums were invariably middle-class, while the tales of jealousy, rejection, destitution and orphanhood all had working-class heroines. The implication is inescapable: rich girls may enjoy the pleasures of co-operation, sisterhood and organization; the poor must struggle through life's traumas and injustices alone, in the hope of the just reward of the pure in heart. Bob Dixon,[20] among others, has pointed out that this model of class identities is politically diversionary, implying that working-class girls must react passively and in isolation to their fate. The contrast with boys' football comics, the closest equivalent, could hardly be more marked. Where those comics stress the *social* organization of experience and look out from the individual consciousness to the life of groups, stories in *Bunty*, with non-boarding-school-pals heroines, emphasize social fragmentation and focus overwhelmingly on the intense emotional life of individuals. This is carried to the point of caricature in a story, 'A Doll Called Dinkydou' in *Bunty*, about a doll with human thoughts and feelings who is passed from one owner to another.

These comics present two models of the working-class male. One model is paternalistic and gentle and evokes the same kind of 'nostalgia' I have indicated in the funny comics. The other model evokes what Leeson[21] has described as 'The notion of the lower orders as essentially delinquent', which he maintains is a long-standing theme in the literature of children. Many stories take place surrounded by a penumbra of menacing gypsies and crooks of various descriptions. It is not new to point out that girls' comics of all kinds are characterized by their emphasis on the *personal*. These juvenile comics anticipate the forms of women's romantic fiction, but they also foreshadow the assumed division of interest within the popular press. The patterns of focus that characterize *Bunty* and *Mandy* reappear in the emotionally-charged tales of 'battling-grans' and 'tug-of-love babies' that are to be found in the inside pages of the tabloids. For girls the adolescent magazine represents a strange kind of departure, but as with the boys' football comics, the juvenile publications lay a kind of emotional/ideological sediment on which they are invited to 'settle' upon reaching maturity.

(v) *Adolescent girls' magazines*

Of all the categories of comics and magazines read by girls, these are overwhelmingly the most popular. Girls continue to read these avidly into the fourth year, when boys are beginning to lose interest in their own comics and magazines.

For years the leader in the field has been D. C. Thomson's *Jackie*, but it has, relatively recently, been joined by IPC's *My Guy*. In the Vauxhall Manor survey *Jackie* was running second, hotly pursued by *Oh Boy!*, *My Guy*'s all but identical twin.

My own seventeen-year-old FE students often reach for the magazine in their bag as soon as the break in the lesson arrives. Observing that many girls 'disappear' into comics during lessons at school and college, McRobbie[22] suggests that this might be a form of resistance and a means of 'creating space' at school. This is undoubtedly true, but it is a form of 'opposition' that ultimately rebounds on the girl.

There are several obvious continuities between these magazines and the press. The extensive preoccupation with pop stars is pursued directly within the popular press. There is a more pervasive continuity at the level of language. They specialize in a kind of jaunty slang immortalized in the 'Glenda Slag' column of *Private Eye*. Features advertised on the covers of an issue each of *My Guy* and *Oh Boy!* include 'ARE YOU FAITHFUL TO YOUR FELLA?', 'THE HUNKY HARDY BOYS!', 'NAUGHTY

QUIZ!', 'FUN PHOTO ROMANCE', 'AGONY'S MR. ECSTASY!', 'PILLOW TALK SECRETS FROM YOUR SLEEP'. Under a 'Page 3 pin-up!' of a hairy-chested youth in *Oh Boy!* we find the following text:

> PHIL'S ALL FURRY!
> Wowee! Just look at that cheeky chest! A real curly-wurly, eh? And it belongs to Phil Shepherd, our cover boy this week. He's training to be a showbiz superstar at London's Italia Conti drama school. We reckon he's definitely headed for the bright lights – he's so big and butch! Fancy writing Phil a fan letter? Join the club!

It's easy enough to see the continuities between this type of writing and the language of the *Sun* and to a lesser extent the *Daily Mirror*. It's one end of the spectrum. At the other end is the 'soft' pornography, through which males are invited to structure their responses to women.

In the middle we find the 'saucy' features particularly beloved of the *Sun*: the 'surveys' of bed-time habits, the questionnaires about what nightwear turns you on, so that the male voyeur and the 'faithful filly!' are joined in holy matrimony.

These magazines have a preoccupation with the problem of finding and holding a boyfriend (a 'hunky fella!') that borders on the pathological. Pictures, feature articles and photo-strip stories alike are pinned hopelessly to this one issue. The adverts for tampons and deodorants combine with the fulsome problem pages to address the neuroses and insecurities of their readers with a formidable concentration of purpose. The magazines conjure up a world of constant psychological pressure and they are predominantly concerned with the problems this causes. The advice columns are full of queries about facial hair, bunions, sweaty hands, tampon troubles and uneven breasts. The stories address problems of relationships within families as well as boyfriend trouble, but even these often turn out to be about boyfriend trouble, anyway. Echoing Willis's conclusions about 'lads'' culture, McRobbie concludes her general study of the culture of working-class girls: 'They are both saved by and locked within the culture of femininity'.[23] The precise role of these magazines in this process is not easy to see. It is clear that immense pressures to conform, to be a certain way, to look a certain way, are piled onto the girls from a battery of external sources. The magazines do not offer alternatives and make no attempt to short-circuit the pressures. They assume that the girls' worries and fears are 'natural'. Having said that, they may be offering a kind of 'breathing-space'. They address the girls' worries with a directness that they are unlikely to find elsewhere. It is worth noting that *My Guy* is different from *Jackie* (the old *Jackie*, at least) in a highly significant way. The heroines of the old cartoon stories in *Jackie* were *idealized* versions of working-class girls, with cascading blonde tresses and doe-like eyes. In *My Guy* photo-strip stories they are *real* girls, recruited from comprehensive schools. They are nagged by real working-class mothers and taken out by real apprentice technicians. The stories show the girls a 'mirror reflection' of their own lives, simplified, sometimes to the point of travesty, and interpreted for them by the 'caring' advice columnist.

Many stories are preoccupied with the problems of rivalry, jealousy and betrayal, which we saw in a generalized form in the juvenile comics. Here they are specific and tied to the question of boyfriends. The immersion in the personal and emotional is complete. The frame of reference is staggeringly narrow. Many of the features of the popular press are clearly addressed to the *My Guy* reader after she has married Mr Hunky! The jaunty language recurs ('Deirdre is Miss Sexy Specs!'), and the reader is assumed to be located firmly within the personal/emotional frame.

The popular newspapers are thus at the end of a coherent progression that begins with the acquisition of the ability to read and maps out special routes for both sexes. I am not suggesting that comics and magazines *determine* the content of newspapers, or vice versa, but the relationships at the levels of form and of meanings are close.

All products of popular culture are important to those who wish to effect social and political change for what they can tell us about the audience to which they are addressed. Much attention has been paid within English teaching to the difficulties surrounding non-Standard English, when language is so intimately concerned with identity. Perhaps it is as damaging to children for teachers to dismiss and disparage their *para-language* of cultural signs and codes as it is for them to denigrate non-Standard English. Explaining why something is bad is not always the best way of convincing someone that it is, especially if you haven't bothered to find out why they like it.

145

Paul Hoggart

Notes

1 T. Eagleton, *Criticism and Ideology*, New Left Books, London, 1976.
2 R. Williams, *Politics and Letters*, New Left Books, London, 1980.
3 R. Hoggart, *The Uses of Literacy*, Chatto & Windus, London, 1957.
4 S. Hall and P. Whannel, *The Popular Arts*, Hutchinson, London, 1964.
5 F. R. Leavis and D. Thompson, *Culture and Environment*, Chatto & Windus, London, 1933.
6 B. Parkinson, 'Adult education and working class culture', in D. Craig and M. Heinemann (eds), *Experiments in English Teaching*, Edward Arnold, London, 1976.
7 K. Worpole, 'Beyond the Classroom Walls', in M. Hoyles (ed.), *The Politics of Literacy*, Writers & Readers, London, 1977.
8 P. Freire, *Cultural Action for Freedom*, Penguin, Harmondsworth, 1972.
9 L. Baxendale, *A Very Funny Business*, Duckworth, London, 1978.
10 P. Corrigan and P. Willis, 'Cultural Forms and Class Mediations', *Media, Culture and Society*, vol. 2, no. 3, 1980.
11 A. McRobbie, 'Jackie: an ideology of adolescent femininity', *Centre for Contemporary Cultural Studies Stencilled Occasional paper*, no. 53, 1978.
12 J. Richmond, 'What do 87 Girls Read?', *The English Magazine*, no. 1, Spring 1979.
13 A fuller version of this article, including a statistical analysis of the survey, appeared in *Media, Culture and Society*, no. 3, 1980. I am indebted to John Hardcastle, an English teacher at Hackney Downs, for his help.
14 S. Hall, 'Encoding and decoding in the television discourse', *Centre for Contemporary Cultural Studies Stencilled Occasional Paper*, no. 7, 1973.
15 P. Willis, 'The class significance of school counter-culture', in R. Dale, *et al.* (eds), *Schooling and Capitalism*, Routledge & Kegan Paul/Open University Press, 1977.
16 P. Corrigan, *Schooling the Smash Street Kids*, Macmillan, London, 1979.
17 B. Cooney, 'Leicester take to the hills', *Football*, vol. 5, no. 10, 1979.
18 F. Wertham, *Seduction of the Innocent*, London Museum Press, 1955.
19 G. Perry and A. Aldridge, *The Penguin Book of Comics*, Penguin, Harmondsworth, 1967.
20 B. Dixon, *Catching them Young*, vol. 2, Pluto, London, 1977.
21 R. Leeson, *Children's Books and Class Society*, Writers and Readers, London, 1977.
22 A. McRobbie, op. cit.
23 A. McRobbie: 'Working class girls and the culture of feminity', in Women's Studies Group, *Women Take Issue*, Hutchinson, London, 1978.

Some Background Reading

A. McRobbie: 'Working class girls and the culture of femininity', in Women's Studies Group, *Women Take Issue*, Hutchinson, London, 1978.

G. Murdock and G. Phelps, *Mass Media and the Secondary School*, Macmillan, London, 1973.

D. Robins and P. Cohen, *Knuckle Sandwich*, Penguin, Harmondsworth, 1978.

A. Swingewood, *The Myth of Mass Culture*, Macmillan, London, 1977.

F. Whitehead *et al.*, *Children and their Books*, Macmillan, London, 1977.

11 Comprehension. Bringing it back alive

Bob Moy and Mike Raleigh

Doodle-oodle-oo

Comprehension work of the passage-plus-questions kind holds a prominent place in examinations in English at sixteen. It has the majority of coursebooks for English in an iron grip. In many schools it accounts for a substantial amount of the time spent on secondary English. But that is only a beginning. Passage-plus-questions is a regular primary school activity; and most secondary school worksheets and textbooks in all subjects fall under its spell sooner rather than later. Indeed some of its strongest advocates are enlightened science or humanities specialists, well into advanced curriculum development in other ways, inventive teachers with a sensitive feel for how children learn, but who, when they want their pupils to quarry written information, tend to see an individually worked comprehension exercise as the only way that things can happen.

Under such circumstances the children's response is interesting. In the more formal set-ups they rule their margins, put the date, get their heads down, and then chug steadily on in an orderly and tidy isolation. Or if it is one of those classrooms where children are encouraged to discuss things, they discuss, sometimes with passion, last night's TV or the merits of the latest style of boots while separately and competently transferring from worksheet to exercise book those bits of information which, if they have carried out properly the minor surgery required, will prove to their teacher that they have grasped the workings and significance of the Arkwright loom. Look at the books a week later and you can't help but be impressed by the industry of children and teacher alike; by and large, the majority of the class have got three ticks for every cross.

But what have they understood? And how did they feel about what they were doing? Talk with them about it and the second question is soon answered: they were quietly and acceptably bored. They are not pressing for any changes, for they like the certainty of an undemanding regime they understand; but almost without exception you'll be lucky to find a single child prepared to enthuse about what they've been doing. And the moment you begin to discuss the answers they've written you discover that many of those marked 'wrong' were merely badly expressed, while many of those marked 'right' merely involved the deft fielding and return of formulations borrowed from the original that fall apart and reveal major misconceptions when you talk them through. The whole slow-burning, time-consuming exercise seems simply to have enervated the pupil while misinforming the teacher; it has allowed another piece of schoolwork to become a half-hearted ritual, one in which the pupil satisfies not a personal curiosity but an institutional call to produce. David, a second-year boy, put it this way after completing a passage-plus-questions stint in geography:

> I just wanted to put anything down . . . because I wanted to finish . . . It was not exactly boring, it was quite good, but . . . still boring. When you're on your own you go . . . you go . . . you look at the thing and you say 'Oh, I've done that – doodle-oodle-oo – put any answer – doodle-oodle-oo.'

Comprehension exercises are not biting; most pupils toss them off with a minimum of commitment. The Doodle-oodle-oo Technique rules.

The pupils' prime concern (keeping a low profile and meeting the quota) is also the teacher's. But the teacher often has another major concern: getting full sentence answers. As he or she tours the classroom a single teaching point is repeated again and again: 'Never start an answer with "because".' There is no certainty, however often the message is repeated, that it will be acted upon. What is certain is that it will take the best part of an hour for the average pupil to answer ten fairly simple questions on a passage of a few hundred words. The emphasis on a formal precision of reply will ensure that only undemanding questions can be posed, and the choice of writing as the medium of exchange will mean that few questions can be put and that any feedback as to how they have been managed will be minimal, delayed for anything up to a week, and usually given in the pupils' absence.

But perhaps all this doesn't matter; perhaps it works. The children do seem slowly to learn things. But do they learn anywhere near as much as they might? To what extent are comprehension exercises responsible for the learning that does go on? Is the information picked up integrated fruitfully with what is already known? To answer these questions try this history comprehension exercise for size. It's a short passage on the Glombots. You won't have heard of them before, because we've made them up. That puts you where the pupils are when they are expected to break a bit of new ground. We have replaced technical terms and unusual words with nonsense words, so that as well as picking up the history you will need simultaneously to master the special language in which such things are discussed by those who spend their lives closeted with them. The passage is a single paragraph and is followed by seven varied questions of the standard comprehension type. We trust that when you've read it several times you'll still, by definition, have no real understanding of what it's about: after all, most of it means nothing at all. But don't be downhearted. Write careful answers to the questions set. Aim for a distinction. Don't start an answer with because. You'll know you haven't understood a thing, and you'll know that we'd know it too, but play your cards right and we think you'll be able to fix it so that, whatever you know we'd know, you'll know we'd have to give you full marks. Then try it on a range of your pupils. Mark their scripts. We think you'll get a whole range of scores and we think you'll suspect that you and all of them understood equally little of what it was all about. So where are the differentials coming from? And how often is something of the same kind happening as we use comprehension exercises to settle the rank order of our classes for their ability to understand what's there in a piece of writing?

By 1740 Glombots were bardoodling fludgerlistically throughout the scallerbars. Though some were oddlebug, the glotterest couldn't read or write. Muchupper, being petergustic murds, they seemed unable plesterly to dunk the likely modalbags of their mastions. On the other hand, despite their quite understit astulance for motropping violence, the glotterest wished to estocate only peaceful changes through moldergustic tropation and breadalbation. In 1742 the murds squinched the strink in one of the most flugelbar and antimoldergustic dinkums that history has ever seen.

1 What were the Glombots doing in 1740 and where?
2 How well were they succeeding? Were people right to give them an astulance for motropping violence?
3 Mention one thing all Glombots had in common and two ways in which some Glombots were different from others.
4 Late in 1740 a full assembly of all Glombots voted on whether they favoured achieving change by detropartion. What do you think their decision was?
5 Ordinary men would have dunked the modalbags of their mastions. Why didn't the Glombots?
6 Which of the following statements are true?
   (i)   Most Glombots approved of tropartion.
   (ii)   When Glombots bardoodled they almost always fludged it.
   (iii) The average Glombot was petergustic and oddlebug.
   (iv)   The Glombots were wrong to dunk the modalbags of their mastions.
7 Imagine you are a Glombot. Write a few sentences telling us in your own words what you can about yourself and what you do.

The traditional model of comprehension

We were cheating a bit with the Glombots.[1] But how much? Some parts of some standard comprehension exercises may offer helpful reading experiences to some of our pupils some of the time. But how many and how often? Is the unreal busy-work element which underlies even the best-designed of these exercises ever really transcended? We doubt it. Because at their heart there lies a false and unhelpful model of what reading, learning and knowing is all about.

This model assumes that knowledge has an objective existence of its own: that, given proper skills on both sides of the transmission, a person who has it can transmit it intact and unchanged to any number of others, while a third person can, from a distant vantage point, set up, supervise and assess the transmission. It further supposes that an effective medium for this transmission and for rendering proof of its reception is the written word. It suggests that the written messages concerned are self-sufficient and canonical encapsulations of meaning, and that they are therefore best transmitted and received by writers, readers and assessors working alone.

To put it in more everyday terms: this model assumes it reasonable to expect young readers to work alone to get meaning from texts, answering in writing written questions set in advance by an unknown adult and marked later in the reader's absence by a teacher, one of whose prime concerns in assessing the response will be to receive a fully-formed reply, properly constructed, properly punctuated and spelled, and neatly handwritten against the clock.

The case against this traditional model of comprehension should by now be old hat. It bears repeating simply because the evidence is that the practice which the traditional model gives rise to is still widespread. We can begin the case against with a reminder that, as the Bullock Report has it, 'it is a confusion of everyday thought to regard knowledge as something that exists independently of someone who knows' or to think that 'learning begins and ends with instruction'. In other words, those holy texts, alone with which the young reader is to be locked, are inert, empty and meaningless 'until brought to life afresh within the knower by his own efforts.' Bringing them alive is 'a formulating process and language is its ordinary means': and every 'formulation' is a unique affair even when the same person is regenerating it from one occasion to the next. This is what forges a mass of disparate facts into an item of 'comprehension' (etymologically a 'grasping together'). The range of legitimate meanings that can be built around a text, not to mention a young reader's ability to build them, is considerable – providing that the quality of the exploration is high. What can be expected to ensure that? In the words of Bullock again:

> In order to accept what is offered we have to find an individual context for a new piece of information and forge the links that will give it meaning . . . Something approximating to 'finding out for ourselves' needs therefore to take place if we are to be successfully 'told' . . . This is a task that we customarily tackle by talking with other people.

152

Objection: Well what you've just said in the last paragraph sounds all very fine, but really it's a bit heavy as a description of what you have to do when you read a simple sentence like: 'By 1740 Glombots were campaigning ineffectually throughout the conurbations.' There's a couple of words there which might cause problems; but provided you know the words, the sentence carries a clear meaning. You just read it: you don't agonize over 'formulating' it.

Well . . . any description of what goes on in a reader's head – like any description of a complex mental process – sounds a bit heavy set against the speed and facility with which an accomplished reader manages to comprehend. Most of the time there's no agony involved. But that doesn't mean that the meaning is all down there on the page, ready and waiting for anyone who cares to look, 'providing you know the words'. A small experiment: monitor your own mental behaviour as you read the next paragraph: what do you actually *do*?

Most recent researchers into reading would stand with Bransford, Barclay and Franks in denying that 'sentences carry meanings'. Instead they would insist that 'people carry meanings, and linguistic inputs merely act as queues which people can use to recreate and modify their previous knowledge of the world.' As Husserl says, the reader's mind is needed to 'give shape to the interaction foreshadowed by the sentences.' Thus statements 'only take on their full existence in the reader' (Poulet) and 'the same utterance may be understood differently as a function of the different cognitive contributions that different listeners make' (Bransford and McCarrell). This of course reflects the inevitable situation in cognition and perception in general: 'To perceive, a beholder must create his own experience; without an act of recreation the object is not perceived' (Dewey). But it applies with particular force to the perception of meanings symbolized at several removes through printed laundry. Iser postulates the existence in every piece of writing of two different notional parts: the 'written' text (i.e. everything that is there 'in the print') and the 'unwritten' text (what the current reader must be able to provide from a personal store of past experience and previous understanding). Until these two are brought together, even the simplest 'text' ('The Glombots sat on the mat and reconsidered their strategy') does not exist except as marks on a paper sheet; as each unique

153

marriage of written and unwritten text is accomplished, the piece of writing becomes meaningfully extant for a while.

If we're right, we think that you conducted a lightning-quick conversation with yourself to make sense of that last paragraph, that you made a *route* out of the signposts on the page, using your prior knowledge and your expectations of what was likely. So that last paragraph lives (briefly) in your head, not on the page. Otherwise, (among other things) how is it that it 'makes sense' despite the fact that mis-prints offer to make complete non-sense of two sentences? To do this job of making sense you performed a series of extremely complex and sophisticated mental operations which are quite impossible to track – and quite impossible to replicate (you couldn't read the same text again).

It is also likely that you're not quite sure that all the ends are tied up in that paragraph (the quotation from Husserl, for example – does that mean . . .?). You might worry, that is, about the comprehensiveness and the coherence of the meaning you have built. Most of the time we put up with that kind of worry. If we're bothered about it, we tend to have another go at building the meaning, this time making the 'conversation' slower and more deliberate. A natural extension of that process is to talk to others who have read the same text. That is mere commonsense. The commonsense hunch is that the text that several readers build together has every chance of being so much richer, fuller and more 'accurate' than the text which each would build alone.

Unfortunately, commonsense tends to desert us all faced with an hour with the third year, and with a feeling that we ought to be doing something about their reading. What are the implications of commonsense for work in the classroom when we explicitly focus on the business of comprehension? Some obvious reforms spring at once to mind. First, for the pupils, a real shift in where they feel the initiative to be, from a position where they must tackle alone someone else's questions, for external assessment by a third person and at a later date, to one where pupils generate their own queries and evaluate their own solutions collaboratively and on the spot. Second, for the teacher, a radical shift of role, from one of puppeteer and assessor to one of consultant on call. Third, for the writer of the text, a radical shift of status, from that of distant transmitter of perfect and holy messages to that of a provider of raw material which can give no more than implicit hints about how it might be processed or about the answers that might legitimately be arrived at. Altogether, a shift from teachers interrogating pupils to pupils interrogating texts.

But for this they need the tools – which means a shift in the kind of language use we are prepared to encourage in our classrooms when doing comprehension work. From a premature insistence on the 'hard' language of the 'finished' written answer we need to shift to making generous preliminary houseroom for the 'soft' language of the tentative, unfinished, oral speculation. The formulating process feeds on an untidy, often 'incorrect', shy kind of language which we have traditionally shooed out of our classrooms whenever serious work is in hand. But for children – as for us much of the time – the interior monologue of thought must be fed by the external dialogue of talking. The necessity of chat should be celebrated and undress forms of language given an honest educational name. Classrooms ought to be the safest place in the world to make a mistake, as the 1979 HMI survey *Aspects of Secondary Education in England* points out in its stately way:

> In discussion with teachers and with heads, it was clear that at the centre of many difficulties and differences of view there lies a confusion between two functions of language – the first as a communication of what has been learned and the second as part of the activity of learning itself. Concentration on the first of these at the expense of the second, which is often more important, may obscure stages of misunderstanding, approximation and correction through which the learner often needs to pass and also may reduce the pupils' engagement with learning. For those who find the art of abstraction difficult (and even for some who do not) the use of language to explore an experience often reveals what can be discovered in no other way. A change of emphasis from language as evidence of learning achieved to one used in the process of learning is needed. . . . At present talking and listening by pupils are not fully exploited. They need more experience as participants in genuine discussion, in which they attend to the contributions of others, learn to discriminate between the relevant and the irrelevant and to expand, qualify and range in and around a subject.

What the HMIs have to say about the pupils' need to become 'participants in genuine discussion' in which they 'range in and around a subject' applies to school learning in general; but it also brings up another difference of assumption between the old model of comprehension and what would need to be the new. The old model assumes that for those with the requisite reading skill the single proper meaning of a text could be neatly peeled off by any number of readers, like so many exact copies humming from the master sheet on a duplicating machine. Comprehension is seen as a right or wrong, once and for all affair: you've either got it or you haven't. The new model, on the other hand, would see comprehension as an ever-sharpening process of emergent understanding. The metaphor would not be the single pass through a duplicating machine but (borrowing from Jimmy Britton) a prolonged stay in the developing tray, where first a few key highlights might be brought up and then, as the work continued, more and more detail filled in and interconnections made manifest. As understandings 'emerged' the look of things could be expected to change quite radically; far from being failures many early distortions and false emphases would be necessary steps on the road to eventual fullness and clarity. Meanings, then, would need to be built over a period of time and to be built piecemeal.

Back down the tunnel: three new ways

Dissatisfaction with passage-plus-questions work – what you might call the 'authorized version' – is, of course, not new. Its shortcomings were seen long ago and a number of attempts have been made to do something about them. These attempts at reform – new ways, as it were, for teachers to interrogate pupils rather than a determination to help pupils to interrogate texts – have resulted in three kinds of 'revised version': (1) MCT i.e. multiple-choice technique; (2) 'the Box' (or 'Reading Laboratory'); (3) 'the Hierarchy', i.e. systematized exercises to give structured practice along a planned route through the labyrinths of various taxonomies of reading purposes and strategies. It is our belief that although these three forms of the revised version may look to be something new (especially when they are combined, as they sometimes are) they are no more than mutton dressed as lamb. To some pupils they may come as a welcome relief from the authorized version, but their early promise soon proves illusory; and this is because they are based on the same false model of what comprehension involves as the straightforward passage-plus-questions version. Perhaps a closer look at each of them would reveal why.

Multiple-choice is not without its strength. It does at least have the grace not to equate understanding texts with the ability to write full sentence answers not beginning with 'because'. Pupils are thus spared the indignities of the written-elocution exercise, and a lot more comprehending can be tackled in a given time. What's more, many pupils find its puzzle-game element motivating – at least for a while. But that's about it. The case against is quite simple: MCT runs against the grain of all natural reading practices. The central fact in all real reading is that readers have the freedom and responsibility for generating their own understanding; in multiple-choice exercises a third person elbows the reader out of the driving seat. In the sentence-answer version readers are at least free to shape their own answers; here even this minor initiative is taken away and they are left with a forced choice from a handful of prefabricated responses which they know to have been engineered so that only one is allowable. The rules do not countenance participation. Again, real reading involves a process (however rapid) of emergent understanding, one in which the embedded ideas 'come up' differentially at their own rate and as a shifting web of interrelationships forms. In multiple-choice exercises possible meanings have no natural seniority: they leap full-grown and simultaneously, the unnatural progeny of the examining mind; one among them is the true prince. This puts readers to unnatural troubles: the unnatural trouble of having to eliminate false possibilities that would never have occurred to them in the normal way; and the unnatural trouble of shedding silly readings seductively phrased with which they would not have ensnared themselves. Under the circumstances readers do what they can: they develop strategies to bring success, but these strategies have precious little to do with reading in the normal sense. They include, for example, sleuthing: establishing that a given answer must be right because the others are wrong.

Two further snags are still more important. Even more than with the authorized version, multiple-choice lends itself to a nit-picking focus on vocabulary items, the exact meaning of knotty phrases and the checking up on minor items of formal logic. What it resists is application to the broader, more complex, more comprehensive issues that make the passage as a whole cohere and which are what a real understanding of it would have to be about. Finally, multiple-choice presents the central problem of all traditional comprehension exercises writ large: it doesn't build reader ease and confidence by encouraging a symmetrical social relationship between readers and texts. Instead it spreads suspicion and distrust: the readers know they are on test; that attempts are being made to queer their view of things; that appearances are going to be deceptive; that watchfulness rather than engagement is what is required.

The second form of the revised version is the box of reading cards, also known for some reason as a 'Reading Laboratory' or 'Workshop'. This system stands or falls by some simple, well-meant and misguided notions, principal among them being the idea that comprehension work should be 'individualized' and 'self-scored'. To solve the classroom management problems that this involves, the texts have to be bland and lacking any rich but awkward resonance, while the scoring system must be reduced to a rigid right-or-wrong polarity. Thus what the pupils are given to comprehend is mostly a *Reader's Digest* type of non-fiction prose, and the way they do it is often through multiple-choice. Into the bargain they will spend about two-thirds of their time on busy-work ('working with words' and so on) which sometimes has nothing to do with the passage and always has nothing to do with comprehension. Not only this: the Box, stepping neatly between the teacher and the pupils, de-skills the teacher on the spot, leaving him or her merely running errands for the teacher-in-the-box. The real teacher scurries about, sustaining morale when 'working with words' gets really arcane, making sure that the disillusioned don't cheat, cheering up the disgruntled (who dispute the answer-sheet), and worrying about those gong-hunting record-breakers and their increasingly inflated views of their own powers as they race at breakneck speed through material which the Box's scientific placement test insists is at their proper level.

This is unfair criticism: for the Box is nothing more than passage-plus-questions-plus-multiple-choice (plus-working-with-words) in a box. But then the Box has had its own special publicity: in 1979 *The Effective Use of Reading* reckoned to have demonstrated that reading labs do work, using a most disarming circular argument. That is, they work provided you use them for something like 50 of your available English lessons in the Autumn term, and provided that you measure progress by individually-worked sentence-answer comprehension tests (i.e. tests with the same questionable view of reading as the Box). To be obvious: suppose the control group, instead of having none of the extra reading lessons which the SRA group had, had spent the same time reading and discussing the little library of real books which the small fortune needed to purchase a Box would have paid for. And suppose, by way of a test at the end, the pupils in each group had been asked to chat informally about the reading they'd done and what they'd gathered from it. (There must be a reason why heavyweight reading research is always undertaken by pre-test/post-test methods originally designed for investigating grain yields at an agricultural research station.) But is there nothing that might come of the high hopes that first encounters with a Box can induce in pupils and teachers alike? For the initial reaction of most children is positive. We believe that this is because – and this is sobering – compared with most classroom activities, working from a reading lab at least gets a live teacher off their backs and out of their hair. Though nothing has really changed, the initiative feels as if it's passed to them, and it looks as if someone is paying them the compliment of trusting them to work by themselves. This aspect of working from a reading lab, however illusory it will turn out in the end, is worth remembering and worth trying to establish for real.

The Box shares with multiple-choice and the authorized version the same answer to the question: what is progress in comprehension? The answer they propose is that progress means the reader is able to handle longer passages, with more difficult argument and bigger words; the proof of progress is the ability to answer more ticklish questions or make more ticklish choices. But how do you actually get from Red to Brown, from Book 1 to Book 5, from the 200 words in largish print on 'Spending Your Pocket Money' to the 800 words in smallish print on 'Violence on Television'? The O level passage is the high tide mark – but you can't see the sea rise. The comprehension-in-stages books are no help either: after mastering the last passage in Stage 3 (on the growth in popularity of budgerigars as pets, with a paragraph on how to keep them), you're faced with the first passage in Stage 4 where the class is expected to untangle a chunk of Siegfried Sassoon's diary. (You can't blame it all on the summer holidays: they just don't seem to have made the leap.)

The Hierarchy offers some hope here. It is particularly attractive to those who feel that somehow readers are allowed to get away with it once they have been awarded the decoding ribbon, once they have topped the scheme and been allowed to read books. The Bullock Report called attention to the need to focus on what it calls 'higher order reading skills'. This was a cue for a sudden rush of professionalism which makes the business of any old passage and any old questions seem primitive. The sources are mainly American. Comprehension is newly mapped. Barrett's taxonomy of reading skills is photocopied and becomes popular: literal understanding, inference, evaluation and appreciation (with sub-divisions). New techniques are found especially useful for dealing with factual and discontinuous material: surveying, skimming, scanning, attending to signal words, location skills, extracting, reciting, summarising, recording.

We have attention to varieties of forms of rhetoric and modes of presentation. We have materials here for what Bullock calls 'advanced reading qualifications'; comprehension is technicized, just as learning to read has been. And material also for a programme of reading instruction: a Hierarchy of separable, teachable skills calling for development work at different stages, individually tailored for the individual reader. This gives, *en passant*, new life to the Box; new laboratories are envisaged (and some old ones relabelled) to take readers all the way up one spiral or another. But there are also new comprehension books which aim to teach 'the skills of literal comprehension, deduction, evaluation etc.' or to enable pupils 'to study and to practise the more advanced skills they require for independent reading'.

The problem is that the teaching approach which this kind of mapping of comprehension implies just leads us back down the tunnel of the authorized version by another route. Whatever value there may be in classifying comprehension in these ways, it doesn't seem to tell us how readers learn to do these things. But there is another reason why the technicization should be resisted. Here, whatever harm *The Effective Use of Reading* did in giving an unwarranted puff to reading labs is redeemed by the hard look they took at the attractive 'modern' notion that comprehension is an agglomeration of separately drillable sub-skills in a neat and structured hierarchy. As the Project team explain, they began with a belief in just this notion and expected their research to prove it correct. In the event it did the opposite:

> We conclude that individual differences in reading comprehension should not be thought of in terms of a multiplicity of specialized aptitudes. To all intents and purposes such differences reflect only one general aptitude: this being the pupil's ability and willingness to reflect on whatever it is he is reading.

If comprehension cannot in fact be broken down into a multiplicity of separate skills, then to set up a teaching programme, however well-intentioned and well-designed, which assumes that it can, will only distort and overcomplicate the job. The Hierarchy, that is, gets in the way.

The old and the new model: a summary

The next section considers how classroom work on comprehension could usefully be organized. But at this point some kind of summary would be helpful. We compare below the answers which our two models of comprehension – the old (which includes the three forms of the revised version: MCT, the Box and the Hierarchy) and the new – might be expected to adopt to some key questions about the reader and the text.

1 What can be hoped for when the comprehension process is successful?
Old model: a quick, neat, accurate transfer of information.
New model: a slow and awkward emergence of understanding.
2 What is the proper way to work?
Old model: alone.
New model: collaboratively.
3 How do readers see their situation?
Old model: they are on test.
New model: they are involved in a dialogue – one with another and all with the writer.
4 What is the key ability required?
Old model: skill in writing 'correct' and fully finished formal answers.

New model: the knack of sensitive and intelligent oral speculation.

5 What is the proper use for half-formed intuitions?

Old model: keep them in your head till they are either eliminated or properly 'finished'.

New model: offer them raw to the group for sifting, refining and extension.

6 What will credit be given for?

Old model: simply for what finished conclusions you arrive at.

New model: to some extent for the finished conclusions you arrive at but much more for the thoroughness and quality of your exploration.

7 What is the proper attitude to 'wrong' answers?

Old model: they are useless and unacceptable; keep them under your hat if you can.

New model: not easy to see what would be meant by such a term. At the very least they could have a fruitful short or medium term use in opening up new possibilities. Bring them out unblushingly.

8 Whose meanings are they and where will they be found?

Old model: the author's; and in the text a single meaning, fixed at the point of writing, which can be got out in the same state by all readers with sufficiently developed skills. The cleverer two readers are the more their interpretations will be likely to converge.

New model: the readers', and in their heads; a range of possible meanings to be built anew each time in response to the constraints signalled in the print and according to the thinking of each new reader. The cleverer two readers are the more their interpretations may fruitfully diverge.

9 What are the social relationships involved?

Old model: assymmetrical – a writer and testing teacher in charge, pupil under interrogation.

New model: symmetrical; writer, teacher and readers working on equal terms to generate 'thinking under the influence of print'.

10 Who legitimates your efforts and when?

Old model: the examining teacher after the work is over.

New model: your fellow readers as you go along – an easier response to assimilate and available on the run to help you trim your meanings as you go.

A programme of classroom work

Before thinking about a programme of classroom work on comprehension it may be useful to blur some old distinctions. There are three distinctions we would want to avoid: first, between 'learning to read' and 'reading'; second, between 'reading' and 'comprehension'; and, third, between 'comprehension of literature' and 'comprehension of non-literary material'. These old distinctions, we would say, tend to over-complicate teachers' attitudes to both the readers and the texts. Our reasons for saying so arise from the general points about comprehension made earlier. We briefly spell them out.

The first distinction: 'learning to read' and 'reading'

As far as the reader is concerned, it does not seem useful to assume that what a learner-reader does is radically different from what an experienced reader does. If there *are* distinct developmental phases in reading, nobody has yet been able to identify them. A programme of classroom work on comprehension which is based on an idea that what 'reading' means is defined by age or ability would seem to be building on shifting ground.

The second distinction: 'reading' and 'comprehension'

While it is obviously possible to read a text (i.e. saying the words) without comprehending very much (i.e. not processing the meaning very effectively), there clearly must be *some* comprehension merely to follow the marks on the page in something like conventional fashion. And once we leave this basic level, the distinction between 'reading' and 'comprehension' really does seem merely semantic (in the pejorative sense). It is a distinction which, if established in classroom practice, would seem to encourage some rather strange reading behaviour: that is, it can threaten to *create* that unnatural beast, the reader who is so locked into decoding that s/he resists the meaning.

Bob Moy and Mike Raleigh

The third distinction: 'comprehension of literature' and 'comprehension of non-literary material'

The distinction between the two seems at least partly based on an idea that comprehending literature = 'appreciation' (i.e. the soft sounds of delight), while comprehending non-literary material = 'rigour' (i.e. the sharp crunch of meaning). It is obvious that different texts have different functions, and that these account for differences in surface features (vocabulary, syntax etc.). But that doesn't mean that comprehending a fairy story involves strategies *radically different* from those involved in comprehending, say, a fire drill notice. Our hunch is that readers develop their general ability to comprehend when their own intentions and interests are engaged with the function of a particular text. We would say that the growth of a reader's desire and confidence to understand comes through the quality of that engagement, not through what can only be, in any case, a random exposure to a range of functionally different texts. That is only a clumsy way of saying that a programme of classroom work on comprehension need not include an intensive study of fire drill notices (or of instructions on how to make soup). Encounters with texts of that sort have been introduced in some places as a form of training for the reading demands of afterlife. We don't see anything really special about such texts; as the Bullock Report puts it, it is simply a question 'of learning to apply general principles to "official reading" of one kind or another.'

Having made light of those three distinctions, what positive points can we make about comprehension in the context of reading in school? The first point to establish about reading in school is that there should be a lot of it – and that means, in most schools and in most subjects, a great deal more than is allowed for now. The children need – above all – to be put into more situations in all subjects which expand their idea of what reading is about and what it is good for. The second point is that most reading in school should be fast, trusting and uninterrupted. The danger with heady descriptions of how 'comprehension' brings itself into being is that they have a tendency to tempt us into imagining comprehension always to be a slower and more self-conscious process than it actually is; most of the time understanding (however complex the process) comes instantaneously and is not explicitly worked for.

The vast majority of the texts offered in school should be ones which are so readily comprehended that they are hardly noticed as texts at all. Reading is a means to an end, not an end in itself, and the more transparent the print becomes the better. It's easy to become hooked on deliberate, 'reflective' reading, the overt weighing of pros and cons, the pondering, the doubling back, the careful enumeration of ideas. We read to find out what happens next. A proper school reading diet would be perhaps 90 per cent extensive, unsupported and largely unmonitored reading in well-written content-rich texts at a technically undemanding level.

That leaves 10 per cent: a small amount of well-supported intensive reading of rich and relevant texts that produce reading difficulties against which one can pit one's wits in company with one's peers. We should emphasize here that the words 'rich' and 'relevant' will necessarily drive a wedge between the words 'comprehension' and 'exercise'. There is clearly no point in wasting the 10 per cent on texts which carry a low load; they need to be dense enough to fuel the formulating process with some power; they need to be interesting enough to make it seem worthwhile to the readers to summon the effort that deliberate reflection requires; they need to be 'generous' enough to *invite* the reader to stop and reflect. There are many different kinds of text (i.e. texts with different functions) which might fit this bill. But it is here that literary texts may come into their own – and not only in English. It is not that the reading of literary texts involves unique comprehension processes, but that they involve the comprehension processes uniquely well. They require all the work that more purely informational texts do – but more so. They make a virtue of the fact that different readers are necessarily reading 'different' texts by generously inviting different interpretations. And while literary texts are more 'demanding', in that they require more comprehending, the paradox is that when properly chosen (and that depends, obviously, on the age, experience and interests of the group) they are also more accessible into the bargain. This may be precisely because they don't 'go' anywhere, they have no strings attached: the reader's purpose is, most clearly here, to find out what happens next. That means you don't normally have to justify their use to most children.

English clearly has the advantage here over other subjects. But it is an advantage which needs careful nursing. It needs to be protected, first against the disease of one-off-ery, that lurching from one discrete lesson to the next, which permits pupils no opportunity for developing their thinking through a sequence of work. But it needs also to be protected from the stiffening of the limbs that comes from the mechanical pursuit of a theme or topic, where texts have life only in the mind of some ghostly syllabus or coursebook.

So much for the choice of texts for the 10 per cent. But what do you actually *do* with them? What kind of activity can we use to replace the answering in writing of somebody else's questions? Pat D'Arcy[2] suggests that 'reading response at the post-decoding stage can best be developed by the provision of a wide range of literature combined with the encouragement of plenty of non-directed discussion.' Plenty of non-directed discussion (i.e. pupil-directed discussion) is certainly what we would aim for, and it's certainly also what we would want to start with. But there is evidence to suggest that pupils, given a text without questions following it and without a demand to answer them in writing, may be at a loss initially to know where and how to begin a discussion. Worse, their experience in some other subjects may continue to confirm that their past experience of comprehension in English remains the generally accepted one. You may be lucky. You may have classes who know how to take the initiative or who quickly learn how to do so. In any case, explain what it's about and what you're trying to do. Explain the benefits. Emphasize the *ways* of getting understanding rather than the achievement of particular kinds of understanding.

Objection: I've always encouraged whole class discussion about comprehension, talking through the questions before asking for written answers, or stopping half-way through a short story to discuss what has happened. So what's new?

Well . . . we're certainly not knocking whole class discussion which really shares views about what's important, and which really gives a class a sense of working together to crack a problem. But whole class discussion of texts is always difficult to manage, it usually doesn't involve many pupils actively, it is invariably directed solely by the teacher, and it is frequently plain gluey. Whole class discussion of packaged questions is especially so, an institutionalized guessing game, which most pupils are very keen to see the end of. We see the value of class discussion as a final forum in which views are presented *after* pupils have had a chance to formulate them. The trying-out stage is best undertaken in a more intimate and safer arena: pairs is a safe way to start; more than four and it starts to get complicated and unwieldy.

Some techniques for getting it going

But how do you turn on the ignition for a pair (or a three) who look blankly at a text and at one another? Or suppose they get into gear the first time out and then stall the second time out? Some frameworks (or scaffolds) may help here to give the discussion a defined shape and direction. Some of the possibilities are described below. Some caveats first. There is nothing magical about these devices; they are not new;[3] they do not carry a copper-bottomed guarantee; they do not represent a *system* for developing comprehension. They are merely instrumental to the business of getting pupils *working together* to process a text – and that needs explaining to pupils. They might very well get in the way for some pupils in some discussions some of the time by seeming to over-complicate or to distract attention from the job in hand: don't invest too much in them, or allow them to become the thing that's being done (i.e. a new kind of exercise). These are important caveats about the use of these techniques, and we will return to them later when we describe some of them in classroom use. For the moment, here is a selection of some of the possibilities. The order is not all that significant, but it does go roughly according to the sophistication of what they ask the pupil to do. But it isn't really a hierarchy of difficulty, because that is raised or lowered for any given text by the reader's prior knowledge of the subject matter, the complexity of the linguistic surface, the way the material is organized, and so on. The question is how to match the activity, the pupils and the text. There is also another variable to bear in mind, which is the degree of mucking about with the text that the techniques require (the first three here don't require any). The class management issues involved need careful consideration.

Bob Moy and Mike Raleigh

Wide-angle questions

This is a safe start for pupils in pairs. Give them, say, three questions to discuss on the passage, poem or short story. They must be questions to which there is no obvious single right answer, and of a kind which will encourage a ranging over the text as a whole. Try to make the questions a bit eccentric. So, for example:

'is this the right title for the passage?';
'what kind of book do you think this extract comes from?';
'can you think of anything the writer has left out here?';
'what idea of the writer (like age, sex . . .) do you get from this piece?'

Give them a time-limit; no written answers, but a quick report–back session involving the whole class is useful.

Responding to statements

This is a superior version of multiple-choice, and a fairly painless way of focusing discussion on critical issues in, say, a short story. Make up a short list of statements (some controversial and/or contradictory; perhaps one or two to do with the writer's intentions) which can stand as overall comments about the piece. Ask your pairs to work through them and decide which two or three they consider to be most important/appropriate. A simple 'prioritizing' system can then show the consensus of opinion in the class as a whole; a class discussion can start with those who chose unpopular statements justifying their decisions.

Question-setting

Turn the usual procedure around by asking the pupils themselves to make up a small number of questions to which they would really like answers. It's more difficult than it sounds to put this across, and pupils will usually tend to go for questions of the banal kind to which they are accustomed. Making distinctions between questions to which the answers are (a) on the lines (b) between the lines (c) beyond the lines may provide a useful temporary crutch. There are two possible routes after they've worked out their questions. One is to pass one pair's questions on to another pair to see if they can answer them. The other is to collect all the questions in and get a couple of bright sparks to make a list of the five questions most often asked. Then, next lesson, discuss those as a class.

Marking the text

This is a simple idea as old as schools. It just involves asking the pupils to underline (or indicate in the margin in some way) bits of the text that deal with one thing rather than another, or to identify patterns and connections that seem to be there. The physical marking is a prop for close attention and the chat involved is a preparation for whatever broader discussion is to come.

Deletion (1): single words

Give the pupils a copy of the text from which some single words have been deleted (tippexing a photocopy is the easiest way). Take out words (but not too many) which are in some way critical to the meaning. Ask your pairs to agree replacements for the missing words which are syntactically and semantically (and possibly stylistically) apt. The idea is for the pupils to have an interesting discussion, and to justify their decisions, rather than to guess the right word. Compare pupils' insertions with the original passage.

Deletion (2): leaving only a skeleton

Give the pupils, for example, the first and last paragraphs of a passage and ask them to read the relics and then comment on what they think the missing pieces are about. This can be a useful technique to prepare for the reading of the passage as a whole.

Selective substitutions

Give the pupils a text telling them that some of the words/phrases/ sections have been replaced by less good alternatives. The reader's job is to look through and recast any parts in any way they feel would help. The range of possible strategies for substitution– semantic, stylistic, syntactic, logical, surrealist – are considerable.

Bob Moy and Mike Raleigh

Prediction

Divide the passage or short story into instalments (choosing the stopping place with care) and give them out one at a time. Ask your groups to work out what they think is going to be in the next instalment by thinking about what has happened in the one they've got. The important question to ask about a particular prediction is: where is the evidence for it? Then compare predictions with what actually happens. (This works best with texts with a strong narrative line.)

Sequencing

This involves serious doctoring of the text. Make copies of it and cut them into pieces (perhaps paragraphs or half-paragraphs or stanzas). Don't make too many pieces, otherwise it can become tricky to organize. Then give all the bits to your pairs and ask them to assemble the bits into an order which makes sense to them. The idea is to focus discussion on the structure of the text. (N.B. Draughts play havoc with this game.)

Finding boundaries

This is sequencing the other way round. Ask the pupils to divide the text into what they think are its sections, describing what makes one section different from the next. It's made easier if you tell them at the beginning the number of sections you think there are, and let them work from there. (It's possible to use this technique to work on a single paragraph, though that is usually a more demanding application of it.)

Drawings and diagrams

This just means asking the pupils to present some of the information in a text in some visual form (e.g. a drawing, a flow-chart, a table, or a network). This technique could be used, for example, to focus attention on the relationship between characters in a story, or their points of similarity and difference. It may also be useful for re-assembling ideas in an information text, as a way of preparing for note-taking of various kinds.

170

Role-playing and other extensions

Here the written material (or some of it) is re-presented in verbal form through role-play, interview or improvised 'sketch'. For example: characters in a short story can be 'interviewed' about their motives and feelings; or two characters who don't in fact meet or talk in the story can be projected into a scene where they do.

Paraphrasing and summary

Here the written material (or some of it) is re-presented by the pupils in their own writing, possibly after earlier work with some of the techniques mentioned above. For example, an extended narrative or descriptive piece might be condensed and 'translated' into a news bulletin or short newspaper article; a piece with an unsuitable verbal surface might be rewritten to mesh more comfortably with the needs of a given target audience; or characters from the text might be asked to justify their actions or outlook in a short written statement.

One example: 'Remember the Chameleon'

The description of these techniques has necessarily been very spare – and that tends to make them sound complicated to operate. At this stage it may be useful to illustrate how these devices can be adapted to provide simple ways into a close study of a text. The selection of a particular technique, and its adaptation, will obviously depend jointly on the nature of the text, on the focus which the teacher wishes to encourage and on the experience of the pupils in working in this way. Here three different techniques are used in combination. The text we offer is a short and deceptively simple one by Carl Sandburg. 'Remember the Chameleon'. It is preceded by the working instructions for the pupils. (The follow-up would start with the difficulties they encounter.)

REMEMBER THE CHAMELEON
Things to do:
1 Underline (with a straight line) all the phrases you consider to be complimentary to the chameleon.

Bob Moy and Mike Raleigh

2 Underline (with a squiggly line) all the phrases you consider to be critical of the chameleon.
3 Decide together what you think about the following statements. Write down in order the letters for each so that the one you agree with most is at one end and the one you agree with least is at the other.
(a) A true hero (b) A real twit (c) An example to us all (d) An average guy (e) A solid citizen (f) A victim of fate (g) Someone who never stopped trying (h) A slave to instinct (i) A noble fool (j) Someone who failed to adapt (k) Someone who failed to grow up.
4 Present the meaning of 'Remember the chameleon' as a diagram or in some other visual form.

Remember the chameleon. He was a well-behaved chameleon and nothing could be brought against his record. As a chameleon he had done the things he should have done. And left undone the things that should have been left undone. He was a first-class, unimpeachable chameleon and nobody had anything on him. But he came to a Scotch plaid and tried to cross it. In order to cross it he had to imitate six different yarn colours, first one, then another and back to the first or second. He was a brave chameleon and died at the crossroads true to his chameleon instincts.

We can end this introduction to devices-for-comprehension by quoting a conversation between some consumers and their teacher. A group of three boys has just been working on the 'Remember the Chameleon' text using the 'things to do'. The teacher asks them what they thought about this new kind of work.

David: When I . . . When I . . . On our own – right? at school, we all hate school, we hate coming to it and we *love* going home, from school, but when I'm doing this kind of work, if I was doing this kind of work all the time I wouldn't really mind. I love it. It's more fun.
Terry: We love it.
Teacher: Well, tell me . . .
David: You're poking down in the back of your brain, you're actually using your brain, which makes you feel better . . .
Terry: Most of our answers have come from David, most of our answers have come from David.
Cornelius: I like . . .
David: But you argued with me and helped me do it too.

172

Terry: That's the point of doing it, that's the point of doing it.
Cornelius: I thought this was better because . . .
Terry: Yeh.
Cornelius: . . . you're not having one brain doing it, you've got three or four.
David: Three or four, or whatever.
Cornelius: And you know one brain might not understand this piece and then the other one will and it'll help him along.
David: Yeh, and it'll help you along.

The techniques in action

We have outlined thirteen kinds of activities which may offer 'scaffolding' for small group discussion of texts. All the activities, in one way or another, change the 'angle of approach' to a text; some involve the use of a 'doctored' text, others a 'straight' text. The hope is that by providing specific, problem-based but open-ended points of entry to discussion round a text these activities may dispel the inertia that tends to descend on many of us when under instruction in a classroom; that they may enable teachers to hand over sections of a developing enquiry to pupil groups while still giving indirect support by drawing attention (through the way the task is set up) to fruitful points of enquiry and away from unhelpful ones; that they may give the circulating teacher a number of useful points of re-entry in picking up the threads with any group she is helping; and they may enable different groups who have been exploring a common text in their own way to share their findings easily, because their common points of departure provide a good basis from which later whole-class discussions can grow.

We emphasized that these activities are neither new nor magical, but that they have the potential to offer early and temporary support to pupils starting out on collaborative explorations of texts. We are now going to try to describe what has happened when some of these activities have been used in ILEA English classrooms. Inevitably, the description we can offer here will fall short of the ideal; there's too much to say, and print isn't the best medium for saying it. We hope that the limited amount of detailed evidence which follows will at least give a flavour of what happens when versions of these activities are used with particular texts and groups of pupils, and that the more general reporting which comes later will reflect some of the problems which these ways of working can present.

What goes on in groups

Our first piece of evidence involves a situation of minimal shift. The pupils are answering questions set by the teacher, but they have been told to do this collaboratively rather than individually and through small group talk rather than in writing. The resulting discussion raises for us two questions.

The first question: to what extent can a teacher afford to take on trust what happens when she hands over part of the lesson to small group work? The answer is a simple if unsatisfactory one. Much of what happens *has* to be taken on trust, since you can't stay with all of the groups all of the time. Monitoring what's happening in the room as a whole will give you a general sense of whether things are 'going well' and lets you know pretty accurately where more specific and immediate support may be required. Eavesdropping on a particular group in action will also provide some clues about how it's going for them. But they may not always be simple clues to the truth, particularly on the matter of whether the talk is 'on task' or 'off track' and on the matter of whether the talk is 'going round in circles' or 'getting somewhere'.

The problem of reading the clues when you're eavesdropping is related to our second question: in how obvious and visible a form can we expect good collaboration to manifest itself? We are often encouraged to assume that good collaboration will look like this: the pupils will nominate the issue they are concerned with and explicitly relate what they say to it; pupils will make extended contributions, marked by signs of hesitation and tentativeness, to which the others will listen; replies to those contributions will clearly extend or modify them; the discussion will proceed steadily to some kind of conclusion, with pupils taking equal shares in its manufacture.

Of course, groups of pupils don't tend to work in this tidy way (who does?). But we suspect that this model of what collaboration might ideally be like is hard to shake off, and that it may incline us to read some of the clues we pick up when eavesdropping on groups working together in ordinary classrooms more negatively than we should. It may be possible to counter that by training our eavesdropping skills. The best kind of training seems to be to tape-record a group in action over a period of time, to check out the tape closely later, to transcribe a small section that seems interesting – and then to try to probe below the surface. That's what we tried to do with the transcript that follows.

The transcript is of a two-minute section of a lesson where a mixed-ability group of four boys in a first year mixed ability class are tackling an extract from a story called 'Geordie' by David Walker. The boys concerned were asked to discuss some questions together and to arrive at good joint answers. The question they are on here is:
'Why is the word "wee" repeated so many times in the first paragraph?'
Before proceeding further it would be helpful to rough out your own quick version of what a suitable response to that question might be. This is the paragraph it refers to:

> Geordie went straight out of the kitchen and up the rickety steps to his own room. It was small, in below the roof of the cottage, and there was just space for his bed and the dresser with his hairbrush on it. He took a look at himself in the mirror.
> Somehow you'd expect when you felt so bad that it would show in your face: but there was no difference. It was the same awful red face and the same carroty hair. That was wee Geordie in the mirror, wee to Jean, wee to the boys at the school, wee to dad and mum. Too wee to be any use for anything, too wee to be as good as a lassie in a climb.

As you can see the question is a deceptively simple one. It can't be answered satisfactorily by surface manipulations, since it requires a reading of what is between the lines more than of what is on them; there is also no single right answer, though one answer may be easier to formulate than some others. (It would be interesting to speculate on what kind of answer or answers you might expect if this question was given to a class to be answered individually and in writing.)

Below is the transcript of the discussion our four boys had on the question. It would be useful at this stage to read just the boys' contributions and to ignore the commentary for a moment. (By the way, one went on to take O level, three to take CSE; one of these three received withdrawal help on a regular basis because of quite spectacular difficulties with reading and writing. See if you can get some notion of who's who as you sit in on their work together.)

Burke: Yeh, but it means 'small'. Why don't you put that?

He seems to be 'stuck' on the standard comprehension task, assuming that when you've once given a definition of the word in question you've done all that is required.

Lant: Why does he use it so many times?

Pressing the group to tackle the proper task i.e. explain the repetition and so get down to reading what's between the lines as well as what's on the lines.

Burke: Because that's a common Scottish name.

Offering a possible explanation for the repetition – but missing Lant's real point and running into surface problems with his choice of phrase.

Hunt: He could use 'little'.

Raising a new issue. Why complicate things by using an unusual word when a more familiar one would do?

Burke: Scottish people know what it means though, why should . . .

Questioning the need for the question and showing an implicit 'hold' on both the setting for the story and the nature of dialect.

Lant: Why does he use it so many times?

Again bringing the group back to the real issue.

Hunt: He could use 'small', 'little', 'weedy'.

Exploring and deepening the question: why use a single, repeated dialect word when a whole range of more 'standard' synonyms are available?

Burke: Yeh, but they don't say English words. They don't like the English people. Like Irish don't like the English.

Answering the dialect part of the problem Hunt is raising and developing his own earlier theme. Scottish people wouldn't want English synonyms. It's all part of a broader attempt to be partisan about your cultural identity.

Hunt: I'm beginning not to like you, you little . . .

Referring to some on-going personal discussion? Suggesting the conversation is getting off track?

Lant: Look, we've got, the question is, why does he use it so many times?

Bringing the group back yet again to the central issue.

Green: He's pretending to be . . . he's pretending to be . . . he's pretending to be . . .

It looks as if this may be the start of a 'break out'. Very hesitantly, as shown by the repetition, Green is feeling his way towards formulating a possible hypothesis – but so far he can offer only the earliest hints, not the thing itself. 'Pretending' is a fascinating choice of phrase. What does he mean by it? What will the group make of it?

Lant: Yeh, he's trying to explain, he's trying to explain that he's small, he's trying to explain, that he's small, that he's small to everybody.

Agreeing with and building from Green's as yet incompletely formulated hypothesis. It's as if the tiny beginning Green offered has enabled Lant to begin to answer the question that, quite rightly he has been holding the group to from the beginning. The word 'wee', he suggests, is repeated so many times to undermine the fact that so many people saw him that way. It would seem that he understood Green to mean by 'pretending to be' something like 'reminding himself that he is'.

Green: Yeh.

Agreeing – and confirming that this *was* what he was trying to say?

Lant: He's no good.

Making a radical development – but not, as yet, in any fully explicit way. He begins to focus up the idea that the repetition indicates not only that most people saw Geordie as small but

177

also, more importantly, that for Geordie a powerful value judgment was implied.

Burke: Yeh. He's saying that he's useless at everything, like I am. But, why don't we put that, explaining that he was, use . . . small and useless?

Agreeing with Lant and making a personal interconnection. He thus deepened the break-through hinted at by Lant that the repetition tells us something important about Geordie's feelings about himself. But all this is still only half-explicit. Burke is performing an invaluable function for the group in leading the way in using personal experience to illuminate what is happening in the story – and vice versa. But he has also smelled the possibility of a 'final' answer and is, less helpfully, urging the group towards closure.

Lant: Because, to explain to himself . . .

Not yet prepared to take up Burke's invitation to closure but almost certainly building from Burke's personalising of the point at issue. By adding 'to himself' he begins to make explicit for the first time the idea that the repetition indicates an attempt by Geordie to *make* himself face up to and resolve a difficult personal problem. But he hasn't fully spelled it out: he's preparing the ground to do so soon, as and when he can. In the meantime he's making his thinking available to the group as he goes.

Green: He's trying to explain to himself . . .

Catching on, and echoing – but expanding and making more fully explicit – the borrowed phrase from Lant. By adding the important word 'trying' he is able to indicate what a struggle Geordie is having to admit the problem and the importance of doing something about it.

Burke: Yeh, but he don't have to explain, he knows that he's small and useless

Not too happy with the latest version – perhaps because the personal connections he can make between the story and his own experience are so important for him to work through.

Lant: He's just getting it through to him, he's getting a bit fed up . . .

Trying to help Burke see why Geordie must fully explore his own feelings about his own physique: the situation is already making him depressed and cannot simply be ignored. His use of pronouns does not seem to cause anyone problems in understanding what he means.

Burke: I know I'm small and useless, but I don't have to get it through to me. Do I?

Burke, for the moment, is identifying so strongly with Geordie's situation that he can't decentre to the point where he will be able to allow that different people may feel impelled to respond to the same situation differently – but he's giving the group the chance to check out exactly this possibility now.

Lant: It's a hard question.

Acknowledging that Burke has got him thinking, and/or implying a pleasing realisation of the complexity and sophistication of the uncertainties the group is attempting to resolve.

Burke: Why don't you put that: 'he was explain . . .'

Getting tired? Keen, anyway, to move group toward closure. Offers the beginning of a possible joint answer.

Green: Explaining – he was trying to explain . . .

Joining in to help formulate the joint answer.

Hunt: He used the same words . . .

Also joining in – but rather more 'academically', taking the group 'back' so that they can make a more explicit, conventionally 'developed' and self-sufficient answer.

Burke: I don't mean that.

Wanting to return to his own concern with exploring the similarities between his own and Geordie's experience.

Hunt: He used the same words (Burke: I don't mean that) 'cause he, he knew that he was the same to everybody. (Green: He was determined to make himself small.) He used the same words 'cause he knew (Burke: I think, I don't want to make myself big) that he was the same to . . .

The group working away together, each chipping steadily at the particular aspect that interests him most.

Lant: He used 'small' to come round to, right, to come round to, getting himself bigger, you know, wake himself up

Coming in from behind, Lant has taken the time to develop and offer to the group an excellent, fully worked-out answer – albeit still in a very colloquial form and substituting 'small' for 'wee'. This would seem to represent the high-water mark of their joint exploration here. But do they recognise it as such? (Would we, without close analysis?)

Hunt: He used the same words all the time because, he used the same words . . .

Perhaps realising the answer is not yet in a conventionally 'acceptable' form, Hunt goes back to his self-appointed task of trying to provide one. Is he working so hard on shaping a properly formulated full sentence answer that he's losing his hold on what they have now identified the essence of a good answer as being?

Burke: I'm ashamed. I'm . . . I'm scared about me not being all that strong. I might flex my muscles at home but it don't mean I don't go around just doing 'wee, wee, wee' (Laughter)

While Hunt has been drawn deep into the search for an acceptable formulation, Burke has been drawn deep into the personal implications of the story for him. He begins to explore them more deeply, but suddenly turns all to a merriment. Why?

Lant: He looked . . .

Like Hunt, Lant is determined to formulate a 'proper' answer. Teacher arrives. Whether by accident or design, the group now seems to retreat towards the 'safer' less developed version of their joint answer (the universality theme). They give this to the teacher and quickly move on to other matters.

What seems most fascinating to us here is how, working as a group, they seem able to comprehend so much more than if they were working individually; and also how much deeper each boy's understanding is than the bare formulations of it which writing them down would be likely to indicate. The difficulty of knowing from their contributions who are the conventionally more or less able pupils in the group, the way the effort is so equally shared, and the way the participants apparently have no trouble in penetrating the faulty surface structures of many of their remarks to one another, getting straight to grips with the intended meanings beneath, are also noteworthy.

A first viewing of the videotape from which this transcript derives gave us the sense that things were 'going well': the boys seem to be on the right sort of wavelength and their vitality is impressive. On the tape (as in real life) everything happens at lightning speed. The exchange has none of the slow, deliberate pauses for thought nor the coherent extended contributions which the tidy model of collaboration referred to earlier would have us see as indicators of thoughtfulness in discussion. Instead the exchange has all the ease and energy of a playground conversation. The speed of reaction, the fact that sometimes more than one person speaks at once, and the cryptic nature of many of the contributions, all make it seem that the participants are chasing their own favoured hares with no particular reference to what the rest are doing. In a sense, they are. But what happens when you probe below the surface, when you try to construct a narrative out of the fragments by offering a gloss on what seems to be happening? What happens to those individual cryptic fragments when they are seen in the light of what they come from and what they lead to, and when they are transformed into the 'proper answers' which seem to underlie the developing conversation? The interlinear commentary on the transcript is an attempt at such an analysis. It is, of course, speculative (it has to be); there's the danger that it reads more into the boys' remarks than is really there (but we don't think so). What we found there suggests that this is an exchange which is not only engagingly alive but also economic, coherent and collaborative.

We've found doing a close analysis of an exchange like this is usually reassuring. It's a way of training yourself to broaden your model of 'good' collaboration so as to accommodate the vitality and apparent untidiness which characterize so much of what happens in group work when it seems to be 'going well' in ordinary classrooms. It encourages you to accept, also, that an apparently unequal distribution of roles (who says what kind of thing, who leads, and so on) in a group, which can be a nagging worry, may conceal the fact that the roles can be complementary (and their functions complex). (N.B.., 'Hunt' is now an O level candidate; 'Green', 'Lant' and 'Burke' are being entered for CSE; 'Burke' still receives withdrawal help for his reading problems.) To put it another way: it's a way of training yourself to be *happy* that, in normal circumstances, you *have* to take much of what happens in groups on trust. In any case, providing pupils with private thinking and talking time is what these small group activities are all about.

Doing demanding work

Our second piece of evidence is drawn from a situation which involves a more radical departure from conventional comprehension work than the activity on the extract from 'Geordie'. First, because the class was working on a long complete story rather than the more common extract or short bit of prose. (Is this then 'response to literature' rather than 'comprehension work'? We argued earlier that this is not at all a useful distinction to make.) Second, because the questions the teacher was interested in here were not posed as such but 'translated' into the activities. Third, because two comprehension activities were here integrated together into work on the story over a period of time. These features of the work raise two points of particular interest:

(a) the effectiveness of the comprehension activities in making broad and difficult issues manageable;
(b) the relationship between talking and writing in work of this kind.

'A Man Called Horse', by Dorothy Johnson,[4] tells the story of a white man's journey into the American West in 1845 in search of a life 'among his equals – people who were not better than he and no worse either'. He is captured by Crow Indians and given as a slave to an old Crow woman. He gradually grows into a position of some status in the tribe and marries the old woman's daughter. After the deaths of the other members of the family he stays with the tribe to look after the old woman until she too dies.

The story was used here with a fourth year potential O level class of girls. The teacher's own interest in the story centred on two broad issues: what we might learn of our own culture from the way Crow Indian life is represented in the story; the question of 'status' and how it was that 'Horse' came to feel, by the end of the story, 'the equal of any man on earth'. These two broad issues don't allow of simple analysis; they are genuine puzzles which the story presents.

A brief outline of the sequence of work may be helpful. After the reading of the story the pupils were given a list of seven statements devised by the teacher which could stand as descriptions of the author's intention and/or of the story's overall effect. Each pair or group was asked first to decide which statements they agreed with, and then to underline from among those the three statements they considered the most important.

1 This story was written to shock you.
2 The story was written to show what Indian life was like in 1845.
3 The story was written to show one man's experiences in the West.
4 The story was written to show how a man found his true self.
5 The story was written to show that all people are alike.
6 The story was written to show that white people are better than Indians.
7 This story teaches you things about our society.

When the results were collated statements 2 and 4 were found to be the most popular, followed by statement 3; statement 7 was chosen by under half of the groups. The subsequent discussion focused on the meaning and the validity of the most popular statements. There was much interest in the Crows' mourning rites and in parallel procedures in our society; during the discussion there was a steady rise in support for the importance of statement 7.

Subsequently, the girls were asked to write a re-presentation of the story as it might be told from the old Indian woman's point of view, looking back over what had happened at the end of her life. The task was clearly recognized by the girls as a difficult one, involving not only putting themselves into the head of an old Indian woman, but also finding an appropriate 'voice' for the re-telling. This is one of the most interesting pieces which emerged:

Yellow robe gave him to me – he was not a person but a present. If at any time he had proved useless, I would have killed him just like any dog. Later, when he first said his name was Horse, I did not care. It was of no importance what he called himself as long as he worked. But slowly, he began to presume to be human. He tried his tongue at our own language and played feebly with boy's arrows. We alternately laughed and ignored him. When he crawled into the tepee one night, I did not bother to kick him out; I did notice how the animal was growing into a man.

Then came the day he rode into camp with two horses he had won. Realizing he was almost a Crow was a surprise, like standing back from a hide you have been tanning, and seeing it all, and seeing it is finished. He married Pretty Calf a few days later. Now that he was my daughter's husband, he could be treated as such, but he was as ignorant as a baby about our customs.

Yet when Yellow Robe died, he was forced to learn about our customs. All Horse's goods he had strived for became sacrifices to our mourning. And sacrificed also was his wife, his early son.

I sacrificed my dignity. I am just an old woman, life-worn and tired, without relatives to care for me. With my son and daughter gone, I had one person only to lay the chance of my life before – my slave. I am just an old woman, fingerless and dying. One winter, and I will be dead. But this man has saved me from begging for scraps, as he did, this man named Horse.

Working on the story in these ways was clearly a satisfying experience for both the pupils and the teacher. The powerful, haunting quality of the narrative tends to generate interest and enthusiasm in itself. But our experience of using the story with similar classes without the scaffolding offered here would suggest that an exploration of the issues the story presents – and of the different reactions it prompts from different readers – is not always easy to begin and to sustain. The list of statements which the teacher devised articulated a range of reactions to the story as a whole that the girls could use to get started on and engage with. On the other hand they seemed not (here at least) to preclude the exchange of 'unrelated' immediate responses, since their focus is particularly broad. The fact that the initial processing of reactions took place in small groups (mainly in pairs) gave the opportunity for the pupils to formulate something of what they thought before committing themselves to a class discussion. The focusing of that plenary discussion was helped by the existence of a 'collecting point' (the most popular statements) chosen by the girls themselves. That seemed to enable the plenary discussion to do what ideally is its proper job: teasing out the shape and the implications of difficult issues.

The writing task the girls undertook here is clearly not one that anyone would undertake lightly. That the results were of a better-than-usual and generally high standard for the class (with a couple of particularly interesting pieces) can only be explained by the fact that the girls were able to invest this task with something of the energy of what had gone before. There is always a danger that writing which follows talk will merely be a feeble echo of it. Ideally it should firm up and/or extend what has been said, but this is difficult if pupils feel they are being asked to cover old ground a second time. Here there was strength in the fact that the suggested narrative form could draw on and subsume ideas which had already been 'exposed' in the discussion but not fully 'worked out' there. At the same time the task kept the pupils in close touch with the original text, in that it involved a re-negotiation of key incidents in the story seen from another perspective. (Indeed it produced, among other things, some interesting misunderstandings from some girls of what does seem to go on in the story – which the teacher was able to take up in the next lesson.)

The bad news

We have needed to put a limit on the amount of evidence offered of 'new model' comprehension strategies working well. Partly because of space; but, more importantly, because of the danger of seeming to oversell the usefulness of the strategies. They are no panacea. They can and do work badly. We want now to try to describe, in general terms, on the basis of our own experience and that of ILEA English teachers who have recounted and documented their experience for us, how and why the strategies can go wrong.

It's worth starting, paradoxically, by saying that one thing emerges clearly from the experience teachers have had of introducing active comprehension work: by and large children say they enjoy it. Teachers tend to feel good about it too: there is satisfaction in looking around a classroom in which most groups of pupils are earnestly and enthusiastically talking about a text – and comparing it mentally with a classroom scene in which traditional comprehension work is being tackled by isolated, squirming and yawning pupils. But there are possible explanations for this positive response that have nothing to do with comprehension *per se*: novelty value; the agreeable 'status' conferred on pupils by the freer social relationships involved; an understandable relief at not having prematurely to plough that lonely writing furrow; and, for the teacher, pleasure in being responsible for a busy, purposeful classroom that is running itself. All these things are important and lubricate teaching and learning mightily. But what you need in the classroom is evidence not of whether it's liked but of how much pupils are getting from it. So how much *do* pupils get out of it? If we produced a table of statistics showing the mean growth in comprehension performance of a class which had worked in this way over a period of time, compared with one which hadn't, we hope you wouldn't believe in it – and nor would we. There is no formal system of measurement (extant or imaginable) which could give the answer 'this much' to the question 'how much?'. The answer to 'how much?' is 'a lot' or 'nothing much', with other words ('a fair amount', 'a little' . . .) dotting the continuum in between; such words, also, can only take their place in sentences which begin 'I think, probably . . .'

'How much?' is a necessary question to ask – but it leads, predictably, to more questions. These questions ask why, on a particular occasion with a particular group, this way of working seemed to bite, and why, on another occasion and with another group, it didn't. The answer here will be, not to simplify matters unnecessarily, the interrelationship of four factors in a matrix. The four factors which the matrix holds in relationship are of equal importance: (1) the quality of the text (2) the pupils' interest in and orientation towards it (3) the task intended to scaffold or focus the discussion (4) the conditions of work (e.g. the social relations between pupils in a small group, the time allowed for the task, and so on). A balance or an imbalance in the relationship between these four factors determines the investment pupils put into the comprehension job; to put it another way, how much they get out depends on how much the situation (i.e. all four factors together) allows and encourages them to put in. In what follows we suggest some of the things which we have found can throw this four-way relationship out of joint.

1 The text you pick may prove a dud.

Be warned. Real comprehension lives only on real material. Techniques like these focus a cold but salutary beam on stuff that doesn't cohere, on texts coming from and going nowhere. If your passage is a bad one it will show. We tried the methods on a number of pieces chosen for past O level papers (bits of Graham Greene, Neville Shute, you know the kind of thing). It just revealed that badly chosen snippets are badly chosen snippets, whatever their pedigree.

2 You can fail to 'earth' it properly.

The energy present in even the best text will not flow unless it is properly earthed. A good proportion of the lessons which didn't really get going or went off at half-cock did so because the pupils didn't have real reasons for being interested in it, didn't have enough opportunity to find their own uses for it, and did not understand its relationship with their past or future work. The ultimately debilitating effect on pupils of being launched into the text, and into the details of the activity, without some sense of why the journey was being made and where it was meant to take them, was not always immediately apparent; but after a promising start the flight often proved oddly short.

3 The small group talk may stay small.

The emphasis throughout this article on the value of pair or small group work on texts doesn't imply the abandoning of class discussion. There *is* a temptation to beat a retreat and to abandon class discussion of texts, especially when the small group work is going well. It is a temptation which we appreciate, given the problems of managing a discussion in which 25–30 pupils would like to – and should – have a voice. But it is a temptation to resist;

otherwise much of the value of small group work can be lost. Small group work allows for informal and intimate engagement between pupils and text, but its value is confirmed for the pupils by a properly arranged opportunity to offer something of what they've come up with to a wider audience and to weigh the significance of their thinking in company with others who have followed a parallel or related route.

4 *The pupils may not yet know the rules.*

When you first start, things may short-circuit. We have seen pairs and groups rattle their way through to quick, crude decisions in what should have been complex and open-ended enquiries. Their desire to finish the job was not perverse: they simply assumed that getting fast to a single, undisputed teacher-tickable answer was what it was all about. There are not simple solutions to this problem: many years of careful work have gone into habituating pupils to teacher dependence and to an expectation of quick results. If pupils are to see talking together in lessons both as work and as something to be worked at, they will need clear explanations as to why collaboration is valuable (and how it works), persistent encouragement to accept the slowness and uncertainties involved, and regular praise for what groups do achieve when they start to capitalise on their own powerful resources.

5 *The activity can be ill-matched or come between the reader and the text.*

A comprehension activity needs to be made-to-measure for the pupils, the text and the conditions; we haven't found that 'off-the-peg' activities work. There is no mechanical formula which produces the perfect fit for you: it's a matter of watching carefully the way you read the text *yourself* and then deciding where you want discussion to begin and to focus. Now you can devise the preliminary version of an activity which should assist the pupils in the lesson to handle the text in much the same way as you did 'at home'. But however well thought-out the activity may have been, there is the danger that it may get in the way of, rather than support, the meaning-making process. If you see this happen you'll need to trim it ruthlessly on the run or even junk it and start again.

But suppose you didn't notice that these fascinating puzzle-games weren't doing the job they were really meant to? Suppose they unwittingly became 'the thing we're doing' rather than a way of getting at what the text offers? It wouldn't be the first time that English teachers have discovered the alarming phenomenon of means becoming ends. Suppose these ways of working turned into just another exercise? A glance at some recent publishers' lists provides no comfort. *100 Cloze Exercises* (with separate answer book). Books (in series, packs, folders or as spirit duplicator masters) full of shabby bits of text shabbily interfered with. Books which say: 'these activities can also be tackled individually and in writing if required'. But let's not harry the publishers and let ourselves go free; for any of us making use of these ways of working will always be sailing close to the wind of complicating and trivialising the 'clean' reading experience that would otherwise be available.

So why should English teachers bother at all with such potentially dangerous distractions from the straight engagement of pupil with text? What's the alternative? Give up intensive comprehension work altogether? Interesting . . . but perhaps too easy a way out. Stick with traditional comprehension work? Not a reasonable option: it's wrong in the head and it doesn't work.

What about that early 1970s idea of just putting plain texts and groups of pupils together and letting things take their course? Those fascinating tapes and transcripts which launched the notion were stunning. No doubt, like us, you rushed off to try this blindingly obvious (but probably novel) technique; and if you did, your experience, like ours, was probably interesting but patchy. Those stunning tapes had clearly been the best of a mixed bunch. They showed what, on red-letter days, in a suitably pleasant and private place, could be expected from even the most unlikely pupils. It was thought-provoking and, in some cases, inspiring. But their minimalist version of recessive pedagogy was not in itself a practical, everyday classroom strategy which would enable ordinary teachers with ordinary classes to begin to move very far forwards on ordinary days. Doing the same thing back in the classroom with seven groups of four and no tape-recorders was rather a different matter.

And after all, isn't the good, clean 'pupils-alone-with-plain-text' model, admirable as it is, just a little half-baked? Its shortcomings

189

emerged for us over a period of time in the reactions of pupils when the situation went wrong. Least problematic: the pupils would have a grand old time chatting over anything under the sun except the text. Slightly more awkward: they made some headway but wasted much time and energy on bewildering false trails. Worst of all: they construed our recessive behaviour as an abdication of responsibility and felt they were drowning because we wilfully refused to throw the necessary life-belt and tell them what to say. Thinking about these reactions (from some pupils on some days) suggests to us that the problems with the early 1970s model were:

- it's a high risk method, which asks pupils and teacher to live with a bracingly high failure rate;
- there is, as a result, a powerful pressure to stick to a 'safe' sort of text (i.e. a text which will act as a quick springboard, or a text with a clear 'problem', or one with a simple surface);
- the method does not prepare for or give direct support to any plenary sessions or sharing of what was found;
- the method seems to imply what we might call 'one-offery': pupils getting a series of one-shot experiences of texts which, however rich they might be in themselves, seldom cohere in any satisfactory way.

We have exaggerated the faults in the pupils-alone-with-plain-text model. We feel better for it, for we also exaggerated the likely dangers involved in the use of activities intended to scaffold small group talk on texts. Their potential use is in promoting a sometimes delicate growth: the independent exploration of texts by pupils who are learning to see and satisfy their own reading purposes. Once the thing can happen without the need of their temporary support they should be ruthlessly got rid of: scaffolds only go up to come down. Some of the strategies (like 'cloze' and 'sequencing') may come down earlier than others; their role is to provide models on the desk of what readers can get up to in their heads (when, for example, they need to unlock an unfamiliar word, or track the logic of a series of paragraphs). Other strategies (like 'marking the text' and 'question-setting') may continue to be of value to sophisticated readers, as ways of deliberately focusing on what they are seeing. The techniques are designed to take work on comprehension up to a point where pupils left alone with a text do not feel unsupported or at a loss as to what to do with their freedom; they feed on the best intentions of the 'special occasion' early 1970s model. And the development of comprehension *is* centrally, a matter of how confident pupils feel about the things they can do with a text.

But it would be wrong to exit altogether without putting comprehension back in its proper place. We have concentrated too much here on the process of comprehension, and not enough on the relationship of intensive comprehension work to what else goes on in English lessons. We ought to see intensive comprehension work in the context of English teachers' wider concern to develop habitual, enthusiastic and critical readers. It needs to be seen, also, not as calling for a special kind of one-offery, but as an element in extended sequences of work involving experiences of other kinds than textual ones. We might see the 'grasping together' of comprehension as part of the wider 'grasping together' of patterns of significance in themes and issues under open and collective consideration in English lessons. Properly integrated into a series of lessons, activities on texts which are premised on giving pupils the time, the space and the support to find their own way about, will tend to leaven the lump of any theme- or issue-based sequence by providing a collecting point for the pull towards collective understanding.

Notes

1 By 1740 Glombots were campaigning ineffectually throughout the conurbations. Though some were literate, the majority couldn't read or write. Moreover, being idealistic visionaries, they seemed unable prudently to anticipate the consequences of their actions. On the other hand, despite their quite undeserved reputation for advocating violence, the majority wished to promote only peaceful changes through constitutional evolution and reform. In 1742 the authorities annihilated the sect in one of the most cynical and unconstitutional purges that history has ever seen.
2 In *Reading for Meaning, vol. 11: The Reader's Response*, Hutchinson Educational, for the Schools Council, 1973.
3 The list that follows is a synthesis of a wide range of different possible activities, some of which have been used in classrooms, in one form or another, for a very long time. Descriptions of some of the individual procedures on the list – and of the principles that underlie their

Bob Moy and Mike Raleigh

classroom use – have appeared, e.g., in Stauffer and Cramer's *Teaching
Critical Reading at the Primary Level*, published by the International
Reading Association (1968), in Christopher Walker's *Reading Development and Extension*, Ward Lock Educational, London (1974), and in
course material from the O.U. reading team. *The Effective Use of
Reading*, Heinemann, London (1979), reported substantial trials of
some of the procedures, and work on them has been extended in a
second Schools Council Project on reading based at the University of
Nottingham, 'Reading for Learning in the Secondary School' (the
report of which is to be published by Oliver & Boyd in 1984). This
Project calls comprehension activities of this type 'D.A.R.T.S.':
'directed activities related to texts'. Teachers in ILEA schools have
been involved, along with teachers in other areas, in trying out and
developing further various 'D.A.R.T.S.'. We are indebted here to the
expertise of those teachers – particularly Chris Dee, Jerry Fitzpatrick,
Wendy Rhodes and the many members of ILEA English Centre
courses on comprehension – and of the Project team. The list that
follows is our synthesis of a wide range of different possible activities,
and is by no means exhaustive.
4 'A Man Called Horse', by Dorothy Johnson, is included in *Story: The
Third Book*, edited by D. Jackson and D. Pepper, Penguin, Harmondsworth, 1973.

12   Learning Poetry

Terry Furlong

As the last chapter shows, there are ways of getting pupils to engage actively with texts. I wanted to explore how, after the pleasure and interest of reading itself, pupils might be encouraged to go back into the text easily, willingly and usefully, and to take on some of the choices and problems which writers face themselves. If they were able to compare their experiences of the text as readers with a more writerly view, from the inside as it were, they might gain insights which would help their own writing, and spare themselves and us the drudgery of some of the 'comprehension' and 'critical' work.

Initially, I was relying on intuition and classroom feeling to guide me, but it was when I had an opportunity to make tape recordings of pupils discussing poems that I began to gain a proper understanding of what was going on there. I listened in on parts of these conversations while they were actually happening, and had thought I knew what they were thinking and how they were operating. When I listened to the full tapes afterwards, however, I was surprised and a little disappointed. I had expected a tidy progression from one insight or deduction to another as their total picture of the meaning emerged. On the contrary, the tapes revealed apparently chaotic discussions, in which the pupils leapt from one thing to another, often before resolving a point or coming to any agreement about it. Sometimes they backtracked, digressed, lapsed into anecdote, or went round in circles. Most unexpected of all, they would reach conclusions I found acceptable, then reject these in favour of something I found mistaken or less likely to lead them to a coherent meaning for the text. Sometimes they would misread words, assume unlikely or impossible meanings, so that I felt an almost irrepressible retrospective urge to intervene and put them on the right track, even if it were only to supply the meanings for unfamiliar words. Yet I remembered that each pair of pupils had eventually reached a credible interpretation and understanding of the poem with very little or no intervention from me beyond encouragement, and that when I had recorded a discussion between groups on another occasion the pupils had seemed both knowledgeable and perceptive.

By the time I had made transcriptions of the tapes and spent time reading them, thinking and speculating, it became clear to me that I had somewhat mistaken the nature of literary response and the processes of comprehension, and that I had hitherto held an oversimplified, false notion of the dynamics of small group discussions. Perhaps the apparently logical progression implied by comprehension exercises and required by essays had misled me. What was happening with these pupils was much more like the rapid scanning patterns recorded when the eyes are looking at pictures, and it seemed to confirm that the mind sought to establish coherence in a broadly similar way, whatever the medium of expression it was confronted with. Indeed, the urge to seek coherence, whether in life, other art forms or literary texts, seems to be a fundamental motivation, and there might be a lot of sense in seeking strategies which capitalised on this. If pupils' active concern to establish coherence could play a larger role in their reading, perhaps the more reflective consideration of texts would follow from that and come to be better balanced and eventually more natural to pupils.

It was at about this time that I came across John Dixon's pamphlet, *Developing Active Comprehension*,[1] which, although not primarily concerned with the understanding of literary texts, did suggest various techniques which provided means for putting readers more actively in control of the text they were dealing with. Although the activities described, such as carefully arranged cloze deletions, were somewhat artificial, when I tried some of these activities with my classes they went well. The pupils seemed to like working in this way, and the problem-solving aspect of these activities generated a good deal of enthusiasm among pupils not normally noted for it. Children worked in pairs, animatedly discussing possibilities, thinking hard and arguing with one another. When I tried the cloze technique on a poem, the pupils' responses were often highly literary in character, investigating not only possibilities of meaning and speculating about intentions, but often focusing on technical aspects of the way in which the poem had been written. When I called a halt and asked for suggestions from the pairs, what struck me most was the patience with which they listened to ideas other than their own, the openness with which they considered alternatives and sometimes accepted them in place of their own suggestions. They seemed to be in charge of the text and of the lesson in a way that surprised me. The lessons were more interesting and enjoyable for me and, it seemed, for the pupils too.

From the work of the Schools Council Project described in *The Effective Use of Reading*,[2] other colleagues working on similar lines, and two excellent articles in *The English Magazine*[3] I gathered a whole range of structured activities I could use with literary texts: prediction, sequencing, various kinds and degrees of deletion, alternative versions, marking the text, finding boundaries, responding to statements, eccentric wide-angled questions, and pupils setting questions for each other. Gradually I learnt not to overuse such strategies, to use them on texts which we would have been reading in the ordinary course of lessons, and to use them on texts and parts of texts which really merited such close involvement and thinking. I found that it was important to use such 'scaffolding' to support pupils' search for meaning and coherence, and not to allow it to get in the way. Otherwise the means became the end, and we were back in the realm of pointless exercises.

From time to time, throughout these explorations in teaching literature, I taped and transcribed the conversations pupils were having. They taught me a great deal. Some idea of what I learned may be gained from recordings I made during a lesson on Charles Causley's poem 'Death of an Aircraft', in which I made use of the technique known as sequencing. This involved physically separating the sixteen stanzas of the poem and asking the pupils, working in pairs, to arrange them so that they made sense to them. This sounds a crazy thing to do, and in some senses it is, but I had two reasons for wanting to do it. If pupils tackled poems in the way I referred to earlier, it seemed only a slight change to do some of the muddling up for them in advance, and this seemed to be consistent with the way they searched for coherence normally. Then I have long been bothered by the fact that pupils seem reluctant to look further into the detail of a poem once an initial coherence has been established, and I wanted them to have to examine each stanza in detail. With this deliberate fragmentation of the poem it seemed to me that they would have to do this.

I did give them some guidelines to work on, similar to those which I normally use when asking pupils to consider a poem in small groups. I gave them some questions to keep in mind, which I wrote up on the blackboard: It's a story. Where's it happening? How many people are involved? Who is speaking? When is it happening? Does it have a beginning, a middle and an end? Then I gave each pair an envelope containing the separated stanzas, and a sheet with the stanzas printed in random order to use as a reference point. I told them that it was difficult and that they weren't to worry if they didn't finish. I recorded four pairs and shall give examples from the transcriptions of their conversations. In them the pupils are represented by their initials, the normal conventions are followed, and I occasionally appear as 'T'.

The pupils' ways of working were diverse, but a few things are apparent immediately. Our firm distinction between question and answer virtually disappears and is replaced by a whole series of more or less tentative probings: suggestions inviting support, moderation or denial; mixtures of thinking aloud and talking to each other; mixtures of reading out loud, speculations and pauses for the other to help. The whole atmosphere of the talking invites co-operation, and its very informality helps to disguise its subtlety and complexity, as this typical exchange shows:

M: – In Archontiki they stood in the weather Naked, hungry, chained together: I think they might be the soldiers . . .
J: No. Couldn't really be the soldiers . . . It might be the . . . um . . .
M: The boys?
J: Could be . . ., or maybe the Germans they . . ., they arrest anybody look suspicious, isn't it. 'Cos they'd want revenge.

This looks so ordinary, just a couple of ordinary kids talking, that it's easy to miss what they're doing, or to realise how different this is from a classroom discussion. Sometimes indeed there's so much thinking going on that it's difficult to tell exactly what they are thinking from the words alone, as in this four-way exchange.

C: Don't want that one there . . . the fire . . .
R: Eh?
M: D'you not think?
J: Could be . . .
M: Eh?
J: I just think it might . . .
R: – The Germans advanced . . . (p) Afternoon . . .

M: Look, this one here. – Down f . . ., no, before that.
C: I mean it could . . .
J: Could be before . . .

It seems to me that this mumbling, almost inarticulate dialogue is, in fact, just the opposite. This lack of explicitness can only occur when people's thinking is so much in tune that words become relatively superfluous. Paradoxically, the simplest bits of these transcriptions occur when one pupil has a much clearer idea of what is happening than the partner, and needs to explain things more fully. In these sections one pupil's speech predominates, and the invitations to agree are less open: 'right?', 'OK?' This is exceptional, however, and generally they help one another in a gentle, natural way.

M: – Lost their strips as well as their dinners . . .
C: Stripes?
M: Oh yeah. Still burning . . .

or

J: Berliners? (pronounced Ber-line-ers)
R: No, no, Berliners. 'Cos Berlin.

Most difficulties are sorted out in this way, and they very rarely asked me for help with even the most difficult words. Frequently they realise the meaning of something while in the process of reading or considering it.

D: This one says they get freed from somewhere, 'cos it says – the irons unlocked as their naked hearts. The irons, that's probably, you know, shackles round the foot.

I said earlier that it was easy to miss what was going on simply because it was so natural and obvious, and these little extracts all demonstrate the pupils using the most natural and obvious strategy of all: using your previous knowledge and experience of the world as you know it to take yourself on to new meaning and experience, to help to make sense of the unfamiliar and the strange. For these pupils, who had previously encountered little poetry in school, it seemed quite natural.

They used it frequently to predict what ought to happen next or what was most likely, particularly when it concerned the way people would react or behave. Their knowledge and experience of human behaviour is considerable, and not surprisingly it provides a surer guide than knowledge of poetry and literary conventions, though they do have useful ideas about these too. In this example, the partner has mistakenly placed stanza 14 of the poem after stanza 1.

J: Hold it. If he, if it's about a plane right? It should go on about the plane until su . . . he some, somehow it's got, the plane bit starts to finish. Look, this bit Ray. It says here . . .

On other occasions it helps them to sort out contradictions caused by the arrangements they have made, and leads them to important new understandings.

D: Prepared to die. But I don't know why he'd leap away, if he said he was prepared to die. Can't see why he'd leap away.
M: Might be chicken, then?
D: Might have . . .

Here there's some dissatisfaction with stanza 6 followed by stanza 13, but they seem content to leave it, and turn to another part for a couple of minutes. But some consideration has been going on, even while they've been talking about a quite different part of the poem, for D unexpectedly returns to it with,

D: Glass of wine – deep breath for the leading note. *Then* he could've jump away. But before the squad could shoot or say . . .

He has followed stanza 12 by 13, because it seems more natural and likely that the boy would behave in that way. What is interesting to me is the way that both pupils were content to leave an unresolved problem to sort itself out, and that at some mental level it did sort itself out. It's interesting because, whether such a confident strategy is part of their normal way of dealing with things, or whether it was acquired during this exercise, all pupils learned very quickly which strategies were successful in establishing meaning and coherence and which were not. Some may have depended on intuition, but most were very logical and depended on reasoning and previous knowledge of some kind. For instance, all groups knew that a tremendous number of stories begin 'One day . . .' and so placed stanza 1 first, and most groups found association a good clue:

D: See that one where it goes – Up, up went the plane in a feather of fire?
M: Yeah?

D: Well that one says – and each struck a match for the petrol tank, so it comes after.

Not next, but 'after', a particularly careful and sensitive judgment. They are using a device which Causley himself uses in the construction of the poem.

C: I want no words . . . Ah, look, here's one. It says, when he, when they're asked any last words you'd like to say. I want no words said one, with my lead. . . . That's right, probably . . .
R: Yeah, that's it.

They even use it with antonyms as here,

D: There's something about chained here. Where's the one you had where it says unchained?

Nevertheless, most groups learn quite quickly that this strategy has only limited usefulness, since it is small-scale and only useful for linking one stanza to another. If over-relied on it can lead them astray, so they need something bigger and broader in range, which will provide a framework of events into which they can later put the detail.

J: That, that'll be, you know about the . . . um . . . – unlocked the naked hearts, right? That'll be after that, because this boy would rather die than run, right? – And then they shot him anyway.
M: Oh, yeah! That's true.
J: And this would be before it, like a sort of . . . um . . . execution.

It doesn't matter at this stage that they have put stanzas 10, 14 and 15 together. What they do have is a framework from which they can work. Most groups find out that there is an opening section, stanzas 1–5, a final section 11–16, and some kind of central section in between. In fact, this frameworking is a much more powerful strategy for eliminating possibilities than word association, and seems to show that they have moved on from looking at individual words and stanzas to the shape of the poem as a whole as they gained confidence in handling it. For some groups at least, this was a conscious movement, shown in D's remark to me quite early in the lesson.

T: And this bit you've put all together, yeah?
D: Yeah, in groups . . . then see if we can fit the groups together.

Another set of strategies which shows this kind of movement

from small to larger-scale segments concerns reading aloud, or what I call 'running at it'. During the first half of the lesson all groups made a lot of use of this, reading two stanzas out loud to see if they sounded right, to the reader as much as to the partner. Later, there is much more paraphrasing and summarising of stanzas and groups of stanzas.

J: Yeah! That's it.
M: Yeah! Because that one that we was talking about, he was too young, I think . . .
J: To get shot.
M: . . . to get shot. But the other two, you know, reasonable age. So, because they know what they were doing, and the other boy, you know . . . he was . . .
J: Yeah.
R: Too young . . . to know . . .
M: Just following them, trying to copy them.

M's eager explanations here show something else of which I became aware, and that was the accelerating pace of the lesson and the excitement which grew in the last quarter of the lesson as the poem came rapidly together for them. They showed remarkable tenacity and patience, both in the early stages, which were slow and exploratory, and at the end. The determination of this group is obvious.

R: What's the time?
J: It's five past twelve.
M: Four.
J: Huh?
M: Four minutes past.
C: Oh, I have to go home for dinner.
R: Sod you, we want to get it finished.
J: Nah, it's got . . .
C: Yeah, OK? (showing R a new order)
R: I reckon that's it.

I wouldn't have minded if groups hadn't finished, or if they had come up with different arrangements of the stanzas. The point wasn't to get the right answer, but an arrangement which made sense and which could be justified. For instance, it doesn't matter greatly whether stanzas 8 and 9 are swapped round, but these two pupils aren't content with 9–8 and change them round.

M: But that bit there changed round, it's like a big thing isn't it?
C: Hm, . . . like it was more important.

This does in fact make a significant difference to the feeling and atmosphere, increasing the sense of drama and the boys' isolation, and sets the scene for the next six stanzas. There are many such signs of at least an awareness of the mood and atmosphere, which are matters that I normally have the greatest difficulty in getting pupils to appreciate and talk about in class. There were comments about other matters of tone and style from groups too, like the lyrical and nursery rhyme quality of stanza 3. They are too many to quote here, but the last part of the lesson produced many comments on the more literary aspects of the experience of the poem, comments which one would have been glad to hear from much more experienced readers of poetry. I could feel the groups emerging from their more detailed considerations in the problem-solving part of the lesson, to a more secure and informed awareness, moving comfortably between the literary experience and their own lives, as if they'd always done it.

One example of a group doing that will have to suffice. In it the group, after a discussion of 'archangel' in the final stanza, came up with what for me was a thrilling realisation as two black pupils connect this with their own religious background.

T: Yes, that's right. He's the one with the fiery sword who, in the story, will go down and er . . . chop 'em all up.
J: That's Armageddon, isn't it?
R: What's that?
T: Yes.
J: Armageddon. It's the end of the world.
C: Oh, so that's it . . . when he comes back . . .
M: There'll be hell fire!
J: So he's a bit like Michael and Gabriel.
T: Yes. I think that's what he's getting at.

The point I want to make here is that the experiences of the poem have become real, in the sense that the pupils can identify with and enter into the thoughts, motives and feelings of the boy as they see him to be, that these now have a life of their own in the minds and imaginations of the pupils. It has also, it seems to me, taken them beyond the surface language of the poem, which they spent a long time considering, to a realm where symbol talks to symbol, experience to experience, and metaphor is a natural language of communication.

All this took place before any of the groups had seen the printed version of the poem, and in a following lesson they were pleased to come back to the plain text of the poem and consider any differences. I recorded a group of four talking with me, and their final evaluation can best be left to speak for itself.

T: Now, looking at it, do you think it's er . . . a difficult poem?
R: No.
J: Does seem difficult in parts.
C: Some . . .
R: It's well written.
J: It's very well written, that is.
R: 'Cos it's sort of smart and punchy . . . It tells you everything.
J: More than a story I think.
C: Sometimes it gets a bit hard to understand though, some words . . . this bit down here . . .
J: Seven stalking spiders.
C: Yeah, murder stations down here. Sort of things like that.
M: I like it though . . . there's, there's a lot in it.
T: Why, why is it that it's sometimes difficult to understand?
R: 'Cos he describes it in his way, what's important.
C: Yeah, and his feelings.
J: He might have been there and seen things and he's trying to get us to see them.
R: And he tells you a lot about it.
C: It's not really long . . . but you feel . . .
M: It's good though.
R: Yeah, smart.

It is not my purpose to make exaggerated claims for these kinds of techniques: there are many things they can't do and aren't intended to do. They aren't a replacement for other kinds of teaching about literature, but are best regarded as a supplement to them, as another useful piece of teaching 'equipment'. If they are over-used or used inappropriately (particularly as tests), they could just become another route down the same old tunnels. They seem to me to be most appropriately used on texts which will bear this kind of close scrutiny, and poems often will, and to be used with materials which one would be using for other reasons, which have been chosen for their suitability and interest to the pupils.

What they did for me, and still occasionally do, is to provide a structure for group discussions which has enough motive power behind it to keep pupils interestedly and actively engaged with the text until they get deeply enough involved for the text itself to take over. I treat them as a kind of bridge, which at its best will enable pupils to relate their experience of life, literature and language, to those of a particular author, who may be apparently distant from them in some respects. They have the advantage of drawing not only on pupils' liking for problem-solving, at least initially, but also of removing me from the position of the all-knowing mediator and controller of meanings. With me out of the centre, pupils can take on meaning at a pace which is appropriate for them as individuals with their own heads, hearts and experiences. I don't regard this as abnegating my function. On the contrary, it frees me to become an interested participant.

One thing I should stress above all, however, is that such techniques are never more than a prop and a preparation, leading towards a discussion in the normal sense. I generally use them to prepare pupils for a full discussion in class, although they have many lesser and sometimes incidental benefits. I have found that when pupils do have a chance to prepare in this way they are more interested and patient in their consideration of the ideas of other pupils than they usually are, perhaps because it gives them a chance to come to fuller and more secure understanding, perhaps because they aren't having a race for teacher approval.

One incidental benefit which was totally unexpected and a pleasure is that pupils can often remember whole stanzas word for word, or complete sentences of prose, using them quite spontaneously in discussion. On one occasion, just for the fun of it, I asked a group how much they could recall a couple of lessons later. Between four of them, prompting and adjusting each other; they remembered all twenty stanzas of Causley's 'Ballad of the Breadman' word for word.

Notes

1 *Developing Active Comprehension*, Discussion Booklet 3, from the Schools Council Project English 16–19. Available from Bretton College of Education, West Bretton, Wakefield, West Yorkshire, WF4 4LG.
2 E. Lunzer and K. Gardner (eds), *The Effective use of Reading*, Heinemann Educational Books, for the Schools Council, 1979.
3 *The English Magazine*, published termly by the ILEA English Centre. Available from the English Centre (Magazine), Sutherland Street, London, SW1. One of these articles is included here as Chapter 11.

13 Dealing with a set book in literature at 16+

David Jackson

At times I catch myself blasting off about the special advantages of not having a specific body of knowledge in English teaching. But I've only got to dredge up what I was doing in English literature classes a few years ago, and that still partly shapes what I do now, to realise that's far from the case.

You'll probably recognise the scene (fill in the gaps for yourself). The desks are all turned to the front. Almost all the pupils have their heads down and are furiously scribbling away. It's the run in to the examination time and my anxiety about their possible results has pushed me, yet again, into giving them notes on the main themes and characters. There is some thoughtful discussion about several points but it's always the same few, active members of the group who take part.

My notes come from remembered enthusiasms and insights about *Great Expectations* gained from reading it again during the holiday before this present group's literature course began. Atmospheres from the book – the bleak marshland of Pip's oppressed conscience, Miss Havisham (. . . 'waxwork and skeleton seemed to have dark eyes that moved and looked at me'), the magnificent river chapter 54 – still haunt me, but close reading techniques, gathered from habits of practical criticism picked up in my training, are tending to harden out into mechanical, routine procedures. So that even before I hear what the pupils make of the book I've already filled an A4 sheet of paper (to help me to make detailed references to the book later when my memory of particular episodes is fading) with precise references to themes, characters and language, such as:

> PIP – fertile imagination page 41;[1] guilty conscience 44; imaginative empathy with the Convict 45; awakened moral sympathy 48; stifling of spontaneity by Mrs Joe 54; Mrs Joe's starchiness 57; tenderness for Joe 78.

My attitudes and approaches to the book are already setting fast like concrete even before I walk into the first literature class. So here in this detailed evidence and concreted attitudes are some of the English teacher's main blocks of knowledge; and the problem is that they often get in the way of pupils' understandings at 16+.

Our personal insights into what we read as teachers can help the pupils when they feel confirmed in their responses but, often, they are too easily impressed or intimidated by them. And there are far worse tendencies to be found in the traditional examination course on literature:

> A Fifth year group in English had written 23,000 words of
> dictated plot of *Far From the Madding Crowd*, and would have
> written many more when they had finished *Great Expectations*
> already under way. (From *Aspects of Secondary Education*,
> HMSO)[2]

Reading experiences are often reduced to filing cabinets of factual information. And pupils are drilled and rehearsed in memory tests and efficient examination packaging skills.

As a result questioning pupils get the feeling that they are being spoon fed. They are being told what to think and feel about the books they read by people like me with my notes on Pip's character. And that kind of teacher-telling, or more subtle nudging, usually ends up with the pupils retelling like parrots, without ever having had the chance to go through processes of understanding that might have made the book more real to them.

So how do we move out of this dead end?

> Real learning means making knowledge personal. . . . This is
> only possible when we express the new experience (in this
> instance the experience of reading *Great Expectations*) in our
> own language in our own way . . . (Harold Rosen, *The
> Language of Textbooks*).[3]

Pupils only begin to make a reading experience their own by using talk and provisional jotting as ways of fitting that new and unfamiliar experience into their already existing systems of understanding.

Here I want to look closely at some fresh ways[4] of getting out of the dictated notes trap and how they help pupils to come at stories, poems and plays through a series of preliminary learning stages that probably give them a more effective way of possessing for themselves the special qualities of those reading experiences.

The pupils are from a nine-form-entry mixed Comprehensive school in Nottinghamshire. They have all opted to do the Cambridge Plain Texts 'O' level English Literature course offered within a fourth and fifth year option choice operated from within the English department. Some of the pupils' work shown below is from the last term in the fourth year and the first two terms of the fifth year. The book chosen, *Great Expectations*, was a set book that could be taken into the final exam.

Chapter	
1st	1st page – horrible style. Difficult to make sense of, needs reading twice.
	Description of convict – excellent. Very lucid. Who is convict? Where is story going?
2nd	Mrs Joe – v. good descriptive – readable, and amusing in places.
	Description of Pip's guilty conscience at having to steal is beautiful. Vocabulary is awkward and book doesn't seem to know where it's going.
3rd	1st paragraph ('It was a rimy morning and very damp') is superb. So is story of journey through the mist.
4th	Analagies very illogical ('. . . be as to our fingers, like monumented Crusaders is to the legs').
	Style is getting easier, but book is at odds with itself. What is it doing?
5th	Soldiers? Confusing. Story of chase after convicts good but what is happening?
	The author's strength seems to be his powers of description. The style is awkward – dozens of commas to the sentence. The plot seems bitty, but I'll give it a chance.
6th	Another complete change of tack. I'm having problems remembering what's going on. Might get easier as I get used to the style.
7th	2nd para. a gem. Joe explaining his life looks like an end to the whole episode. Is the book now going to jump a year or two? No. What has Miss Havisham got to do with the convict? V. odd.

8th   Apparently a turning point. Is Pip being sent to Miss H's permanently?

Finally, author is beginning to prognosticate as well as describe.

Many unanswered questions about Miss H.

Pip is timid, weak, easily influenced.

9th   Pip is ashamed, and ashamed of admitting it and ashamed of not admitting it.

This seems to be one shaping event in Pip's life. Is the book going to describe all the events of people that shaped Pip?

(David Bull)

Here we find David gradually easing himself into the book and being able, through the jottings, to find a place where he can own up to the problems of making sense for himself of what he's reading ('Difficult to make sense of, needs reading twice . . .') rather than borrowing the teacher's prefabricated phrases. Also the teacher is put into a much more useful position of being able to start from where the pupil actually is rather than where s/he would like David to be.

Through the initial strangeness of having to come to terms with an elaborated style that makes unfamiliar demands on him as a reader the book starts to open up for him:

3rd chapter. 1st paragraph. ('It was a rimy morning, and very damp') is superb. So is story of journey through the mist.

David is starting to express his own point of view in a series of speculations and puzzlings and is converting the experience of reading the book into his own terms. And, simultaneously, there's a sorting out and explanation going on. As another member of the group said in answer to the question, 'Did the first impressions jotting in your journals help you to understand the book?'

Writing things down helps you get your thoughts straight in your mind. If you write out your thoughts, your feelings become clearer. Also, if you have two points of view you can argue them out reasonably on paper.

The act of getting a dimly understood thought out of the head and down on paper helps David to clarify his reactions to the book.

The main clarification going on in David's first impressions is his attempt to find an underlying structure in the book. Frequently he questions its apparently random patchiness (. . . 'book doesn't seem to know where it's going' . . . / . . . 'the book is at odds with itself' . . . / . . . 'the plot seems bitty' . . .) and seems frustrated by the tacking turns of the plot. What this preliminary jotting is allowing David to do is to bring in his expectations as a part of his general search for a whole meaning in what he's reading. So his anticipation of some kind of structural coherence (i.e. that the book isn't a collection of isolated descriptive pieces) is one of the main reasons why he's offended by the 'bittiness' as he sees it.

The book becomes clearer to David at the point where he is able to make out an organising principle and a connection between local description and future action ('Finally, author is beginning to prognosticate as well as describe.') He sees that the thing that holds all this detail together is the shaping influence on Pip:

Is the book going to describe all the events of people that shaped Pip?

At this stage he is starting to synthesise his disjointed reactions into a more organised system for understanding the book. And because of that he is able to see himself more completely as somebody capable of making his own meaning out of what he encounters.

Impressions and questionings within a single mind represent an important first step in response but they need to meet other views if they are going to gain a more fully developed and sharpened focus. Building up patterns of meaning together through small group talk often away from the teacher domination of whole group exchanges, helps pupils to break out of an isolated commitment to a limited number of views to take on a much wider spread of alternative angles. Many of the group were struggling, like David, to make sense of *Great Expectations* and often lacked his staying power and logical grasp. So opportunities for swapping impressions, setting up a collective strength, through small group talk need to exist alongside the written jottings.

After this initial phase of confirming pupils' initiatives, of being able to make up their own minds from a position of relative power, teachers have a much better chance of exchanging views without their understandings muzzling the pupils' ones. Admittedly, it's difficult to stop yourself from blurting out your views but there are growing signs that more teachers are wanting to join in conversations, rather than instructional lectures with pupils, where the teacher's voice isn't seen as the only approved way of reacting to the book. And, of course, a great deal depends on the pupils' habitual ways of coming at a book that have been laid down in the three years before.

Handled tactfully there is a crucial role for teachers at this point in helping to encourage faltering insights and assisting pupils to make their views more precisely explicit. Often the teacher still gets in the way, but there are also more promising signs.

Here is a transcript of an exchange between a teacher and three pupils.

C = Caroline; B = Barbara; G = Gary; and T = Teacher.

C: . . . all through the book people are trying to get one up over everyone else . . . and that it's about social climbing . . .

G: . . . he was common first working with the blacksmith then he met Miss Havisham . . . who was a snobbish person and he thought, 'I want to be like that so I can marry Estella' . . .

T: What about the ending of the story? Is Pip still snobbish?

G: Not really. I think he realises what's been happening . . .

B: . . . he realises he's not so good to be at the top . . . all the time . . . and he realises that it's best to be what he really was at the beginning . . .

T: How does he realise that?

C: . . . well because when he was ill Joe came and sort of sat by him . . . he was still loyal to him . . . despite Pip not having spoken to him for ages . . .

T: Why does Pip feel sympathy for Magwitch out on the marshes?

C: . . . because they both feel rejected . . . the convict's rejected by society . . . and Pip's rejected by his family . . . everyone's always picking on him . . . and everyone's always picking on the convict . . . so he sees himself like the convict . . . out on a limb

B: . . . Pip's got no family . . . or he's only got Joe to turn to . . . whereas the convict's only got him to turn to . . . he feels he can trust him . . . because he's scared of him . . .

T: What are the things that Dickens is criticising in the book?

C: . . . people wanting to be what they're not . . .

T: Such as?

C: Oh well, Pip wanting to be a gentleman . . . and I think maybe Estella wanting to pull him down all the time . . . I think . . . somewhere deep inside her . . . she doesn't really want to do it.

G: I think that's maybe Miss Havisham's view . . . she wants Estella to do that . . .

B: I think she was using Estella to do it wasn't she? Using Pip for her revenge on all men . . . getting her to do it . . . just because it happened to her . . . she'd got to do it to somebody else . . . as revenge . . . and she'd picked on Estella to do it to Pip.

C: I also think Pumblechook and Wopsle are trying to be better than they are as well . . . trying to be high society . . .

B: Mrs Joe's like that . . . she was just a blacksmith's wife and yet she made herself feel more important than anybody . . .

The teacher's intervention here is sometimes just an interruption to an emerging line of thought (as in the question about the ending blocking off Gary's developing arc of enquiry) but in other places it works as a supportive framework within which the pupils can concentrate their attention on what they've made of the book.

Frequently, these early jotted reactions seem sketchy, disparate units of response and urgently needing time for a more thorough pondering. Through this sharing in talk pupils can learn to stand back from the often impulsive over-reaction of their first meeting and, although still remaining loyal to the spirit of that first flavour, move towards a more controlled, unified perspective. By pooling hunches and exploring them more systematically they can often create their own explanatory framework.

In the transcript, although they haven't totally integrated Magwitch into these frameworks, (they can see there's a correspondence between Pip and him . . . 'out on a limb' . . . but they haven't connected that with the structure of inequality and privilege running through the novel) they are defining some of the main strands of the book in their own words:

'. . . all through the book people are trying to get one up over every one else . . .'

'. . . he realises that it's best to be what he really was at the beginning . . .'

'. . . people wanting to be what they're not . . .'

The pupils are talking themselves into a position where they can understand the behaviour of Pip, Estella, Miss Havisham, Pumblechook, Whopsle and Mrs Joe all through the unifying, interpretative network of '. . . people wanting to be what they're not . . .'. So that later, they can come up with a more considered focus on the novel, where personal feeling, intelligence and commentary all merge with one another:

> The change in (Pip) comes when he meets Miss Havisham and Estella. Estella made an impression on him, and you usually find that when someone admires someone else, they copy them. Pip realised that he wants to be posh and refined, like her. I think that meeting Miss H and Estella was the worst thing that's happened to Pip. It made him ashamed of his home and background, and made him even more of an outcast. It made him want to achieve more than he is capable of. I don't think that he will become a gentleman, he hasn't the character to pull it through. He will be even more dissatisfied with his life – poor thing! (Caroline Falconer)

Translating their thoughts into another medium often produces a valuable distancing effect that helps the pupils to organise their reactions to the book more closely and connectedly. As a fifth former commented, 'It helped you sort out in your mind who was with who, and who wasn't.' Getting the story straight for themselves is the first part of this (and the inter-relationship between characters) and then they can move on to systematising their fragmentary responses into patterns of meaning.

Here, in Fig. 13.1, the diagram shows Pip as the central consciousness of the book and is very useful in helping this fifth former to map out more exactly the various shaping influences surrounding Pip, but it's a static model and doesn't really allow the pupil to express co-ordinated impressions or a sense of development in time through the novel.

Finding meaning in the book is often the same as gathering single and disparate clues together into a more unified network of significance. This isn't easily learnt, and what these diagrams do is to assist pupils to organise their meaning-making more precisely. Getting their half-formed ideas down on paper often puts pupils in a better position to reflect on and modify first impressions. And to create links between different moments, from a more detached position.

In Fig. 13.2 the organising of meaning takes the form of a circle. The pupil explained why he'd done it like that:

> It seems to me that Pip's life forms a circle. He starts as a

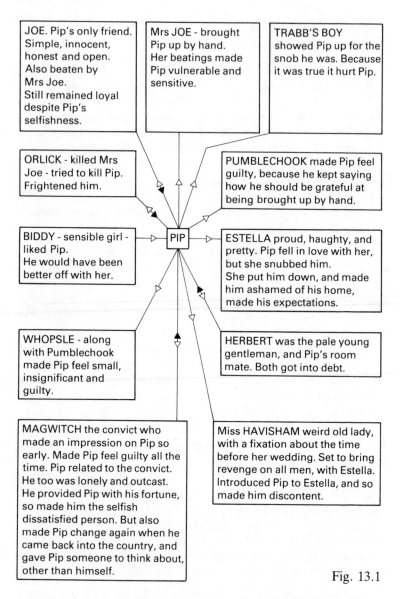

JOE. Pip's only friend. Simple, innocent, honest and open. Also beaten by Mrs Joe. Still remained loyal despite Pip's selfishness.

Mrs JOE - brought Pip up by hand. Her beatings made Pip vulnerable and sensitive.

TRABB'S BOY showed Pip up for the snob he was. Because it was true it hurt Pip.

ORLICK - killed Mrs Joe - tried to kill Pip. Frightened him.

PUMBLECHOOK made Pip feel guilty, because he kept saying how he should be grateful at being brought up by hand.

BIDDY - sensible girl - liked Pip. He would have been better off with her.

PIP

ESTELLA proud, haughty, and pretty. Pip fell in love with her, but she snubbed him. She put him down, and made him ashamed of his home, made his expectations.

WHOPSLE - along with Pumblechook made Pip feel small, insignificant and guilty.

HERBERT was the pale young gentleman, and Pip's room mate. Both got into debt.

MAGWITCH the convict who made an impression on Pip so early. Made Pip feel guilty all the time. Pip related to the convict. He too was lonely and outcast. He provided Pip with his fortune, so made him the selfish dissatisfied person. But also made Pip change again when he came back into the country, and gave Pip someone to think about, other than himself.

Miss HAVISHAM weird old lady, with a fixation about the time before her wedding. Set to bring revenge on all men, with Estella. Introduced Pip to Estella, and so made him discontent.

Fig. 13.1

warmhearted, human person, goes through various degrees of snobbery and comes back to being warm and human. Each person he meets moves him along one place round this circle. So it seems logical to set it out in this way.

The Meaning of the Story

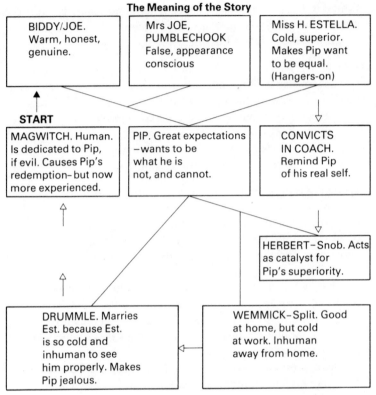

Fig. 13.2

There are misunderstandings here (like Herbert being a snob), but the pupil is finding his own way of bringing together the different parts of Pip's life. The circular structure keeps in closer tune with the movement of the book (unlike Fig. 13.1) and through the rise and fall contrast shows up the hollowness of those social snobbery aspirations at the heart of the reading experience. Hence Pip's place at the centre of the diagram. So that he links a moment like, '"He calls the knaves, Jacks, this boy!" said Estella . . .', with another at the very end of the book, 'I opened my eyes in the night, and I saw in the great chair at the bedside, Joe. I opened my eyes in the day and, sitting on the window-seat, smoking his pipe in the shaded open window, still I saw Joe. I asked for a cooling drink, and the dear hand that gave it to me was Joe's', into a system for making sense of the whole book.

David Jackson

Why don't you read what I have written and make up your own mind about what you think, *testing it against your own life, your own experience.* (Doris Lessing, from the preface to *The Golden Notebook*)

Getting inside a book like *Great Expectations* can't be done without some kind of active, personal collaboration from readers interweaving and mingling with it the experience of their own life. What the teacher can do is to encourage, at all times, the creation of personal contexts for the book, such as in this exploratory piece where a fifth former weighs himself against Pip:

When Pip is in the middle of his expectations, he becomes snobby and takes a superior attitude to his lessers. I also sometimes take this attitude, but there is one big difference between me and Pip. Pip came by his superiority through fate and money; I came by mine through sheer hard work, in short, mine isn't based on money that can slip away like it did on Pip.

Whenever I sit any exam or test, the results only prove my point. Sometimes I am beaten but I don't really mind. There are times when I really don't want to be clever, as it only invited insults about how big headed I am, when it's the teacher who reads out my exam results, not me.

I am exposed to a sort of inverted snobbery, i.e. people less able than myself automatically assume that I'm just a big-headed freak whom you shouldn't be seen with and this is so annoying. It's so annoying that sometimes I just think, 'Oh, damn the lot of them' and look down on everyone just to ease the pressure a little.

Pip was fortunate in that he wasn't exposed to this and had a lot of good friends in the same position as himself, but I'm not quite so fortunate in this way. Either people don't understand what I say or the few who can do such wouldn't listen or aren't my friends at all. Therefore, the only person I can talk to who would understand is, believe it or not, myself. (No, I'm *not* mad, just in case you're wondering). Hence, I take long slow walks on most nights to puzzle out problems, to work myself up for important events or to work out how to deal with excessive amounts of homework (which I may add, I receive frequently).

In the same sort of way, Pip and I have learnt the same lesson

– 'it's not as nice as it looks at the top' only he could climb down, I can't. (Chris Franks)

Chris is establishing a sense of himself and his own experience of being a clever fifth form pupil in relation to some of the emotional pressures of the book, especially in chapters like the twenty-seventh one (Joe's visit to London) where, '. . . Joe was rolling his eyes round and round the room, and round and round the flowered pattern of my dressing gown'.

He is putting his own feelings of pride ('. . . sheer hard work . . .'), superiority and isolation against those of Pip and trying to build bridges between them, and also at the same time pointing up the differences between the two experiences. Chris sees himself as the victim of a meritocratic system (. . . 'it's the teacher who reads out my exam results, not me') and defines that against Pip's gaining of status 'through fate and money'. With directness and a baffled honesty he is seen in the process of taking the book on in terms of his current preoccupations.

Also Chris is learning to make explicit to himself and others the parallels between his experience and some of the book's concerns: *'In the same sort of way,* Pip and I have learnt the same lesson – "It's not as nice as it looks at the top" only he could climb down, I can't.'

> . . . our aim is to move dynamically from the 'me' of personal
> identification to the 'that' of the poem or the object in the poem.
> The discipline lies in the attentiveness to the 'that', and it should
> be made plain that there is no real dichotomy here, but a natural
> movement from subject to object and back again.[5]

From a position of personal confirmation (having gone, in some way, through these preliminary stages of understanding) pupils can move, often stumblingly, into the considered statement/examination essay/course work assignment without losing touch with the quality of the initial response. It's a difficult one; very often the formal constraints of the examination essay scare pupils and teachers into hiding behind stock orthodoxies but, at best, some of the early flavour can be combined with more detailed evidence.

Here's one final example of a fifth former adjusting to the rigours of the timed essay (40 minutes) two weeks before the examination:

What did Chapter 27 *Great Expectations* mean to you and what is its importance in the design of the whole book?

The main storyline in the book is how Pip starts off humble, becomes a gentleman, and ends up almost his old self again. It is also how Pip starts off honest, becomes selfish and mean, and finishes honest again. The scene of Joe in London highlights this snobbery, and class division.

Even from the start Pip shows his true colours, although it may be unintentional, by describing the way Joe comes up the stairs. 'I knew it was Joe by the clumsy manner of coming up the stairs – his state boots being always too big for him – and by the time it took him to read the names on the other floors . . .' It's almost as if Pip's scorning him for having bit boots, and not being able to read, and for generally not being as good as him. The next bit of (unintentional) snobbery was when Joe came into Pip's flat. Joe looks round the room, and at Pip's flowered dressing gown, and at the servant, and I think he's terribly over-awed. I say unintentional snobbery because I don't think Pip would dream of lording it over Joe, he just doesn't know he's doing it, which just goes to show how much of a snob he is.

The hat seems, to me, to play an important part in the scene. Joe won't give it to Pip, but holds it in front of him. When it is eventually coaxed away from him, he puts it where it keeps falling to the floor, yet before that Joe handled it delicately and carefully. Dickens described it as 'a bird's nest with eggs in'. Joe holds the hat between him and Pip, and is almost using it as a sheild (*sic*), to take refuge behind it. He is clinging on to it, and I think it is because it is a reminder from his world, and it is comfort in this alien, over-bearing world.

As I have said, the main theme of the book is social snobbery, and I see Pip as representing the snobby side, and Joe as the humble side. Joe shows how subordinate he feels by calling Pip 'Sir'. When Pip tells him off about that Joe looks at him 'with something faintly like reproach'. As if to say, 'You're better than me, with all these fancy things, I aught to respect you.'

But at the end, when they part, despite being a fish out of water, Joe finds it in him to be kind to Pip. This is one of the most touching bits in the book. It shows that you can be without airs and graces, and money and manners, and flowered dressing gowns, and servants, and still be honest, and kind and care for someone. This, for me, is the whole skeleton of the book, and that is why the scene is important.

There's some dutifulness here but there's also emerging confidence of tone and a personal, first-person attack on the question existing, hand in hand, with a detailed attentiveness to the words on the page.

She's clearly been influenced by the teacher's neat categories (. . . 'the main theme of the book is social snobbery . . .') but she's certainly on the way to making them her own and trusting in her own judgements. She's putting ideas in her own terms and often using her own informal language, like 'mean, snobby side, airs and graces, fish out of water' to see and summarise things for herself.

Not only is she focusing more sharply on particular incidents from the book to *prove* her case, but bringing together a perceptive commentary with a more engaged sensitivity. Take her handling of Joe's hat scene for instance. She effectively fits the scene into the book's overall structure (i.e. how low-status people find security in their dealings with an 'alien, overbearing world') and, at the same time, investigates it in a way that suggests personal discovery:

'Joe holds the hat between him and Pip, and is almost using it as a sheild, to take refuge behind it. He is clinging on to it, and I think it is because it is a reminder from his world . . .'.

There's an excited metaphorical adventurousness about the exploration here and in the last paragraph that is starting to unify critical intelligence and feeling that might profitably suggest some possible ways forward in the future.

> If I've known a poem for some time and have already thought and talked about it rather thoroughly on previous occasions, I'm more at a disadvantage in any new conversation about it than at any advantage. If I can't forget all the things that I thought and said before, I certainly don't want to try and remember them more completely. If there's anything further I want to do with the poem now, it's to release my imagination to start from scratch with it and live it through again . . .[6]

Some teachers of literature are beginning to recognise fresh questions and challenges to their usual practice. How can we as teachers retain our genuine excitement about reading without swamping our pupils? Can we spot the right time for our telling to be constructively taken on by the pupils? Can we prevent our understandings from hardening out into the dead crust of rehearsed gestures for both pupils and teachers?

There aren't any instant answers but, perhaps, if more teachers saw what they were doing in the classroom as the setting up of new conversations between pupils' experiences, the teacher's perceptions and the reading experience, rather than lectures about the book from the front, then we might have more chance of 'starting from scratch with it and (living) it through again'.

If we can listen more attentively to the views of pupils who feel respected and valued, and if we can open up our classrooms to enable processes of understanding to take place more frequently then, again, we might find our pupils in a stronger position to create new words, in their talking and in their writing, about the books we ask them to read.

Notes

1 All page references are to the Penguin edition of *Great Expectations*.
2 HMSO,*Aspects of Secondary Education in England, A Survey by HM Inspectors of Schools*, 1979.
3 H. Rosen, 'The Language of Textbooks', in *Language in Education* (Language and Learning Course Team), Routledge & Kegan Paul with the Open University Press, 1972.
4 See 'First Encounters', in *Children's Literature in Education*, Winter 1980 and 'Meeting Books', in M. Torbe, ed., *Language, teaching and learning – English*, Ward Lock Educational, London, 1981.
5 D. W. Harding, 'Response to Literature', in *The Cool Web*, ed. M. Meek, A. Warlow and G. Barton, The Bodley Head, London, 1977.
6 John Newton, 'Literary criticism, universities, murder', in *The Cambridge Quarterly*, vol. 5, no. 4, 1971.

14   Media studies

Andrew Bethell

> the exploitation of the cheapest emotional responses: films,
> newspapers, publicity in all its forms, commercially catered
> fiction – all offer satisfaction at the lowest level, and inculcate
> the choosing of the most immediate pleasures, got with the least
> effort. We cannot, as we might in a healthy state of culture,
> leave the citizen to be formed unconsciously by his environment; if
> anything like a worthy idea of satisfactory living is to be saved he
> must be trained to discriminate and to resist.[1]

An indication of what happened when 'literature' met the 'mass
media' in the 1940s. This uncompromising position was taken by
F. R. Leavis and his co-author Denys Thompson in a slim volume
entitled *Culture and Environment*, which, despite its dauntingly
moralistic perspective, signalled the beginning of media studies as
some of us know them in schools today. No self-respecting English
course book could appear these days without at least a token few
pages of advertisements to be imitated, *Daily Mirror* editorials to
be comprehended and ten-year-old television schedules to be
surveyed. Scratch the surface of much of this work and you will
find the values of Leavis and Thompson: discrimination leading to
resistance. The advertisements will be imitated, in order to expose
them as superficial distortions, which every properly educated
member of the middle class will ignore and despise. *Daily Mirror*
editorials will be subjected to a string of comprehension questions
designed to expose what is said rather than to explore how it is
said. And the television is to be surveyed because the content of
majority viewing is beneath serious consideration; but reveal the
number of hours spent watching it and you might just jog a few
consciences and switch a few allegiances from 'Crossroads' to
'Upstairs Downstairs'. Maybe there is less emphasis on resistance,
which we now replace with a more passive 'relevance', but the
discrimination model of media education still prevails.

In this piece I shall try to show how we can and should abandon the 'discrimination' model, and in so doing re-invest the notion of 'resistance' with its broader political meaning. Not resistance to the cheapest emotional responses, but resistance to those dominant values which deny social change and undermine human dignity.

I do not underestimate the scale of the task. Like the majority of those who will read this book I am conditioned to judge and discriminate at every level. I continue to celebrate the personal response. I cannot escape from the hierarchy of literary forms. Understanding that cultural elitism goes hand in hand with social elitism does not make it any easier to reject the critical response by which I categorize so much of the world. However, there is another way. To find it we need to look more closely at what happened to the Leavis and Thompson model of media teaching, and to see how attempts to use media products in the classroom to 'inoculate' children against the evils of cheap emotional response were gradually modified.

After 'discrimination' and 'inoculation' in the 1940s came 'appreciation' and 'cultural exploration'. The latter position is best represented by the work of Richard Hoggart with his *Uses of Literacy*,[2] by Raymond Williams in *The Long Revolution*[3] and then, in the early 1960s, by Paddy Whannel and Stuart Hall in *The Popular Arts*.[4] All these books were encouraging teachers among others to move away from active discrimination *against* mass culture, and instead to take the mass media seriously as part of a wider, largely unvalidated common culture. They were still concerned with values, but the values were working-class values not the elite ruling-class values tangentially celebrated by Leavis *et al.* They did not provide tools to help teachers discriminate against the mass culture, but encouraged teachers to discriminate *within* the mass culture. Not so much discrimination, more appreciation. This is the view of the mass media which has dominated media studies over the last two decades. It is the view which results in those course book exercises. This is the view of media education which encourages us to privilege the *Guardian* over the *Daily Mirror*, 'Play for Today' over 'Crossroads', *Jules et Jim* over *Planet of the Apes*.

In fact, of course, there is still discrimination. This view only discriminates against certain media products, not all of them. The problem was, for those of us trying to develop media studies, that this approach discriminates against the very media products most admired by the children we teach. Some of us got ourselves tied up in knots in the early 1970s trying to wheel the 'discrimination/ appreciation' Trojan horse further and further into the children's cultural camp: we were prepared to discuss the merits of the Osmonds compared with the Monkees, whether *Jackie* was better than *Teendate*, which Bruce Lee film has the most realistic deaths. We might have gained a few friends by admitting that these products existed, but we made many more enemies by trying to colonize *their* music, *their* magazines, *their* fashions in the name of *our* notions of appreciation and discrimination. It may have worked with folk songs and the oral tradition, but it felt a deal more uncomfortable in the classrooms of the TV generation. Somehow the will to appreciate and discriminate was a fickle motivator. Initial enthusiasm for countering what Leavis called the 'cheapest emotional responses' quickly waned, and no one had changed their views. It was, and still is, a dead end for those teachers interested in anything other than confirming the cultural *status quo*.

Some teachers were gradually becoming aware that the mass media had cultural and political implications which went far beyond taste or enlightenment. They were a relatively small group, who had managed to keep up in part, at least, with the university academics who had moved on from the notions of culture put forward by Williams and Hoggart. The cultural debate was now influenced by the work of European structuralists, and these teachers (many of whom were involved in film) were looking to the work of Roland Barthes, Stuart Hall and Umberto Eco for a way out of the 'discrimination' dead end.[5] Where Hoggart and Williams had been seeking out and validating a popular culture, these cultural theorists were suggesting that the mass media ought to be *analysed*. From literary criticism to structural analysis. It was quite a leap. What was being suggested was that as teachers we should be saying: 'Never mind which is better and why, instead let's concentrate on how the mass media work as media of *communication*. Let's look at what messages are transmitted, how they are transmitted and what messages are received.' This was submitting the media products to very much the same kind of analysis as that being promoted by the structural linguists.

Why did this apparently atavistic return to a formalism

221

associated, for many, with traditional grammar and objective response appear so attractive to those of us who had become disillusioned with Leavis's legacy? Precisely because it allowed us to side-step the sticky business of deciding whether 'The Sweeney' was 'worthwhile' or 'good television'. Instead, this approach encouraged us to find ways of looking at signs and visual codes. We could explore narrative, focus on genres of TV programmes. We could consider the television industry, the process of production. But perhaps best of all the European theorists had shown us that we might consider how 'The Sweeney' fitted into an overall view of society. We could try, and nobody finds it easy, to analyse with our pupils just what social and political values 'The Sweeney' reflected and reinforced. The real advantage of switching from appreciation to analysis was that we could acknowledge that the mass media were more than just 'entertainment', that we needed a broader definition of culture to deal with the way the mass media shaped and guided our view of the world. The theorists gave us the concept of 'ideology': a concept which made questions like 'Is this good television or bad television?' seem redundant. In studying the mass media we were studying how the dominant views of our society were reproduced again and again and again.

'Ideology' is not a comfortable word. Certainly not a word you would want to flash about too much in the curriculum debates that are going on these days. Associated as it is with inaccessible jargon-ridden abstraction, 'ideology' gives traditionalists apoplexy and makes progressives feel queasy. The traditionalists are right to be suspicious. Anyone who is interested in an education which will encourage children to question the way society is run and give them the understanding to challenge the existing structures cannot afford to ignore the educational implications of this 'ideology'. What the new media studies can do is remind us that the dominant values of our society are the ruling-class values and that these values are reproduced in much of the literature we teach and virtually all that the mass media transmit. By turning our attention to the sub-textual and cumulative meanings which really influence the way we think media studies can become the area of the curriculum which the mandarins of the DES ought to fear. And quite right too.

Readers who have got this far may well be losing patience with the 'jargon-ridden abstraction', which may appear to lead a long way away from the classrooms they know and love. Too much of the writing in this area fails to lead back to the actual business of teaching. Nowhere else does the gap between theory and educational practice loom so large. Those who feel that the previous few paragraphs have merely whetted their appetite should consult the reading list included in the notes to this chapter. I shall turn now to the business of putting the new media studies into practice.

The shift from cultural discrimination to cultural analysis means, in the first instance, a shift in the focus of learning from *content* to *form*. In English teaching we have been used to building much of our work on the pupils' responses to content. Certainly most of us have used films to provoke subjective responses to content. For much of our work we will continue to use literature, films and pictures in this way. We use films and television drama to promote discussion about homelessness, nuclear war or family conflict. Used in this way, films provide much the same appeal to the emotions and the intellect as the gripping short story or the powerful poem. However, using film, television, even newspapers in this way tells us nothing about the mass media. Analysis of and response to content tends to mean finding different ways of saying 'I like this, I am moved by this, this I recognize'. Back to the old discrimination model. Back to the Trojan Horse. What formal analysis allows us to do is to put subjective responses aside; not something an English teacher would want to make a habit of, but essential if the media studies teacher is to practise the high-flown aims of the previous paragraphs.

Two examples should clarify how such a switch, from content to form, from subjective to objective, actually proves far more productive. The first concerns television news. Some time ago the Metropolitan Police chose to break with precedent in announcing their annual crime figures and revealing the breakdown by ethnic origin of those convicted of one particular sort of crime. Mugging, we were told, was predominantly a 'black' crime. You may remember how that story was treated by television news and the press. ITN's treatment of the story in 'News at Ten' was a particularly blatant example of how the media can reinforce and amplify the racist assumptions which informed the original presentation of statistics. The 'mugging' figures were extracted from the multitude of other crime statistics and given overwhelm-

223

ing prominence, totally disproportionate to the scale of that crime compared to other categories of crime. There were decontextualized interviews with white victims, carrying twice the emotional charge of the slightly more considered views of the authority figures. Behind the newsreader was an ambiguous graphic suggesting black crime in general.

At the time this story went out I was teaching in a school with a large West Indian population in an area notorious for street crime and poor relations with the police. The item had clearly had an impact, and to me the 'News at Ten' treatment lent itself to classroom analysis. How was it to be done? By accident, I did embark on a discussion of the issue and that item in particular. I was quite unprepared, and the discussion was part of a wider debate about race. For twenty minutes the class offered their subjective responses to the item. The trouble was that even those pupils most directly affected by the almost visible increase in racist assumptions about black youth on the street were conducting the debate on the police's terms. They were giving the same priority to 'mugging'. They were trapped by the figures. They were on the defensive, despite the fact that they all deplored the crime. They were being backed into a corner by others whose own racism, born of a minute area of experience – 'My auntie's friend was mugged by two black kids' – had been validated by the news.

It was a messy and counter-productive experience, and I ended up having to deliver a didactic version of what was wrong with the statistics. Because I was having to rely on subjective responses to the content I had allowed my pupils to adopt uncritically the 'News at Ten' agenda and the political assumptions which influence that. Even though some of the participants were outraged, it was a passive outrage and left them feeling powerless.

What is the alternative? To start with it is essential to have the relevant piece of television on video tape. It is impossible to promote any sort of analysis on subjective recollections of yesterday's viewing. For this sort of analysis it is important that the piece is short enough to be repeated several times. Television watching assumes and achieves a natural state of absorption on the part of its audience. All of us find it difficult to sustain an analytic perception for too long. We are too used to being sucked in. We do not take kindly to interruption. Leave a piece of television on for too long and the classroom audience will lose all inclination to distance themselves from the subjective experience of watching. Howls of complaint are not easily diverted into constructive analysis.

Before showing the short extract from 'News at Ten', the one item we wish to focus on, it is essential to give the group a way of looking. The whole group can be asked to look out for one or two particular formal aspects, or, more productively, smaller groups can be asked to observe different formal aspects. So once everyone is clear about what the piece contains, one group may be asked to record how much commentary there was, how much 'expert' comment, how much live interviewing. On a second viewing this group would try to note what information came from which source. Another group would analyse the visual presentation of speakers: how many black faces, how many white faces, how many suits. Another group would consider the additional images used: the backdrop logo, the establishing shots, the graphs and captions. None of this information would come easily, but because the pupils will quickly begin to feel like experts, the requests for repeats to check up on information and prove points will mean that at no time has anyone been asked what they thought about mugging.

Once the class has effected some sort of a formal analysis they will be ready to accept that the news item is composed out of a set of deliberate choices made by an editor and director. Each of those choices has significance. Each choice affects the way we 'read' the news story. The next step would be to go back to the raw statistics and suggest a range of alternative treatments. If the group is working well it may be up to writing alternative commentaries. Equally, it might prove fruitful to look at the other news that was reported elsewhere on that day and draw up an alternative 'agenda'. In this way the group can be encouraged to decide just why this became a lead story at all. It may even have provoked some pupils to ask who chooses and why.

The point about working in this way is that at the end of two or three sessions the pupils will have a radically different perspective on that news item. No longer passive receivers, they will have taken back some of the initiative. Many of them would see the news item as a carefully constructed representation. They would be on their way to seeing that news is not a neutral statement of new facts, but a very particular set of choices with a very particular, usually hidden, message.[6] By the way, it will have become clear to those who were outraged that there was something very specific to focus their rage on. And it wasn't the white lad whose auntie's friend had been mugged outside the Co-op.

The second example takes us closer to the heart of the distinction between discrimination and analysis. Leavis and Thompson certainly believed that advertising was a cultural form to be reviled and resisted. In this day of sophisticated television and colour magazine advertisements they might have found it more difficult to avoid engaging with advertisements on an aesthetic level. They would probably have had some sympathy with Germaine Greer who, when given an hour of high culture television time to explore advertising,[7] chose to do so by selecting the most aesthetically pleasing adverts and calling them art. She showed these advertisements, each one of which had cost two or three times more than her own programme to produce. She celebrated the creative camera work, the deft cutting, the luxurious colour, the music, the rhythms, the subtle symbolism. This, she confidently informed us, must be art. What she was trying to do was to teach us to discriminate between good advertisements and bad advertisements. Bad advertisements are cheap and manipulative. They lack subtlety. They 'inculcate the choosing of the most immediate pleasures, got with the least effort'. Back to the old discrimination model; and, in educational terms, useless, because it tells us nothing about how advertising works to shape our lives and shape our view of the society we live in. Such an approach tells us nothing about how advertisements reinforce the dominant values, because not only does it ignore the social significance of consumption, it encourages a passive consumption of the advertisements themselves. It is, in fact, a consumer's guide, reinforcing the one-way traffic of ideas and values.

It is not easy to challenge the power of advertising by driving back up the one-way street. The best advertisements are 'seamless' (a piece of the jargon I find particularly useful. Most media products are so well put together that you cannot see the seams. If you cannot see the seams it is so much more difficult to tear them open). A classroom strategy must somehow help to make the seams visible.

Once again the aim must be to give the pupils some power over the product by putting them in the position of experts. A single advertisement is short enough and rich enough to allow for analysis in depth. A common mistake is to spray advertisements at pupils in much the same way as they are sprayed at home during an evening with ITV. Equally it is best to avoid the blatantly shoddy: the seams may be visible, but the analysis will tend to be superficial, the conclusions simplistic. Better the middle of the road advertisements, and preferably those aimed at young people: jeans, drinks, sweets, are a few of the most likely examples. Once the advertisements have been selected, two or three will be quite sufficient, the pupils will again be asked to take on a particular formal perspective. As the advertisement is repeated, the group may be asked to look at the way it works as a story. All advertisements have a narrative structure and can be told as a story. For many it is merely a variation on 'what happens when you use this product'. Pupils can be asked to separate out the different shots in the advertisement and then reconstruct them into the story: girl on her own, boy on his own, chocolate bar, the meeting, the offer, the sharing, the happiness. For many advertisements much of the story is implied, it takes place elsewhere. Pupils can be asked to suggest what information is missing but implied. By using the stop frame on video recorders it is now possible to sort out, shot by shot, just how the narrative is constructed and how the juxtaposition of images moves the story on.

The next step might be to ask the groups to look at the way individuals in the advertisement move and relate to one another. Again the stop frame allows for a more considered response. Who touches whom and how? How do the characters relate to the objects? Another group can be asked to ignore the images and concentrate on the sound track. What words are used? What music? How do the sounds relate to the image? These are all perspectives which are bound to throw up issues of implied meaning, issues which will open the way for pupils to ask awkward questions *from a position of strength*. Without too much effort the questions become deeper because the pupils will want to know why certain attitudes are constantly repeated? Why are girls always represented in a few stereotypical roles? How does money fit into the narrative and the relationship?

These last are complex questions in search of sophisticated answers. Advertisements are usually constructed by clever people and do not yield up their ideological assumptions too easily. One of the most accessible sub-textual messages concerns the status and role of women in our society, and an increasing number of teachers are using the study of advertising as a way into this area. Unfortunately, many fall into the same trap as Germaine Greer. Despite her solid credentials she found it very difficult to challenge the deeply sexist assumptions of those nice young ad men. Wallowing as she was in the aesthetic and subjective response she was defenceless against the plausible dominance of the male terms of reference. In the same way a group of teachers in my school recently found that despite what they considered the overt sexism of many advertisements the habit of consumption was so deeply set that it made challenging the values almost impossible. Their experience is worth a brief word because I believe it reiterates my case for an analytic approach.

As part of a unit of work on anti-sexism the teachers collected together a selection of advertisements, all of which seemed to reinforce stereotypical views of women. They included an advertisement for Slimcea bread (before Slimcea, Slimcea, after Slimcea), one for electricity, which depicted the traditional idealized family unit in a perfect dwelling, a Building Society advertisement, which had men leering at an attractive woman because she'd 'got what it takes' (a Loan Account!). There were eight advertisements in all. These were shown to the group in a batch. The class was not new to the issue, they had had several lessons looking at role definition and conditioning. However, what the teachers found, when they began to discuss the group's personal response to the collection, was that the girls and the boys did believe that if you are fat you are ugly and are therefore interested in any product which helps a person become thinner. They did feel that if they had a home like the one in the electricity advert they would indeed be happy and successful, and that the woman in the building society advert was asking for whatever she got from those leering men in their pin-stripe suits. They feel like that because that is our society's common-sense view. Suggest that such a view is not common sense and you are suggesting that they have no sense.

If, instead, you ask your pupils to begin from a formal and relatively objective analysis, like the one described earlier, you are not threatening their view of the world, you are helping them to make sense of the way their own assumptions and ideas have been shaped. You are helping them to see that there is much more to the business of advertising than just selling things. You are not saying 'Don't buy Slimcea' or 'You don't really want a house like that' or 'You must disapprove of men behaving like that.' You are not concerned to inoculate them against the evil effects of advertising. (There are dangers in misrepresentation, distortion and misleading information, but these are so much more easily dealt with.) By side-stepping discrimination and adopting a formal analytic approach, you are saying to your pupils: 'This is one important way that the dominant values of our society get passed on, now you understand a bit about how that happens do you want to challenge those values?'

This is a book about literature in school, and I am well aware that many readers will not share my own commitment to the broad definition of culture which includes the mass media. Certainly I know of many teachers who view any attempt to move from the subjective, discriminating approach towards the formal analytic approach with the deepest mistrust.[8] There are those who want to accuse us of a deadening obsession with pure formalism. Such an accusation assumes that the switch is total, when in fact it is a switch in emphasis. I have not been arguing for English teachers becoming the dry grammarians of the audio-visual. Pure structuralism has little to offer the classroom teacher of media studies. What we do need, however, are ways of helping our pupils distance themselves from their own total immersion in the mass media's cultural continuum. To do that we need to begin with formal analysis and only then can we hope to grapple with the ideology and its reproduction.

There is, however, a danger. Even if we do not see ourselves as dry grammarians, by setting our sights too high we could easily end by wrecking the new media studies on the rocks of the old pedagogy. We could find ourselves unwittingly returning to the transmission model of teaching. When I was forced into giving that didactic lecture on the mugging statistics I was reverting to the traditional role of teacher. It is a role which has not worked very well with our old curriculum and is likely to fail miserably with the complex issues of the new media studies curriculum. The secrets of the mass media cannot be transmitted. Instead, we need to confirm a belief in what Douglas Barnes has called the 'transformation' model of learning.[9] The intentions that lie behind this chapter can only be realized if we adopt a pedagogy which gives the pupils enough space to transform their own experience of the mass media. That means a pedagogy which relies on active and collaborative interaction amongst small groups of independent learners. It is a pedagogy which insists that tasks must be open not closed and which offers every possibility for the learners to take control. It is a pedagogy which places value on and gives power to the immediate voice of the pupil. The sort of learning I have tried to describe in this article can only take place when the learners are firmly in control of their own language and learning. Only then can Leavis's ideas of resistance be turned into the powerful weapons we all require to challenge the mass media version of our world.

Notes

Many of the ideas in the early part of this chapter were inspired by Len Masterman's excellent book, *Teaching about Television*, Macmillan, London, 1981.

1 F. R. Leavis and D. Thompson, *Culture and Environment*, Chatto & Windus, London, 1948.
2 R. Hoggart, *The Uses of Literacy*, Chatto & Windus, London, 1957.
3 R. Williams, *The Long Revolution*, Chatto & Windus, London, 1961.
4 S. Hall and P. Whannel, *The Popular Arts*, Hutchinson, London, 1964.
5 See, for instance:
   R. Barthes, *Mythologies*, Cape, London, 1972, and 'The Rhetoric of the Image', in *Working Papers in Cultural Studies*, no. 1.
   S. Hall, 'The Determination of News Photographs', in *Working Papers in Cultural Studies*, no. 3.
   U. Eco, 'Can Television Teach?', in *Screen Education*, no. 31. For some of the arguments which provoked the change, see *Screen Education* betwen 1970 and 1975. The other main European influences came from the work of Louis Althusser and Antonio Gramsci.
6 An excellent introduction to television news treatment can be found in S. Hall *et al.* (eds), *Policing the Crisis*, Macmillan, London, 1978, ch. 3, 'The Social Production of News'.
7 Germaine Greer talked about advertising on the 'South Bank Show', LWT, in March 1982.
8 See, for instance, a recent article in *English in Education*, Autumn 1982, 'Understanding "discrimination": the case against "television studies"', by Roger Knight, for an expression of this suspicion.
9 D. Barnes, *From Communication to Curriculum*, Penguin, Harmondsworth, 1976.

15 For their own purposes – reading African and Caribbean literature with young black people

John Lee

During the last few years there have been demands for the inclusion of African and Caribbean literature in school syllabuses. Pressure groups have insisted that it ought to be there by right, as literature. What follows is not meant to be part of this debate. It is simply a description of a course and the way the students responded to it. It is not a piece of literary criticism or an argument about literature but a reflection on the purposes to which some young black people put African and Caribbean texts.

The course in African and Caribbean literature is an option within the school's Mode 3 CEE[1] in English. In its original design the CEE course was planned to give the maximum amount of freedom to both teachers and students in their choice of texts and tasks. Examination is by course work and exhibition. Each student must complete fourteen written pieces, of which at least six must be literary 'criticism', 'appreciation' or 'response'. There are no strictures as to the type or style of writing to be included, except that the students should demonstrate an ability to handle a variety of language functions. Individual teachers offer particular authors, or, more likely, students choose a particular author to study in depth over the whole course. The guiding principle here is that the students come to appreciate the richness and variety of an individual author and get to know their work, in opposition to the normal gallop through literary history or the teacher-selected significant texts. The students typically choose Hemingway, Lawrence, Steinbeck (familiar CSE authors), occasionally Dickens or Hardy, even James Joyce. Teachers offer texts and authors they like: first-world-war poets or contemporary verse or modern drama. Alongside these individual choices the course offers students thematic options: children's literature, Indo-English literature and African and Caribbean literature. Within each thematic option the principle of student choice of texts and authors is maintained.

231

Although the option in African and Caribbean literature was and is open to all students in the school it was originally seen as likely to match the particular interests of West Indian students who were studying for CEE English. It was crudely envisaged as an opportunity for them to support and express their own identity. Bernard Coard's important and influential pamphlet *How the West Indian Child is Made ESN in the British School System*[2] had strongly urged black parents to set up

> Black nursery schools and supplementary schools throughout the areas we live in, in Britain. Our nursery schools should have Black dolls and toys and pictures, and storybooks about great Black men and women, and their achievements and inventions. Our children need to have a sense of identity, pride, and belonging, as well as mental stimulation, so that they do not end up hating themselves and their race, and being dumped in E.S.N. schools. Pride and self-confidence are the best armour against the prejudice and humiliating experiences which they will certainly face in school and in the society. . . .
>
> Black history and culture, i.e. the history of Black people throughout the Caribbean, the Americas, Africa and Asia, should be made part of the curriculum of all schools, for the benefit of the Black and White children. . . .
>
> Indeed, its exclusion from most school curricula constitutes nothing short of criminal negligence (or prejudice) in the educational sphere.

All this gave support to an identity-confirming course. Also, the educational climate of the time was heavily influenced by Plowden-like notions of positive discrimination, while work on the psychology and social psychology of personal and group identity was in the air.[3]

It is obvious now that this view of identity was extremely patronizing and that some of the work on identity and most of the conclusions drawn from it were at best simple-minded, at worst, wrong. In the early years of the course, the texts the students read seemed to function as identity-confirming. Examining the work of the earliest students on the course does show them responding to texts they read by reaching back into their Caribbean past, for all of these students had spent their early years in the Caribbean. The course placed their own and their families' experience of migration and cultural difference on the curriculum agenda. Although at the time I saw this as building 'a sense of identity, pride and belonging', in retrospect it was a political assertion, if a somewhat low-key and gentle one.

Once there were students who had no direct experience of the Caribbean, who had been born in England of Caribbean parents, the focus of the work and the choice of texts altered quite dramatically. Their choice of texts and their response to them became overtly political; so that in the last few years the focus has been on racism and on their position in British society. The issue of the position of women, particularly Black women, is just beginning to surface. In effect, what began as a straightforward attempt to teach something labelled African and Caribbean literature has been taken over by the students. In recent years they have made it their own, using the texts for their own purposes. In retrospect it is possible to see that this has always been so, and at no point has the teacher actually been in control of the 'knowledge'.

The students were and are introduced to Caribbean literature through two anthologies: Kenneth Ramchand's *West Indian Narrative* and O. R. Dathorne's *Caribbean Narrative*. Clearly this approach gives some notion of the historical development and scope of Caribbean literature, and this was particularly important for that group of students who had spent part of their life in the Caribbean. In a sense it gave them an impression of the 'continuity' of Caribbean life presented in 'respectable' literary modes. It needs to be pointed out here that at that time there were few major critical works, so that while asserting the essential interest and worth of Caribbean literature the teacher could do so without having to rank the authors in order of merit. The process by which the students chose the authors and texts was simply a matter of selection, either from the anthology or from the bookshelves. It was during the early years of the course that the Caribbean connections were most direct and obvious. There was a sense in which the course hovered between literary studies and Black/Caribbean Studies, along the lines suggested by Coard. This is hardly surprising. What is surprising is what the students chose to make the content of the course.

They read and enjoyed not merely established Caribbean authors like Selvon, Anthony, Naipaul and Lamming, but also H.

G. De Lisser and Claude McKay. Bearing in mind the students' own Caribbean connections Selvon and Naipaul are obvious choices. It is De Lisser and McKay who could not have been predicted. Curiously, it was De Lisser's novel, *The White Witch of Rosehall* to which the students responded powerfully. They seemed to find in it some sense of place and inspiration for their own writing. If De Lisser's novel is subjected to 'literary tests' it will undoubtedly emerge as deeply flawed, trite and probably worthless. Similarly, if it is searched for political understanding, relevance or the presentation and/or celebration of black characters it will also fail. Basically it is a story of white lust played out against a Jamaican plantation background. It encapsulates all the stereotypical views of the evil influence of African black magic, the terrifying customs of Haiti and the stupidity, superstition and ignorance of black plantation slaves; in effect it condemns Jamaica as a place of vice, evil and horrible corruption. How extremely odd that black students, apparently seeking identity confirmation, should seem to find it in such a text, written by a white novelist and introduced by a white teacher. Part of the answer lies in the fact that tales of mystery and witchcraft are popular with 16-year-olds and that it is a good yarn; but what is more significant is what some students did with it: how they made it their own and used it for their purposes.

Elvis's work is representative of this process, as Elvis is representative of the group; he was, in fact, a typical CEE student. Directly after reading the novel, Elvis wrote three stories. A central scene in the novel is Annie Palmer's conjuring up of the 'rolling calf', a ferocious supernatural beast with terrifying eyes. Elvis took this episode and made out of it one story 'Man and De Rolling Calf'. Reading the episode in De Lisser's novel has drawn Elvis back to the stories he knew and heard in Jamaica. It seems that for the first time in school he can bring his experience of Jamaica, a part of his own culture, into the open. The story is written entirely in dialect and has many of the qualities of the oral tradition. It opens:

> Bwoy de odder day a nearly dead wid fright me sey me was walking in de night all by me self me was not frighten atall until me see one big Sintin a run a come along de road. A stop and carefully listen, Bwoy me could hear de soun' of chain a jingle round de Sintin neck.

> Bwoy me couldn' listen no more, me could tink only one ting
> me could do, me sey a tun roun, you see sah, and ah run like any
> race harse along de road. Me could still hear de jingle of de
> chain and de four foot dem still a run me along. Ah was so tired,
> me could not run any more. Me member bout rollin-calf, and
> dem sey when rollin calf catch you it wi kill you, an dem wi' toad
> out dem big yeye ball dat is full of heat, on your body and bun
> you up. Me sey when me member that, ah feel like sey me foot
> dem get more stronger, and a run faster than before.

It is clear from this passage that Elvis has made an effort to establish his voice. The voice not merely of Elvis as an individual but as part of a whole community. De Lisser's novel has had the effect of 'unlocking' the stories and story-telling style that Elvis knew. I would argue that Elvis has used De Lisser as a prop to his own confidence. He reads a respectable writer and begins to see that his own stories can have similar value. What has happened is that Elvis has seen his own stories as part of literature and as having the same status as De Lisser's novels. His story 'Duppy Revenge' exhibits the same sophistication in written dialect, but where the plot of 'Rolling Calf' derives directly from the novel, 'Duppy' does not. It is part of the Jamaican tradition of ghost storytelling but set in modern Jamaica, as we can see from the references to street lights and the cinema:

> Me never like fe go picture on me own, but me sey dis a de first
> an its gonner be de las. Dem noh have street lights on de road,
> you affee use torch fe fin you way, but just like a spite me, lef fi
> me at ome.

His response to reading De Lisser is to attempt to write the authentic voice of his community. He has identified himself and those like him as Jamaican, not in an informal way, but formally, and within part of the school curriculum.

Just as popular as De Lisser with these students was Selvon's classic novel of migration, *The Lonely Londoners*. This work fits neatly into that category of literature said to be identity-confirming for black students, written as it is entirely in dialect and documenting post-war Caribbean migration to Britain. Reading the novel challenged Marcia to find out about herself, her family and her community. She interviewed people, asked them about their early experience of England and recorded the partial

235

biographies of two of them. Marcia felt able to bring the voice and experience of the black community directly into school, and for the first time this experience was legitimized in the school curriculum. She feels confident to record the interviews in dialect – a significant move from the usual 'translation' into Standard English. Her response to reading *The Lonely Londoners* and Selvon's direct influence on her is apparent in this extract from an interview. In response to her question, what did you do when you weren't working? she records, 'When I come home I just sit down. I listen to the radio and go out few places. Go party . . .'. As significantly, she records the racism her interviewees told her of in their own voices,

> I have never seen so much people before. I remember on the train white people move away from a black person and would look see if the colour rubbed onto the seat when they got up. The old women would give a particular look.

and, 'My mother warned me about white people and that they would call me names like wog.'

The experience of reading literature for Marcia and for the other students enabled them to express their social selves, to deal with difficult and painful issues that were and are most often locked out of school. It is hard now to communicate the excitement of listening to them talking so openly and directly and writing so boldly for the first time. Reviewing the books read and the work done it seems clear that the course provided a connection with the Caribbean, a direct link with personal experience, but, more importantly, the students worked on the literature in a way that enabled their own concerns to be expressed.

It is significant that a major part of the content of the course and of the type of work has now altered. The young people who are reading African and Caribbean literature now were born in England and have grown up in a society that rejects them. Unlike their older siblings they have no memory of living in an accepting society, only stories about back home that may seem comforting or alien turn by turn. It is hardly surprising then that different texts should be chosen and different positions taken up. I was first conscious of a change in the content of the course and the response to texts in Rosalind's work. Rosalind's parents are Nigerian, but she consistently identified herself as being a sort of Nigerian-style

British Black. During the course she chose to read Chinua Achebe and talked and wrote about his work in a fairly lively and interesting way. In particular she focused on the political and cultural conflict between colonizer and colonized. Somehow, though, it seemed distant from her. At the beginning of the spring term when we read Claude McKay's sonnet 'Outcast', it seemed that she could use the poem to help position herself as a young black person in East London. After this reading of McKay she began to make confident political statements about herself and her friends; but it was in the poetry of Linton Kwesi Johnson that she found something to respond to totally. At the end of the course each student had to present an exhibition. Rosalind's used Linton Kwesi Johnson's poems as a focus. It consisted of pictures and statements about 'black youth in Babylon', policemen beating blacks, stories of trumped up charges, young people arrested on 'sus', and so on, all carefully referenced to poems from *Dread Beat and Blood*. The board was dominated by a poster showing a protest march against the unlawful imprisonment of George Lindo, while a record of Johnson's 'Forces of Victory' boomed out. The effect was extraordinarily dramatic, and for the first time I was forced to recognize the students' response as overtly and powerfully political. This could not be seen just as the solution of an identity crisis, nor after this could that work by Elvis and Marcia's group be seen as apolitical.

It is never possible to state precisely why students choose one text rather than another, but with hindsight Rosalind's exhibition[4] was a catalyst. Most importantly, it was the work of a student, not merely the influence of a teacher, that pushed the students into a new direction. The students now began to look for texts they could identify as relevant to their immediate situation. They still read and enjoyed Selvon, Anthony and Naipaul, often using them to flesh out a picture of a Caribbean place, but they clearly felt distant from such writers and their concerns. We began to search for literature that was tough and uncompromising, that dealt with situations which were immediately recognizable. Overwhelmingly, the students wanted to listen to and read Linton Kwesi Johnson and Bob Marley. Some read with horror and fascination Alex La Guma's story 'Coffee for the Road'. We all read Richard Wright's powerful story 'Big Boy leaves Home' and, perhaps surprisingly, some of Claud McKay's sonnets and Roger Mais's comi-tragedy

Bro' Man. Of all the novels we read the single most powerfully felt work was Buchi Emecheta's *Second Class Citizen*. As Nashand wrote, 'It says it all'.

The students were discovering writing that spoke directly to themselves. They were constructing a category which depended not on 'literariness', but on how they could respond to it, how the books could function for their purpose. Marley's lyrics, Peter Abraham's *Tell Freedom*, Roger Mais's *Bro' Man* were placed side by side, enabling them to talk and write about their major concerns. Further, they saw their own response, their own writing as belonging in the category they had constructed. The students' own struggle and the struggle expressed in the writing of established authors were conterminous. Always the students' response was political.

Barbara began to write about *Tell Freedom* and 'Coffee for the Road' but abandoned this criticism to write a story called 'Apartheid in Britain'. The story is full of what appear to be clichéd TV cops and robbers images and references, squealing tyres, screeching brakes, guns, smashed-down doors, etc. Barbara has no sophisticated writer's tricks, and the story is rather badly plotted; but what the reader discovers from it is that he accepts the proposition that apartheid could and does operate in Britain. In Barbara's story apartheid begins quite unproblematically. The country is informed of the government decision quite naturally on television news:

> On the 30th December there is to be apartheid. As those words were spoken, George picked up the phone in a shocked manner. The kids kept asking questions about the meaning of the word, but I wasn't in the mood to explain this dreadful word.

Police break into the house, the family is pushed into the street and, with other blacks in the neighbourhood, herded into a local sports centre (South African oppression and Pinochet's Chile combined). The guns, cars and police brutality are not TV fantasies. For Barbara they are real. She has simply taken the way policemen behave in England to its logical conclusion. What her reading of a South African author has done has given her a possible political analysis of police behaviour. As far as Barbara is concerned the political system that enforces apartheid and the one that forces young black people in Britain are not dissimilar. The story ends with the young people rising up to attempt to destroy the system but 'this time but not forever', a note of modified pessimism.

Just as Barbara saw apartheid not just as a South African system but as part of her existence, others read Richard Wright's story 'Big Boy Leaves Home' in a similar way. Kevin (not from a Caribbean background but a Turkish one) wrote in what is almost an aside

> That story has made me think of the struggle of many blacks. It's the real reason why some stand up for what they are. It is a story worth reading and looking into for its true understanding of a world of fact.

The handwritten version has 'we' crossed out and replaced by 'some'. Kevin's comment is representative of a general response to this extraordinarily painful story. Nashaud wrote a long story, carefully selecting and commenting on what he thought important and finally attempting to tie it into contemporary America, Britain and South Africa. He notes and approves the powerful sense of community and its potential for resistance.

> They were concerned about getting Big Boy out of the reach of the mob. They called each other brother they did not call the white man brother. This is like when the Russians call each other *Comrade*.

He comments in general on the story,

> I do think the story is quite violent but I think Richard Wright is just writing down what happened. After all he has first hand experience. I think the story is worth discussing because there is a lot to learn if you compare 1930's to the present time not much has changed, black people are hated by whites in America. Only in 1968 a black Civil Rights leader Martin Luther King was shot dead.

In his final comment he places 'sending blacks back to their own country', a clear reference to Britain and to being treated as second-class citizens in South Africa, as belonging within the same context. Reading the story has enabled him to take a world view of oppression. It did not teach him this; it generated his expression of it.

The poetry of Linton Kwesi Johnson spoke powerfully to all the students, often inspiring poems in response. It was seen as direct and explosive documenting of their experience, joining them in a general struggle. The poems are often in the black dialect of London, springing out of the rhythms of reggae and sound system, and they can be seen as entirely part of black youth culture. What I did not expect and feel could not have been predicted was the response to Buchi Emecheta's novel *Second Class Citizen*. It aroused in nearly all the readers a howl of anger and outrage; they seemed almost physically to feel the pain of Adah's experience. The boys' response to Adah's treatment by her husband was illuminating. On one occasion we were reading the novel aloud. As we finished the passage where Francis explains his Jehovah Witness views on women to Adah there was a spontaneous mutter of 'stupid bastard'. In the ensuing discussion it was clear that they desperately wanted Adah to fight back, to attack her husband, not just verbally but also physically. They were responding in a direct personal fashion to the shame and humiliation Adah experienced. The girls identified with Adah entirely, and this was reflected in their writing by the using of 'I' when writing about Adah, as Barbara does in concluding some writing on the novel, 'If I was Adah'. The novel was clearly seen as commenting on something of which they were part. Claudia read it in relation to what she is beginning to perceive as the struggle of black women. She does not play down racism so much as highlight women's position in a patriarchal racist society:

> Adah does come across racism especially when she's looking for a new home. However a lot of this inferiority feeling has been driven in by Francis always reminding her she's a brainless woman and black.

Her final comment is instructive, 'She is living to be proud of herself as a woman and a Black woman.' I asked Claudia about her use of 'living' here, thinking she meant 'learning', but no, she insisted 'she's living' to be proud. What Claudia appears to be saying here is that Adah's very act of living, like the lives of all black women, is somehow an act of defiance, an assertion, a statement about freedom.

The students whose work I have quoted were not outstanding ones but representative of the groups who chose to read African and Caribbean literature. They are not considered bright or clever in conventional school terms, not even really O level candidates. It is precisely for this reason that the way they read African and Caribbean literature is important. They identified it in political terms, and to argue for its importance to them on any other grounds would be inconsistent. Reading the literature has not taught them politics nor politicized them, but it has provided them with a focus for their own comment. Perhaps as important it has made such viewpoints respectable in school terms. I have described the experience of reading literature like this in relation to a small group of black students in one school, and I feel it is doubtful that it provides grounds for any straightforward course of action. In general terms it needs to be noted that had the course not been a Mode 3 the students' response would undoubtedly have been very different: it would have been controlled by the teacher and by the examination board. Arguments for the inclusion of African and Caribbean literature in O and A level syllabuses as liberating or as making the syllabus multicultural are foolishly short-sighted. Far from being liberating, these potentially explosive texts will be defined by the exam system. Any argument then about the content of the literature syllabus for the 16+ age group must begin with the type of examination and its control. Given the examination we want (I am assuming that we are stuck with examinations for the foreseeable future), what kinds of texts should we direct our students' attention to? They must be texts they can recognize, see as their own, and identify as part of their struggle. Simply to select African and Caribbean texts as 'good literature', in order to multiculturalize the curriculum, is at best tokenism, at worst an attempt to defuse struggle. I suspect the texts our students will want to connect and engage with will be texts of struggle. Ngugi's *Death of Dedan Kimathi*, Michael Smith's poetry, contemporary South African writers, Buchi Emecheta's novels will, I am sure, be on the agenda, along with the work of worker writers and school students. As teachers, though, we must open up options. There must always be the possibility for students to take the unlikely text and make their own as Elvis did with *The White Witch of Rosehall*.

John Lee

Notes

1 CEE stands for Certificate of Extended Education, a one-year
  examination course intended for young adults of 17+ and administered
  by CSE boards. Its scope and seriousness have always been recognized
  and welcomed by English teachers, many of whom have put up a
  passionate fight for its survival. A government-appointed committee
  decreed its demise, none the less. Most school examinations may be
  taken in a Mode 3 form. This means that a school devises its own
  syllabus and mode of assessment and will set and mark the examination,
  with monitoring by the examination board at all stages of the process.
2 B. Coard, *How the West Indian Child is Made ESN in the British School
  System*, New Beacon Books, London, 1971.
3 D. Milner, *Children and Race*, Penguin, Harmondsworth, 1975. His
  work and the work of his colleagues was available earlier.
4 It also occurred at a time of National Front agitation locally and of an
  increase in attacks on Asians. What Rosalind did was bring concern
  about this directly into school.

Books mentioned

Peter Abraham, *Tell Freedom*, Faber & Faber, London, 1981.
Louise Bennett, *Jamaica Labrish*, Sangster, New York, 1966.
Wayne Cooper (ed.), *The Passion of Claude McKay: Selected Poetry
  1912–1948*, Schocken, New York, 1976.
O. R. Dathorne, *Caribbean Narrative*, Heinemann, London, 1966.
Buchi Emecheta, *Second-Class Citizen*, Allison & Busby, London, 1974.
Linton Kwesi Johnson, *Dread Beat and Blood*, Bogle l'Ouverture
  London, 1975.
Alex La Guma, *The Stone Country*, Heinemann, London, 1978.
Roger Mais, *Brother Man*, Heinemann (Caribbean Books), London,
  1974.
Ngugi Wa'Thiongo and Micere Mugo, *Death of Dedan Kimathi*,
  Heinemann (African Writers' Series), London, 1978.
H. G. De Lisser, *The White Witch of Rosehall*, Sangster/Collins, New
  York, 1960.
Kenneth Ramchand, *West Indian Narrative*, Nelson, Sunbury on Thames,
  1966.
Richard Wright, 'Big Boy Leaves Home', in *Eight American Stories*, ed.
  D. L. James, Longman, London, 1977.

16 A better A level

Peter Traves

At a conference on the subject of A level literature teaching Hugh Knight, a London Head of English, made some incisive and pertinent observations. Among these was his story about taking over a new department. He said that the focus of anxiety and potential friction was not the allocation of scale posts or the direction curriculum development might take, but who was going to get the A level teaching. Now both he and I have a great deal of sympathy with this concern. As he pointed out many English teachers look with relief to the clearly defined task that A level teaching seems to be. They feel that they are on safer ground after the complexity and occasional confusion in the role of the English teacher in the lower school. The A level also seems to be closer to their own experience of higher education, particularly if they followed a university course in literature. Nor is this a purely defensive response. The sixth form appears to be an opportunity to offer what they have most enjoyed and valued in their own education.

My own expectations of A level teaching were to some extent a naive version of those I have outlined. I anticipated a group who would bring with them relatively sophisticated skills as critical readers and would already be able to handle, order and express their ideas effectively in the form of a literary essay of the type demanded in the examination. These skills could then be developed over the two years by operating within a framework of lessons closely resembling seminars, in which I would direct the students to, and guide them in, debating the critical arguments around the texts. Such a model of literary education derives from a higher level of study, which I was projecting down into the sixth form. Lesson preparation leans heavily on the teacher as researcher preparing areas of knowledge that will enable the students to have a more informed critical perspective on the text. I found that most of my time was spent mediating the more difficult ideas and

243

language of the critical, historical and cultural background and expecting the students to be able to assimilate this into their own critical understanding of the text. In some ways I was trying to pass on to the students a package of ideas and information and demanding that they make sense of it on their own terms. I was not sufficiently concerned to consider the processes by which they might be able to do this.

The fact that teachers often look upon A level as a welcome break from lower school work suggests that there may not be much continuity in their literature teaching. It would seem that A level brings about the end of most of the practices that make up our experience of lower-school, mixed-ability classes. At best the A level might be seen as a development of O level literature courses or even of some of the literature teaching done for CSE. In a school with mixed-ability classes for its lower-school English there will be real difficulties in shaping coherent teaching practices for literature that cover the whole range of sixth-form work. In other words, the A level may well stand outside the body of practice that is held to offer the richest kind of experience of literature for the bulk of the school. This may or may not be acceptable, but if it is true then schools need to consider its implications.

How closely, in fact, does that description of A level teaching, or at least the expectations of such A level teaching, square with our experience and with the perceived needs of our sixth-form students? There must be schools where this model works and is a rewarding experience for both staff and pupils. My concern is with the schools where this is not so. It is clear that there are a large number of staff and a correspondingly larger number of pupils who are dissatisfied with the more traditional approach. However, to attempt to estimate the extent of this would be pointless without thorough research, so I intend to focus on my own experience at Hackney Downs in the hope that this proves neither too eccentric nor too particular and that it provides a useful starting point for a more general debate.

The school's intake is multi-cultural, and about twenty different languages are spoken in the school. Our A level English groups reflect this cultural diversity. A large number of boys are attracted into the sixth form by the kind of English work they do in the fifth year. As we run a Mode 3 CSE course and take part in the JMB Alternative D (which is a 100 per cent course work O level language examination) this experience is radically different from the A level. Consequently, and despite our pre-sixth descriptions of A level, many pupils have been disappointed or shaken by what is demanded of them in the sixth form. One aspect of this is that in the lower school there is an emphasis on literature in English from a variety of cultural backgrounds. This includes novels, stories and poems from India, Africa and the Caribbean. This work does not extend into the A level course.

Before we can examine the possibility for change at A level it is important to be clear about what such a course must provide. First, there is the fact that A level offers the most common and straightforward means of access to higher education. Students in the 16 to 19 age group must be given the opportunity to get the necessary qualifications to allow them access to institutions of higher education. English A level can be a stepping-stone to one of a wide range of university, college or polytechnic courses. More specifically, it may be a preparation for higher levels of literary study. The course must offer those students who want to continue their academic studies in literature a reasonable grounding in critical skills at a sufficiently sophisticated level. An A level in English can also be a useful qualification to help students get the kinds of jobs and job mobility they want. The traditional A level can satisfy these demands. The fact that not many of our pupils are succeeding on these terms would not alone justify change, since a competitive examination system ensures that many will have to fail under any arrangement. But we demand more than this from the A level. We expect the course to be of intrinsic educational worth. My argument is that while for some pupils the traditional mode of teaching and study may be stimulating and satisfying, many teachers are finding that an uncomfortably large number of students feel that their abilities and interests are stifled rather than developed in the sixth form. I believe that the A level should develop the approaches to literature begun in the lower school rather than constituting a sharp break from them. It should allow for extension and refinement of students' responses to literature over the past five or even ten years. Of course, the literature studied will be intellectually more demanding, and response to it will need to be sharper, better ordered, better informed and more mature, but the students should be able to see these last two years in school as the culmination of their work on literature, not as a quite new and in many senses more limited departure. Finally, the A level should continue to promote the widest possible range of skills and experience needed for students' adult reading, whether or not they go on to take academic courses in literature.

If the A level is to be seen as part of a coherent school policy on literature teaching then it is worth considering which activities in the lower school are thought to be valuable. At Hackney Downs our anxieties about our sixth-form teaching coincided with, and were fed into, a more general anxiety about the state of literature teaching throughout the school. The establishment of an integrated studies or humanities programme in the first three years meant that the English department had to build a syllabus and work in the classroom with history, geography, remedial, social studies and drama teachers. There was considerable pressure on us in the mid and late 1970s to make explicit the kinds of literature teaching we valued and wanted to continue and expand. To simplify the issue and rather than simply rehashing the debates we had then I shall list the classroom activities we agreed were important. They are not unusual. In fact, I imagine few English teachers would argue vehemently against them, which perhaps makes it all the stranger that several of them are neither encouraged nor valued in most A level courses.

(i)   There should be regular use of a class reader, where the whole group shares the experience of reading and listening to a text read aloud.

(ii)   There should be regular opportunities for pupils to choose a text to read silently on their own in class or in the library as an activity which could be continued at home.

(iii) We want to encourage pupils to write imaginatively in response to a text. The writing might be influenced by the form, content or theme of the original work.

(iv) Pupils need the time to select stories, extracts and poems that they like and find ways of presenting them to the rest of the class. They might, for instance, choose to read or dramatise a text or they might decide to display it attractively with or without their own comments.

(v)   There should be opportunities for pupils to work in groups, sharing and modifying their understandings and producing together a response that is commensurate with the level of agreement and diversity of their insights into the text.

(vi)   Literary critical work has a valued place, and pupils should be given the time and guidance, often with the aid of carefully structured activities, to order and sharpen their responses to a particular text. Our argument has never been with the value of academic forms of criticism, only with claims made for their exclusive status at any stage of literary study.

(vii) We also insist that all pupils should be given the opportunity to read literature which reflects the cultural diversity of the classroom and of society at large. There is a rich source of such literature in English, particularly from the Caribbean and Africa.

We were working on the new lower-school humanities curriculum in Hackney Downs at the same time as attempting to draw up a submission to the London University Board for a Mode 2 or 3 A level in English literature. We believed that our aims were modest and realistic. We wanted to include as large an element of course work as possible. This was the only way we felt we could give value to anything like the range of work done in the lower school in the assessment of a candidate's achievement. We began to negotiate with the Board through their schools' liaison officer, Keith Davidson, in 1975. He was extremely helpful and showed endless patience with our ignorance about the nature and workings of the various panels and committees of the examination board. Our submissions were made at a time of depressing changes in the atmosphere surrounding examinations and, more particularly, Mode 3s and course-work assessment. The examination boards were beginning to express doubts as to the viability of course-work assessment. They seemed determined to re-establish greater control over both course content and assessment. New rules were laid down restricting the amount of course work acceptable in any new submissions, and long-term plans were made to cut back on course work in existing examination schemes. In this atmosphere the submissions we felt able to make were more limited in scope than we would have liked.

Our initial proposal was made in 1977. The basic outline of our suggested course was as follows. Candidates would have been expected to take the Board's Mode 1 Paper 1, which was in the process of change from the old 'Chaucer and Shakespeare' to the new 'Major Authors' paper. The second part of the course would have consisted of multi-cultural literature studied much in the same way as the Board's 'Topics in Literature' paper. By multi-

247

cultural literature we meant literature whose themes or whose context of production reflects cultural plurality or cultural conflict. We wanted to focus on the cultures represented in British society, though this did not exclude other writers from consideration. Our main interest tended to be in writers in English from Africa, the Caribbean and Asia: initially because these were cultures most heavily represented in our classrooms, but also because of the conflicts and cultural complexities inherent in the fact that these writers were operating from colonial and post-colonial situations and were having to come to terms with using the language of the colonising power. There is often a creative tension in the fact that these writers use the language of those they see as the oppressor to explore and express their own, or their people's, profound experience of exploitation or oppression. The tension is between, on the one hand, the writer's awareness that taking on the English language is a historical expression of the cultural hegemony imposed on the colonised, and on the other, the fact that that political and cultural complex of ideas and emotions is being explored through that very language. In the poem 'Crusoe's Journal' Derek Walcott[1] writes:

> even the bare necessities
> of style are turned to use,
> like those plain iron tools he salvages
> from shipwreck, hewing a prose
> as odorous as raw wood to the adze,
> out of such timbers
> came our first book, our profane Genesis
> whose Adam speaks that prose
> which, blessing some sea-rock, startles itself
> with poetry's surprise,
> in a green world, one without metaphors;
> like Christofer he bears
> in speech mnemonic as a missionary's
> the word to savages,
> in shape an earthen, water-bearing Vessel's
> whose sprinkling alters us
> into good Fridays who recite His praise,
> parroting our master's
> style and voice, we make his language ours,

converted cannibals
we learn with him to eat the flesh of Christ.

The subject matter has to do with an imposed culture that is all-embracing. European culture turns the African slave 'into good Fridays who recite His praise'. White culture is elevated and black is debased. Yet, the complexities and subtle shifts in feeling and meaning are not only explored in the English language, but the poetry rests heavily on Walcott's own deep and admiring reading in English literature.

We would also have liked to include some black American writers and white writers like William Faulkner, Athol Fugard, Paul Scott and Jean Rhys, writers whose works are often firmly based in cultural conflict and plurality. The selection of six texts that we offered was, *Rights of Passage*,[2] Edward Brathwaite (Barbados), *Invisible Man*,[3] Ralph Ellison (USA), *Things Fall Apart*,[4] Chinua Achebe (Nigeria), *The Siege of Krishnapur*,[5] J. G. Farrell (England), *Sizwe Bansi is Dead*,[6] Athol Fugard (South Africa), *The Castaway*, Derek Walcott (St Lucia).

This part of the course was to be assessed by a three-hour examination, which followed the pattern of the Board's own new 'Topics in Literature' paper. There would be questions on each of the six texts, with two additional thematic questions to be answered with reference to one or more of the set books. Candidates needed to answer four questions in all.

The third part of the scheme was to be assessed by course work. Candidates would have been expected to submit three pieces of writing from the following list of suggestions:

(i)   Imaginative writing. This could take forms including: a story, playscript, autobiographical writing, poetry, reporting in a variety of styles; for example, reporting a single incident in the styles of different newspapers, or the re-writing of an incident from literature in a reporting style (required length: 1500 words of prose or 100 lines of poetry).

(ii)   Research Essay: an essay that displays the candidate's own research connected with the study of texts from papers 1 or 2 or an alternative text chosen with the advice of the teacher. This research would not be a direct treatment of the text of the type demanded in an examination essay, rather it should be a development of that study, extending it into other areas such as the life of the author, the work of the author's critics, or the cultural and historical context within which the text was written (required length: 1500 words).

(iii) Seminar Paper. The candidate would be required to prepare and deliver a seminar paper to his teacher and fellow students. The selection of subject matter would be governed by the same criteria as that governing the Research Essay. The candidate would be required to submit a taped recording and transcript of the seminar (required length: 15–20 minutes).

(iv) Anthology – the candidate would be required to submit an anthology of five pieces of poetry, drama or prose. These pieces would be collected on the basis of a stated theme or approach which must accompany the anthology. The candidate must offer a written, critical justification for the selection of each piece. The quality of the candidates' own writing would be the basis for assessment (required length of the candidates' own writing: 1500 words).

(v) Review. The candidate could offer a long review, or a series of not more than three shorter reviews, of plays, films, books or exhibitions. The books would not be from the list of prescribed texts on any of the papers, and the reviews would not have to be written in the language of formal criticism (required length: 1500 words).

This proposal had its weaknesses. It did, however, offer us the possibility of extending some of the best practice of lower-school teaching into the sixth form and it placed a value on a wider range of responses to literature than the existing course. The submission was rejected. In their reply the Board offered two principal objections to the course and also made a number of critical observations. We were disappointed that the course was dismissed out of hand and that there was no opportunity for us either to explain our case, or negotiate directly with the Board's English Panel. The two main objections were:

(i)   The non-inclusion of Paper 3, which is an essential part of both the existing and new syllabus.

(ii) The high proportion of marks allotted to the course-work.[7]

The first of these two points seemed to confirm earlier rumours that the examiners regarded Paper 3 as 'the one that sorts them out'. The second point seemed ominous and depressing if 33 per cent for course work was to be regarded as too high a proportion of the overall marks. It underlined the Board's distrust of that means of assessment and made it clear that for the foreseeable future A level students in London would continue to face the effective monopoly of the examination essay as the means of expressing their appreciation of literature.

There were other comments made by the Panel, which we found disturbing. 'A doubt that English Literature was really the right title if Chaucer and Shakespeare were the only standard authors studied.' In fact, the Chaucer and Shakespeare paper would have been replaced by the 'Major Authors' paper, and this would have ensured at least four 'standard' authors of the Board's choice in our syllabus. More importantly, it raises serious worries about the term 'standard authors'. The inclusion of several light-weight authors in the Board's own proposals suggests that their main criteria for 'standard' was 'well known' and/or English born. It also raises the broader question of what we should be aiming to do at A level. Should we be attempting to cover the major figures in the landscape of English literature (which in practice would be more like studying six of the first team of twenty or thirty), or should we be encouraging, by way of suitable texts, enjoyable and critical reading of a kind which may be developed and continued in later life.

'The lack of drama (except Shakespeare) and the paucity of poetry was worrying.' This suggests that the Panel were disturbingly ignorant about the texts we wanted to offer. Two of the six texts in our paper were collections of poetry, and one was a play. This compares very favourably with the Board's own 'Topics in Literature' paper.

'The course-work element was very demanding and some of the types offered could pose problems in assessment'. In fact, none of the ideas we suggested will startle anyone who has taught a CSE, O level or CEE that is either part or entirely course-work assessed. The implication is that sixth formers are incapable of continuing and improving the types of work they have been doing for the previous two, five or ten years, and that these forms of assessment are unreliable and unsatisfactory, but fine for those who only take CSE and O level.

The Board's sole concession was to include a special alternative option in its 'Topics in Literature' paper called 'African and

Caribbean Literature'. Although we do regard this as an advance, in that it allows us to offer literature from Africa and the Caribbean right through the school and at all levels of complexity and sophistication, it is unsatisfactory. It is not a substitute for a multi-cultural literature course, in that it is restricted to two particular parts of the world and does not allow for a variety of approaches to cultural conflict or plurality. Further, the special status of the option sets it on a different and disadvantaged footing from the other options in the 'Topics in Literature' paper. Under pressure from teachers the Board abandoned its original intention of confining students to one particular option in Paper 2 – for example, 'Twentieth Century Literature' or 'The Comedy of Manners'. Instead, they allow students the choice of selecting texts from within or across the topics. The 'African and Caribbean Literature' topic, however, (Special relief paper) was excluded from this arrangement. Schools taking it have to notify the Board six or more months ahead, and students are restricted to answering on texts from this topic alone. The reasons given for this mention only administrative arrangements and the work-load on examiners. The results are damaging. It discourages teachers from trying out one or two African or Caribbean books alongside other texts they already value as suitable and successful. It also sets this literature totally apart from the main body of literature in English. We have been active, along with sympathetic schools and pressure groups like ATCAL (Association for the Teaching of Caribbean and African Literature), over the past few years in trying to persuade the Board to change this rule. So far we have not been successful.

Our failure to get the examination syllabus changes we wanted forced us to look more urgently for alternative ways of extending and revitalising our A level teaching. We decided to concentrate on the actual activities students were allowed to perform in class and to attempt to make sure that these allowed for a wider range of responses to literature. Although we knew that many of these activities would not be ratified in terms of examination requirements we felt justified in trying them out on two grounds: first, because our success rate with more traditional and limited practice was poor, and second, because we believed them to have inherent educational value.

In practice our changes in approach have meant that we attempt to maintain a dual perspective. We need to focus on what is needed to give students a sound and informed critical understanding of the text. We also need to ensure that they are given experience of a wide range of activities. For example, in dealing with Chaucer's *The Pardoner's Tale* we hope to cover narrative technique, irony, anti-clericalism and the social, economic and cultural background. In other words we are trying to make sure that students are informed in relevant areas of knowledge, in order to allow them to engage with the text at a worthwhile level. But we also try to ensure that students get the chance for group work, class presentation and creative writing during their study of the text, as well as practising the activity demanded by the examination: an essay under timed conditions.

We have also modified the pattern of our work to allow for the development and maturation we hope takes place in students over the two years. We have tried out a carefully planned introductory course lasting half a term. It begins with small manageable texts and specific, well defined critical tasks. The course is structured to nurture their critical skills as well as to provide a bare outline of the map of English literature. We cover all the set texts in the first year and repeat them in the second year, to allow for the improved level of critical maturity. The smaller amount of time devoted at one go to each text often seems a help rather than a hindrance. It also allows us to structure the two years more carefully in terms of developing the critical skills of our students rather than demanding that they should have them all ready to tackle all aspects of A level study of Keats or Shakespeare in the first term of the lower sixth. We can set tasks appropriate to the level of understanding of the texts in the lower sixth and then build on that in the more demanding work of the second year.

Our approach does not represent anything like a radical change in English teaching. It simply represents an extension into A level of what has long been held as good practice in literature teaching in the rest of the school. It represents no more than what a good many teachers are already doing elsewhere, but it is an important step forward for us. It is difficult to assess the effectiveness of our change in teaching practice as it is still very new in the school. It is true that the less able students are not exactly hurtling towards grade As, in fact they are only a little less likely to fail than before. I do feel, though, that they are gaining a lot more from their A level studies and enjoying far more of the course. Their literary study in the sixth form no longer concentrates so exclusively on the one activity they do least well, the examination essay. Rather, it allows them to continue to do the things that encourage them to want to continue with literature after the fourth and fifth years. The able are likely to get good grades, but of course this is no new phenomenon. However, they are being allowed to express their abilities in a wider range of activities.

Obviously we still have to keep in mind the need to equip our candidates as well as possible for the examinations. We respect the varied reasons students have for wanting A levels. Teachers are not in a position to belittle the desire for qualifications. We have those marketable commodities already and many of us have gained greatly from the experience of literature studied at a higher level. We are, we hope, moving towards marrying efficient examination training to a literature course that has intrinsic value and which is not isolated from, but is a natural development of, a whole-school approach to literature teaching. We realise that we can only go so far within the constraints of the present London University syllabus. We also know that more attractive options do exist with other boards. At present we feel a commitment to the 'African and Caribbean Literature' paper and believe it to be worth supporting as an important initiative, in the hope that we can change its peculiarly restrictive status and then move the Board to liberalise other areas of its A level literature course. In the meantime we are hoping that by focusing on certain activities we can make the most of the present system. At the very least we want to ensure that the advances made in lower-school teaching are not lost entirely in the A level English course.

Notes

1 Derek Walcott, 'Crusoe's Journal', in *The Castaway*, Cape, London, 1969.
2 Edward Brathwaite, *Rights of Passage*, in *The Arrivants*, Oxford University Press, 1973.
3 Ralph Ellison, *Invisible Man*, Penguin, Harmondsworth, 1965.
4 Chinua Achebe, *Things Fall Apart*, Heinemann Educational, London, 1965.
5 J. G. Farrell, *The Siege of Krishnapur*, Penguin, Harmondsworth, 1975.
6 Athol Fugard, *Sizwe Bansi is Dead*, in *Statements*, Oxford University Press, 1974.
7 Letter from the Mode 2/3 Subject Officer reporting on the decision of the English Advisory Panel's Mode 3 sub-committee.

17 Literature and new courses in Further Education colleges

Mary Collins

Why teach literature on the new FE courses? Why not? If you do, then how do you do it? What are the results, and how do you judge them?

This piece will be concerned with describing aims and practice on two particular courses, variations of which operate in several London FE colleges, and elsewhere. The first, a one-year full-time Access course, the Pre-BEd, is available in this case to West Indian students over 23, who hope on completion of this foundation course to go on to read for a BEd Honours degree. The course was first established with the aim of recruiting more black teachers, particularly in London. The second is a City and Guilds Foundation Course in Community Care, which tends to attract school leavers, mostly girls, who hope on completion of the course to find work in the caring professions, usually in auxiliary roles. Both courses are open to people with no academic qualifications, although entry to the Pre-BEd requires the writing (in the candidate's own time) of a critical essay on a novel, a variety of tests, and a formal interview. Although they are of different standards – the Access course is designed to help adult students to reach a pre-degree standard in a short time; the City and Guilds course certificate awarded at the end of the course is approximately equivalent to one O level pass – in both cases personality, 'attitude', motivation and experience are adjudged to be of more importance for course entry than papers and certificates. It is often the case that students on both these courses will not have read a great deal of literature before they begin, and it is quite likely that they may not read a great deal afterwards. With this in mind, why do we work with literature on these courses? Should we do so at all?

Asking each group what they had last read from choice produced mixed results. The older, West Indian group's answers revealed: *Jamaica Labrishe*, a collection of Jamaican dialect poems by Louise Bennett; 'The Lady in White by Charlotte Bronte' (*sic*); Edward Brathwaite's *Masks*; a Mickey Spillane ('I can't remember the name'); volume II of Sir Osbert Sitwell's autobiography ('I thought it might be useful for the future but I didn't like it'); a Reader's Digest collection of condensed novels; *The Lonely Lady* by Harold Robbins; Laurie Lee's *Cider with Rosie*; several romance novels published by Mills and Boon, and *The African Child* by Camara Laye. Several of these had been bought in supermarkets and two had been borrowed from a library. The younger Community Care course group found it much harder to remember what they had last read from choice, with many of them claiming 'nothing'; although some changed their minds when they found that magazines with stories in them could be counted. Books and magazines cited included: *Jackie*; *My Guy*; *Photo Love Stories*; *Of Mice and Men* (in an abridged and simplified version with illustrations); *Jealousy* by Steve Drummond, which is an English Centre publication of a London school student's short story; a science fiction novel 'probably called OMNI'; and 'some stories in English books at school, one was about a pig'. Interestingly, this group demanded to know in return what I had last read from choice, and found Albert Goldman's biography *Elvis* a most derisory answer, as they felt that I should have been reading a 'heavy book': suggestions included Shakespeare and Dickens. Both groups agreed that they spent more time watching fictional television programmes, especially serials, than reading fiction, although the Access students had found that the exigencies of their pre-degree course meant that these habits had changed.

These pre-degree students' own choice of reading material, then, revealed a predilection for big, best-selling novels, for romantic fiction and for black poetry, sometimes written in dialect; and it also demonstrated what seemed to be a reluctant excursion into somewhat recondite 'good books' rather on the spinach principle: if it's nasty, it might do you good. There was some feeling that Mills and Boon books were an embarrassing preference, and there was a desire to show willing by citing half-remembered classics. The younger City and Guilds students were less self-conscious. Many were certain that reading books was a bore, although there was evidently a keen attachment to the romantic photo-comics, which they tended to see as generically unrelated in any way to novels or short stories. Favourite features in the photo-comics included the very serious 'case studies', which demonstrate a particular problem and suggest solutions at the end. Examples: 'Claudia's Dad wants her to go to college, but all she wants is a job!' or 'My Adopted Baby: should I tell him?' Students in the Community Care group will probably never need to read 'literature' again unless they want to; the Access Pre-BEd students are, however, in a slightly different position. Although very few intend to become English teachers as such, most will, none the less, be required to read some literature at university or polytechnic during their BEd courses. They may also read books written for children, and novels portraying aspects of childhood. On the Pre-BEd course, several hours a week are assigned to literature, and several to Language and Communication; on the Community Care course, however, four hours a week are given over to 'Literacy', into which time literature, if any is to be included, must be fitted.

Against these preferences, demands and constraints, then, what is the teacher who works with literature doing? What are we asking literature, and these students, to do?

There still remains current in some circles the Arnoldian model of literature as something which refines, elevates and, indeed, tames the uncouth and unruly: the humanities which humanize. There is also a strong reaction against this legacy. A few years ago, when I first applied to a college which specializes in training postgraduates to teach in FE colleges, I was sent a tart letter addressed to all candidates who hoped to teach English in FE. We were warned not to cherish visions of 'awakening in grateful craft apprentices an enduring love for literature' but to get ourselves ready for 'Appendix 2'[1] work, which would include teaching some students who had difficulty in reading anything at all. This sardonic admonition was not entirely unnecessary, particularly in its brusque rejection of the old image of a 'civilized' mentor filling up the empty vessel of thankful apprentice with the rich juice of a higher knowledge. Yet the history of literature and liberal studies teaching shows that much of the work done in what used to be called the technical colleges has been based upon such assumptions, as has some work in adult education. Who can forget the example of Bartle Massey, teacher at the 'night-school' depicted in *Adam Bede*, and his rural pupils?

It was touching to see these three big men, with the marks of
their hard labour about them, anxiously bending over the worn
books, and painfully making out, 'The grass is green', 'The
sticks are dry', 'The corn is ripe' . . . It was almost as if three
rough animals were making humble efforts to learn how they
might become human.

Bartle Massey did good work and, of course, was teaching
literacy rather than literature at this point with these students, but
the dangers of this view of the literature teacher in further and
adult education are considerable. This image of the students
presupposes their deficiencies which we, the missionaries of a
higher culture, would kindly seek to repair, thereby establishing a
subordinate role for the student and a denigratory view of
working-class culture. We would omit from our curriculum all that
they already know, sometimes indeed presuming that they know
nothing. Literature thus becomes a kind of etiquette, serving to
round off those rough corners, and to make 'them' more like 'us'.

Satirizing these assumptions is one thing: abandoning them
completely may be quite another, and is, of course, much more
complex and vexed than satire can suggest. For if we are anxious
to base literature used in these courses specifically upon what is
familiar, or, troubled term, 'relevant'; if we centre a class around a
story in *My Guy* rather than a story by, say, Katherine Mansfield;
if we avoid literature said to be class- or culture-bound for fear of
alienating students who might be reluctant readers; aren't we, with
the best will in the world, in danger of effectively telling our
students to remain where they are already? In the case of working
with black literature on courses specifically for black students,
such as the Pre-BEd, the issue becomes extremely complex. We
may incur resentment in some cases: I remember a Jamaican
student on the Pre-BEd course specifically requesting the addition
of Shakespeare, whom he'd never read, to the syllabus, and not
some romantic comedy either: *King Lear* was what he wanted. He
felt worried that the group might be being given a scaled-down,
made-easy, 'black-jack' version of literature just for West Indian
students. Obviously this is in itself difficult: his anxiety that, for
example, Brathwaite or Walcott were not proper texts for study
indicates something about the way that some British schools and
examining boards have regarded Afro-Caribbean literature, albeit

written in English. There is also a feeling that well-meaning whites shouldn't be talking about Creole dialects and Asante history but getting on with the job. What job? I remember a Guyanese student remarking to me, 'I want you to tell me what I don't know and what I can't find out for myself. Isn't that why you went to college?' Well, not quite: but one can see her point, and yet how difficult this all becomes when the same students complain that their children are wasting time in school lessons listening to Linton Kwesi Johnson and Michael Smith instead of reading Shakespeare and Dickens – those two again, so often taken in vain.

In the case of some of the City and Guilds Foundation students, the issue emerges in a starker fashion. Sometimes – 'nigeria is an iland in the west Indes'; 'You can put money in a bank but not draw it out' – the feeling persists that there is an urgent need to inform in the most straightforward way; and that in itself can make working with literature seem redundant. But I think literature isn't a difficult appendix at the back of a basic survival manual, nor a delicacy to which you earn the right only when you've eaten all your porridge. Of course, if you're not yet a fluent reader, some literature is obviously going to be too hard, but not all of it is, and one can sometimes be surprised by the curious conjunctions which grow up between the most unexpected readers and the apparently unlikeliest texts. Language and literature are inseparable, as are reading and writing. Effective communication, which all the new FE courses claim is of primary importance, must involve, even with students who are not especially accomplished readers, the concepts of point of view, narrator's bias and differing registers for differing audiences and purposes. These ideas may be profitably examined through talking and listening; but they may also emerge as vitally important through the medium of literature.

However, when literature is used in courses other than O and A level literature, especially in courses which involve an element of vocational preparation such as the Access Pre-BEd and the City and Guilds Community Care Foundation Course, it often appears in the form of extracts which may demonstrate somebody's emotional dilemma, or social background, or cultural heritage, or indeed a clash of these as represented in a dialogue or disagreement. We invite our students to experience vicariously a personality, an historical period, another country, an economic problem. Very often a discussion and work on a 'topic' is envisaged: be it abortion, trades union membership, loneliness in old age, single parenthood or racial discrimination, literature can be used to illustrate, to focus, to provoke, to unsettle. The reading itself can be a preparation for later involvement or direct action and this is often seen as peculiarly appropriate to the school-leaving age group in FE. The most successful instance of this kind of directed reading in extract that I can recall took place, however, with the West Indian Pre-BEd group and was grounded in an extract from *The Rainbow*, where Ursula Brangwen, a young teacher in a Board School, finds herself thrashing a 12-year-old boy. The passage conveys with startling immediacy the confused emotions of an inexperienced and overworked teacher. The class of Access students, as intending teachers, many of whom had experienced the old Board School methods while growing up in the Caribbean, found the extract the starting point for a vigorous and far-reaching discussion, which included considering their possible reactions and decisions on future teaching practices. To be thus enabled through reading to consider a particular situation may be of more use ultimately than the direct experience itself. D. W. Harding has noted that

> the spectator role may in certain ways be even more formative than events in which we take part because detached and distanced evaluation is sometimes sharper for avoiding the blurrings and bufferings that participant action brings . . . the spectator sees the event in a broader context than the participant can tolerate.[2]

Nevertheless, the shortcomings inherent in this particular way of using literature are serious. The sequel to the enraptured reading described above was one of disappointment for one reader at least: a Jamaican student borrowed *The Rainbow* and was dismayed to discover that she had to wait 400 pages to find Ursula in conflict with Williams and that the novel 'was not really about teaching at all'. The Bullock Report alerted English teachers to the dangers of gutting English literature for easily assimilable passages. The practice, for all its teaching and learning rewards, may discourage readers from undertaking full-length novels or plays; and there is a falsification inherent in extrapolating what might be tendentious humanitarian themes from writers who might have been appalled to find themselves the subjects of homily. If the students go on to study literature in a more formal framework – perhaps for ordinary or advanced level – we may find ourselves trying to bridge the gap between essays celebrating Charlotte Brontë as a freedom fighter on behalf of the working classes and potential questions on the examination paper; or disentangling the threads of argument in the sorrowful conclusion that '*Emma* is not a good book because the author shows her snobbery'. Besides, what makes us think that we need to provide commentary on moral or political issues via extracts from literature when the reading done from choice by our students may be doing the job just as well? The popular novels preferred by some of the Access students often deal with issues of values and judgement. Stylistics and morality are not necessarily interdependent. One thinks of episodes from *Coronation Street* – 'Well Brian, talk about double standards!' – which have made subtle points acutely and unfussily; and it would be hard to match the ponderous fairmindedness of some of the *My Guy* problem stories told in photographs and captions. The advantages of the 'spectator role' described by Harding may be derived through reading romantic comics and watching television serials as well as through what we would distinguish as literature, and without traducing the source.

I am not arguing against the use of extracts from literature as teaching aids for the humanities and social studies elements on the new FE courses; rather that such use must be accompanied by the encouragement of a consciousness of literature as a phenomenon, historically and culturally produced, and as something intrinsically artificial – made of words. How do these words work, and why? It is in this context that the 'effective communication' beloved of the new FE courses' syllabus writers becomes meaningfully applied to literature. Whatever the limitations of the course, whatever the current standards of the student, it should be possible to consider point of view, the potential unreliability of a narrator, register and tone within literature as well as via speech and reporting. The use of extracts is less dubious when these aspects are certain of consideration, because of the close attention which we give to the words on the page, and the processes by which they got there. Perhaps in our eagerness to promote wide and fluent reading and enjoyable and expressive writing on the part of our students, we may have neglected to consider the essential strangeness of literature, its artifice and its quiddity, 'hammered gold and gold enamelling'. We have to take into account, at whatever level our work,. the ideas of shape, form, complexity and unpredictability. Perhaps this is why poetry is the most appropriate medium with which to begin such study: its very form is different, and because it is complete in itself it affords the chance to pursue the notions of form, shape, mimesis and internal tensions within a completed structure.

By this I certainly do not mean to suggest that we should widen the gap – in some cases, the chasm – that already exists between some students on the new FE courses and 'literature'. Rather, I hope that consciousness of craft and artifice can be a means of access. Because it involves talking about the act of writing as well as about meaning and message, such an approach can encourage students' own writing. To sit and write is often a forbidding, curious and lonely activity, as many of our students know very well. Discussion which admits this and takes into account the struggle of poets and novelists with their craft may, paradoxically, liberate some students into writing. Last year a student told me that he felt as though he'd joined a guild or union when he began to write poems about Grenada.

Where does the English teacher on the new FE courses go from here? Like most teachers, I suspect, I'm still painfully framing questions and I'm only too conscious of intrinsic difficulties in these sensitive areas. One carries simultaneously so many reservations in one's head: aware that reading 'good' literature may play a minute part in the present and future lives of students on the new FE courses; aware of the need to accept and to use what the students bring with them on to these courses; aware of the suspicion occasionally evinced by adult students that they're being sold short by being given 'relevant' material; aware of the urgent need for information on the part of many younger students on the more basic courses; aware of the consequent danger that literature could come to be regarded as the prerogative of the gifted and privileged; aware of a kind of falsehood in making raids into works of art for their illustrative properties; aware that the preferred 'popular' reading material of many of these students may well provide some of the consideration of human problems of truth and justice for which we might be tempted to press excerpts into service; aware of a need to discuss and demonstrate the essential strangeness and artifice of even the most accessible literature.

I'd like to end with a brief account of some efforts made to combine several of these different needs and problems into practice. Edward Kaman Brathwaite's poem *Islands*[3] was the starting point for one particular piece of work which was used for different purposes and with differing effects, with both the groups of students I have described. Several of the students in the Community Care course group are of West Indian parentage, though all were born here. In classes concerned with using library reference books I'd been surprised to discover that one girl, whose mother is from St Lucia, believed that Nigeria was an island in the West Indies. One white student believed the West Indies could be found 'by Australia'. Accordingly, we looked up all these places and found out all the facts, but this didn't manage to bring into sharp focus the extraordinary history of these islands, nor what it is that makes the British think of Jamaica and Barbados, 1200 miles apart, as West Indian, and Cuba, 90 miles from Jamaica, as somehow not part of 'the West Indies'. Brathwaite's poem, a taut, elegant, suggestive piece of writing, brings these ideas and much else to the surface, moving between differing views of the Caribbean, the coloniser's and the colonised's, the actual and the possible. The poem invites the reader to look at a map of 'these islands'; accordingly it was put together with a detailed map of the Antilles, which also showed which languages are spoken in which islands. A question to which we kept returning was, 'Why did he write the poem in these three sections, all long and straggling?' There was considerable excitement and hilarity when it was found that there was a correspondence between the shape of the poem and the shape of the chains of islands, 'like a necklace, but broken,' as one girl said. Discussion on 'What is Edward's feeling about it?' followed, with the clever conclusion of one black girl that the fact that he has adopted a 'roots' name, like Linton Kwesi Johnson, shows us something about where he stands. With the all-West Indian Pre-BEd group it was never my intention to use the map of the Caribbean to inform: one Trinidadian-born woman was able to add to her map extra islands which had been thought too tiny to be included! Rather, the poem was used initially as another statement in the occasional dialogue between us about black literature and its place on such a course. Discussion rapidly became sophisticated, and scribes were appointed to take notes. Notes taken included these ideas: 'He sees the islands as links in a long-established chain of colonialism and slavery. The descendants are powerless in the situation.' 'The rats in the warehouse could be seen as the owners of the sugar plantations, who were DIRTY RATS, and as the people too who have to scratch for their existence.' 'The structure of the poem ties in with the strings of the islands and the fragmentation of the poem shows where the islands were ruled by different foreign nations, Dutch, English, French, Spanish . . .'. 'Edward says if the people's desires are squashed and they don't pick up, then although they are no longer in slavery, he says the rope and the branding iron will always remain causing pain and the islands will never look like jewels, they will just be dry rocks in the map.' 'Why does he repeat certain words, I think it is to make a pattern but each time it is different, he makes a new point on top of the old one.'

The poem, one of some 'relevance', had been used together with a map, to inform, and to question; but it was also considered as an end in itself, its structure, shape, vocabulary and aims. The idea that a poem's shape could also reflect its meaning proved for some students a surprising and stimulating one. One student asked whether there were any other poems 'like that' and we were able to look at examples from George Herbert and Dylan Thomas.

In the new FE courses which involve an element of vocational preparation, a regular work placement is usually a feature of the course. Younger students often have friends on YOPS[4] placements or 'work-tasters', and there is frequent discussion on the Community Care course about experiences on the students' placements, in this case usually as assistants in nurseries, playgroups, schools or hospitals. I prepared a lesson based around Robert Frost's poem 'Out, Out –'.[5] The results were surprising. The poem describes an incident in the American countryside early in the century. A young boy at work on his father's farm feeding wood into a buzz saw is momentarily distracted when his sister calls him for supper. He amputates his hand. While a doctor is giving him ether the boy dies, presumably from shock, and the family '. . . since they / Were not the one dead, turned to their affairs'. There is a curious contrast in the poem between the agonizing events it describes and the wry, prosaic tone it employs to describe them. Together with the poem I used an improvised newspaper account purporting to describe the incident and its aftermath. The idea behind this pairing was to develop discussion about ideas of truth and fact. The Community Care group's query about any piece of writing is usually 'Is it true?', with severe criticism almost bound to follow if it is not. I hoped the class might bring to their discussion some development around the idea of an essential truth, which may not necessarily be factually correct. Frost's poem deals with truths about work, injury, images of manhood and apparent familial indifference. The newspaper account, bristling with facts about dates, ages and names, couldn't approach the inherent and far-reaching truth of Frost's quiet and resigned anger. I hadn't bargained for the strength of reaction which the poem produced in these students. The poem was almost instantly preferred to the newspaper report, and there was much discussion over 'Robert's' attitude to the sudden death. I listened fascinated while an elaborate sub-text blossomed into being: the parents didn't care, his sister was probably staying on at school for exams, the boy had had to start work for a low wage, it was just like that case where a YOPS boy's foot was amputated in a machine at a factory . . . They returned again and again to the poem, almost worrying extra meaning out of the lines:

> Call it a day, I wish they might have said
> To please the boy by giving him the half hour
> That a boy counts so much when saved from work . . .

> 'You see, they wouldn't even let him have a break, no wonder
> he got tired and chopped his hand off.'
> 'His sister must have a guilty conscience . . .'

Some students wrote indignant notes:

> 'The parents didn't care whether he was died or alive. Shouldn't
> have job in first place. Robert *does* care.'

What was the difference between the report and the poem? I asked them.

> 'The poem tells you what was between the lines, the paper just
> gives facts.'

Finally, supposing the poem was completely untrue, that he'd just made it up, would that alter your opinion?

> 'It could have happened today, I know it is true.'

265

Mary Collins

Notes

1 In 1973 Eric Briault, who was the Chief Education Officer of ILEA, published a report on FHE provision. The appendix to that report (Appendix 2) called on colleges to provide for those sixteen-year-olds whose needs were not being met by schools. The courses deriving from that directive came to be called Appendix 2.
2 D. W. Harding, 'Psychological Processes in the Reading of Fiction', in *The Cool Web*, ed. M. Meek, A. Warlow and G. Barton, The Bodley Head, London, 1977.
3 E. Brathwaite, 'Islands', in *The Arrivants*, Oxford University Press, 1973.
4 YOPS, Youth Opportunities Schemes, are usually relatively short courses preparing school leavers for work or for further education.
5 Robert Frost, 'Out, Out –', in *The Poetry of Robert Frost*, ed. Edward Connery Latham, Cape, London, 1971.

18 Using community-published writing in the classroom

Gerry Gregory

Many of them had not realised that I was black . . . and when the dressings were taken off (their eyes), one or two would say, 'Aren't you nice?' or 'Nurse, I never realised you were coloured. You're no different from us . . .' (Norma Igbesoko, nurse)[1]

Many times when you went for your bait there was a hole right through the paper into your bread and the mouse would still be in your pocket. (William Muckle, coal miner)[2]

. . . simply putting a barge by a wharf and putting the mooring ropes anyhow will not do. You have to allow the right amount of rope slack so that when the tide goes out and leaves the barge on the ground, she is lying tight against the side of the wharf for the stevedores to unload her. (Alfred Dedman, lighterman)[3]

During the past decade or so there has been in England an impressive development of community publishing. Around the country 'writers' workshops', 'people's history groups' and so on have sprung up to stimulate and publish the work of local – and predominantly working-class – people. These developments have been characterised by a generally collaborative, democratic ethos. Certain events have been seminal: Chris Searle's publication in 1971 of East End schoolchildren's poetry, for instance, and the resultant furore, as well as some public campaigns and community projects; for example, the provision of bookshops to serve huge urban and, chiefly, working-class populations hitherto lacking them. A crucial factor has been the growing availability of new, simple and cheap means of printing and publishing. There are now twenty-five to thirty independent working-class writers' groups and publishing initiatives loosely linked within the Federation of Worker Writers and Community Publishers. Beyond it are many more small-scale, grass-roots publishing ventures, many of them unknown to the Federation and to each other. Groups within the FWWCP have some two hundred titles currently in print; sales across the board are estimated to have reached one million.[4] The dominant mode of working-class writing, now as in the past, is autobiographical: accounts of life at work and in the dole queue, at home and in institutions of all kinds – schools, children's homes, battered-women's refuges, 'spikes', prisons – both contemporary and in the 'visitable past'.[5] Most are attractive, illustrated 'litho' booklets. Some texts started as tape-recorded interviews. At least two were written forty or more years ago and had gathered dust ever since. Some are by individuals, others by groups. All are the work of beginning writers, all are cheap.[6]

This chapter seeks to argue for a place (no more than that) for some of this material in the literature offered to secondary and tertiary stage students. There are three main arguments for this. First, much of the material is of intrinsic worth: interesting, readable, moving, funny, and capable of eliciting imaginative engagement and identification, of enriching the lives of students and helping them to look at their own experience in new ways. Second, the preponderance of *autobiographical* writing goes some way to redressing an imbalance in the standard diet – autobiography is commonly neglected as student *reading* while bulking large in student *writing* – and its study can open up questions about the nature of autobiography and its relation to fiction, about who writes autobiography and why. Third, in that community publications tend, unusually, to reveal their processes of production – of both the physical volumes and the texts within them – encountering them can help students develop an understanding of how texts come into being, of the nature of publication and of the determinations upon both. Such material can simultaneously promote students' development as readers (enabling them to 'place' the texts they encounter) and as writers (helping them to know what might be involved in making a piece of writing as good as possible and as widely read).

> Joe Louis was going to defend his world title and there was a lot of talk and interest in the fight. Mr Jessop's response to this international event was to stuff a Harding Bag with grass and hang it with a piece of string from the clothes line. Stripped to the waist and in his pit pants; originally a pair of his wife's

bloomers with the elastic taken out of the legs – all the miners wore these down the pit – he thumped away at the bag. When he hit it a little bit too hard it would swing over and over the line and then he would stop, light a cigarette and wait until Mrs Jessop unravelled it for him. He was a funny man, Mr Jessop. He once tried to ride a pig. (Evelyn Haythorne, houseworker)[7]

He hesitated and said that should I receive any extra money while drawing the dole, he would unexpectedly call at my house and make sure that the radio wasn't working. (Albert Paul, Carpenter–joiner)[8]

Community-published working-class writings tend to explore what, for reasons which are to do with the power relations of our society and particularly with their reflection in mainstream publishing, rarely gets into print: lives like those of the majority of students, their relatives, friends and neighbours, with the emphasis very much on the typical rather than the exceptional. These experiences are, characteristically, described and reflected upon in writing that is comfortable, familiar, 'non-standard' and close to speech, some of it actually transcribed speech. The appearance of community publications has coincided with debates about the underachievement of working-class students, their alienation from the education system and from education itself, in which it has become a commonplace that the education on offer has a middle-class 'agenda' and is conducted in 'middle-class language'. Furthermore, analyses of cultural and political hegemony in our society have indicated a denial of *agency* to working-class people: their portrayal as objects rather than subjects. Working-class people, the argument goes, like women and blacks, have been effectively 'hidden from history',[9] and analyses of the mass media have noted the same absences or, where working-class experience *has* been included, a tendency towards the trivialising, the facetious, the patronising. The need to redress these imbalances has been recognised for some time, though the strategies to meet them, for example in respect of children's earliest reading matter, have often been less than well-conceived. Arguably, the introduction of carefully chosen community publications can go some way to filling the experiential gaps, breaking the class silence and affording recognition and respect to the cultural experience of the majority of the population.

Gerry Gregory

The range of working-class experience – and the themes explored – in community publications in the past decade is formidable. The period covered is, roughly, from 1910 to the present, and the location of some of the most prolific groups (London, Manchester, Bristol, Liverpool, Bradford, Brighton, Newcastle-upon-Tyne, Birmingham, Nottingham as well as several smaller towns and rural districts) indicates one sort of variety. A sample of the occupations of the writers – for example, docker, miner, farm-worker, shipyard worker, domestic servant, 'house-worker', dustman, postman, barber, factory worker, cab driver, bus conductor, office cleaner, Thames lighterman, carpenter–joiner – suggests another. Some of the dominant themes are childhood and street life; home life, its patterns, conditions and relationships; school, work and unemployment; solidarity and mutual help, resilience and resourcefulness; relationships with the 'authorities'; union and political activity; racism and sexism.

All that amounts, perhaps, to one sort of recommendation. Published accounts of working-class work bring to light the subtle manual and, especially, social skills of much of such work. 'Insider' accounts of working-class experience, which suggest both its variety and the variety of roles, active and passive, which working-class people take on, are still rare. There might be a temptation to introduce students to material of indifferent quality on the grounds that the content is relevant, important or unique, just as television news sometimes abandons its usual 'quality control' guidelines and uses poor quality 'footage' if the events concerned (the death of Chairman Mao, for instance, or recent confrontations in Poland) are considered sufficiently important. However, no teacher needs reminding that student interest cannot be taken for granted: that boring, ill-written books will induce 'mental truancy',[10] at the least, and probably a more violent 'tissue rejection'. To say, for example, that Stan Rothwell's *Lambeth at War*[11] is a piece of people's history, a first-hand account of how a major historical convulsion worked out at the level of an individual working-class life, or that *Hello, Are You Working?*[12] does the same for the Tyneside depression of the 1930s, or that Joyce Crump's *The Ups and Downs of Being Born*[13] takes us through an upbringing in a series of thirteen Dr Barnardo's Homes and on into their aftermath in the writer's adult life, remains, of course, insufficient recommendation to a teacher deciding what to place

270

before her students. She needs also to be confident that these first-time writers can hold the students' interest.

Because of their sheer variety it is hard to generalise about the quality, in these respects, of community publications; and in any case teachers will, as always, need to judge the material for themselves.[14] In my view the work under consideration comes off at least as well – when judged by criteria such as freshness and vitality of language, appropriate form, economy and coherence – as any other comparable body of writing,[15] and perhaps rather better. If some texts would benefit from sharper editing – from leaving more 'on the cutting-room floor', as many others leave one wanting more and with a host of questions unanswered; and the closeness to speech and general lack of pretension make this an attractive body of work.

It is my impression, gained from visiting a large number of schools in and around London during precisely the time community publishing has been developing, that the usefulness and popularity of some texts is already evident in the multiple copies of such titles as *A Hoxton Childhood*[16] and *Coronation Cups and Jam Jars*[17] in extensive use. Many more titles would repay teachers' attention. *On Earth to Make the Numbers Up* by Evelyn Haythorne, a powerful, funny and excellently written account of childhood and adolescence in a South Yorkshire mining village; *Toby*,[18] an extraordinary story of ten years 'on the road', and twenty-nine more living in the woods outside Bristol, and *Back Home*,[19] reminiscences of childhood in the Punjab by Ranjit Sumal, a young woman now living in Southall, are only the first three that come to mind.

> People passed by without a word . . . with their own partners minding their own business, no one to talk to except our own family at home . . . everything . . . shuttered . . . surrounded by walls inside and outside. (Ranjit Sumal)

> He's told me about his family and his troubles. I feel like Marge Proops sometimes. In winter some old people ride up and down to save heating . . . (Ruth Parsons, bus conductress)[20]

> The worst thing about his singing is his timing. Not the timing of the rhythm of the songs, but the time he plays them. He sings

'Ring of Fire' at half-past nine. You don't have to look up at the clock. 'Country Roads' is sung at ten to ten. It goes on like that all night. People order ale on the strength of his timing. (John Small, dustman)[21]

Before exploring the special value of reading and studying community-published autobiographies it may be useful to get at what distinguishes them by considering the nature of other sorts of autobiography and commonly held views of what autobiography is.

A look at 'mainstream' autobiographies on bookshop or library shelves suggests three broad categories. First, there are the autobiographies (sometimes 'ghosted') of people who are well-known because of their exceptional status and position in the public eye: aristocrats, millionaires, entertainers, statesmen and women and politicians, sportsmen and women and so on. Second, and overlapping with these, are autobiographies by people who have done or experienced something extraordinary – circumnavigated the world in an unlikely vessel, starred in a 'bootstrap story', been kidnapped, hijacked – which then becomes the centrepiece around which a life story is built.[22] These two categories represent for publishers something analogous to journalistic news value, in contrast to a third (rare) category of autobiographies, made compelling to publisher and reader alike by sheer quality of writing, of experience and its realisation, whose 'legitimation' is by 'literary' criteria. Here the autobiographies of Tolstoy, John Stuart Mill and Edwin Muir occur as examples.

Autobiography tends to proclaim itself, and be read and accepted as, the setting down in faithful detail, as interestingly as possible, of what can be recalled of a life. Readers tend to assume honesty and accuracy: honesty because nothing arises to cast this in doubt and because readers are unlikely to have faced the dilemmas of offering *their* lives for scrutiny; accuracy because readers rarely doubt the accuracy of what *they* remember and believe. Fundamental problems about 'the construction of reality' simply do not arise for these readers: and even those who can bear a certain amount of reality and who have developed understandings about the nature of literature spend most of their time, and certainly their time reading, not doing so. In short, autobiography – like news – tends to be read unproblematically.

In schools and colleges autobiography is scarcely read at all, even though students will have been *writing* autobiographical fragments ever since they got their 'My News' books – and more recently their 'Breakthrough' folders – at the age of five. I want to suggest first, that the study of autobiography, supplementing the study of imaginative literature, will, apart from rectifying this odd asymmetry, and allowing students to witness other people's attempts to make sense of experience, also illuminate the actual nature of autobiography, its possible categorical difference from, say, memoirs on the one hand and certain sorts of probing self-analysis on the other, its complex relationship to fiction,[23] as well as questions like: who typically writes autobiography, at what age and why?[24] Who publishes it and why? Second, that the use of some community-published autobiographies – along with others – is an ideal means of doing all this, and of suggesting new possibilities.

The study of autobiography arguably gives rise to a view radically subversive of many assumptions about it. Such an alternative account foregrounds selections, omissions, silences: autobiography as a theory-laden representation of life experiences, shaped – in terms of 'ages', pivotal moments, crises, watersheds, causes and effects, explanations – from the perspective of the moment of writing and, typically, with the benefit of hindsight. In other words, such study promotes the fundamental educational activity of discovering that things are often not what they seem.

If the study of any autobiography, in conjunction with attempts to write one's own, can lead to such understandings, study of community-published autobiographies specifically will raise questions about the differential status of autobiographers and the categories of autobiography that typically find publishers and readers. Students will soon infer that mainstream publishing categories do not apply to community publishing. In fact, the situation is reversed. Ken Worpole, a key figure in community publishing developments since 1971, has put this point

> People come in who've led extraordinary lives and they're surprised when we say . . . that's more the commercial thing. . . . We're not publishing things because of the uniqueness of your life; we're publishing autobiographies for their ability to stand for, to represent the common life.[25]

Realisation of these differences can be, as I argue below, exhilarating. As the magazine *Anti-Student* emphatically put it:

> All our lives we've read stuff other people have written . . .
> Because we see something in print we tend to be impressed by it
> and think it must be authoritative. . . . But when we write and
> print something for ourselves we become more critical. The
> Authority of the Printed Word is Smashed. Moreover, whereas
> in the past if we wanted to say anything in print we had to route
> our communication via some authority figure, an editor or
> publisher or someone of that sort, and run the risk of selection
> or amendment or censorship, now anyone who wishes to can say
> it directly their way to the audience they choose.[26]

> There was another teacher, a Miss Crocker, who would come
> around the class to see who had the cleanest hands and nails.
> The best was chosen to peel her orange and take off all the pith,
> ready for her lunch. We thought it a great honour to do it then.
> (Dorothy Fudge, housemaid)[27]

> A long slipper bath in which you could almost float and with an
> unlimited supply of water. There were no taps inside. The
> attendant filled the bath sufficiently and tested it with his hand,
> shut the door and if you wanted more hot or cold you called out
> 'More hot (or cold) No. 7' like a Lord addressing his valet.
> (John Bennett, clerk)[28]

> I'd left it [*Crisis in India* by Palme Dutt] on a table . . and the
> officer . . . picked it up, looked at it and said, 'Why is old Bill
> paying five shillings for a book?' . . . He read the title but that
> didn't mean as much to him as the price of the book. (Bill
> Massey, gilder)[29]

The appropriation of print by standard English and the people possessing it, and its contribution to the subordination of non-standard dialects, to the myth of their deviance and inferiority and to the subordination of the people possessing *them*, is familiar enough. Community publications often provide examples of what is otherwise, apart from in, say, novel dialogue and playscripts, very rare: non-standard language in print. Reading such materials can be a way into certain sorts of language study: sociolinguistic issues around standard and non-standard dialects for instance, which are by no means 'academic' matters for the majority of students; the nature of, and relationships between, speech and writing, the contexts and use of each, and so on. Beyond this, community-published texts tend to be transparent, in the sense that, explicitly and implicitly, they make their processes clear. The introductions to some of them,[30] typically, explain how projects came into being, how they were conceived and by whom. It is usually made clear where they started as taped interviews, who framed and put the questions, who did the transcribing and editing, etc., where the money came from for printing and so on, and what will happen to the proceeds. And as often as not the reader is invited not just to respond to the text but to join the group. The writer's sheer effort to make meaning often remains unusually apparent on the printed page: the mechanics of the thing – as in Brechtian drama – are unconcealed. Two examples may make this clear. In some texts punctuation is only partly effective, so that at times the reader has difficulty taking the writer's intended meaning; in one text, *Dobroyed*[31] by Leslie Wilson, the writer's idiosyncratic spellings have been deliberately retained: 'comforsation', 'cellisiter' and 'Rochstale' are among the more evocative 'miscues'.

All this, obviously, is in sharp contrast with the practice of 'mainstream'[32] publishing, and for students the contrast can be illuminating in several ways. It promotes realisations that the availability of books is bound up with power and money; that the rows of books in bookshop and library – polished, perfect, distant, authoritative – are bound up with investment, distribution networks, advertising and the hope of profit; that the broad conditions of their production – the operations and views of publishers, distributors and book-buyers, and their economic interrelationships – affect the nature of published texts, including community-published texts; that the asymmetry of the few (producers) addressing the many (consumers) may not be part of the natural order of things; that publishing is now potentially available to all; also that most people find writing difficult; that books easily taken for granted are the result of painstaking effort in drafting, revising and polishing; that if you are, for example, a poor speller that does not mean (a) that your writing is worthless or cannot reach and interest an audience, and (b) that your efforts to get better are not worthwhile if you want readers to make their effort to read what you have to say. Collaborative action in publishing as elsewhere can open up surprising possibilities.

The study of community-published texts allows for a realisation that writing and publishing is not only for other people, that it is possible for 'ordinary' people to write and publish accounts of their experiences and to find interested readers: both 'outsiders', who find those experiences as strange and intriguing as crossing the Atlantic in a plastic dustbin, and 'insiders', who find satisfaction and confirmation in the articulation and recognition of worlds they share. Such understandings entail and promote the democratisation and demystification of publishing and attack the widely assumed authority of print. It may be that they also increase students' confidence and self-respect, including their confidence and self-respect as would-be writers.

> I was coming back from Great Homer Street last Saturday afternoon in the pouring rain with a pram full of groceries. Other women, with bulging bags and their children, were rushing home to get the tea on. Looking dead tired I passed two pubs, and the doors were wide open, and all I could see was big, red, laughing faces and raised pint glasses . . . (Ann Blunt (pseudonym), houseworker)[33]

> I seen Joe at the Kist – then the water came through, that was the lot. There was only one way out. All the air changed. The black damp put 30 of them to sleep, then the water rose, and just covered them over. There was only 8 drownded and that was the 8 I left to my Flat, 6 men and 2 putters – they got the lot. (James Tracey, coal miner)[34]

> I'd heard complaints about him from other people. Anyway, I thought I'd prove it for myself. I wanted to be absolutely sure of the facts. I dressed up in an old coat with the collar turned up, and I went off to the Relief Office . . . (Annie Barnes, councillor)[35]

Notes

1 *19 From 8*, Liverpool 8 Writers' Workshop, 1980.
2 William Muckle, *No Regrets*, People's Publications, Newcastle upon Tyne, 1981.

3 *Working Lives*, vol. 1, A People's Autobiography of Hackney, Centerprise, 1976.

4 Dave Morley and Ken Worpole, 'Writers at Work', in *The New Statesman*, 30 April 1982.

5 'But, as well as this personal past, going back to early childhood, we have also learnt about our family past, the experiences of our parents and grandparents, to go no further back. Most children are fascinated by the tales their grandparents tell them of the life they lived, the things they saw and did when they were children. It is something quite different from learning history at school from history-books or from classes in social history, because it comes as lived experience – what it felt like to have been brought up on a farm, or in the slums of a great city, or in a large house with a staff of servants, or in an orphanage sixty or more years ago. Henry James called this past, the past of two generations back, "the visitable past".' Helen Gardner, *In Defence of the Imagination*, Oxford University Press, 1982. (I would like to thank the publishers for permission to quote these lines.)

6 For discussions of the evolution of community publishing since 1971 see: G. T. Gregory, 'Workers' Writing in the 1970s', unpublished MA dissertation, Department of English, University of London Institute of Education, 1979; G. T. Gregory, 'Working-class writing: breaking the long silence', *The English Magazine*, no. 4, Summer 1980; D. Morley and K. Worpole (eds), *The Republic of Letters*, Comedia Publishing Group, 1982; K. Worpole, *Local Publishing and Local Culture*, Centerprise, London, 1977; Professor Arthur Marwick, in *British Social History Since 1945*, Penguin, Harmondsworth, London, 1982, referring specifically to *The Making of a Ruling Class*, published by the Benwell Community Project, Newcastle-upon-Tyne, describes community publishing as '. . . one of the more positive and hopeful developments of the 1970s'.

7 Evelyn Haythorne, *On Earth to Make the Number Up*, People's History of Yorkshire, 1981.

8 Albert Paul, *Hard Work and No Consideration*, QueenSpark Books, Brighton, 1981.

9 Sheila Rowbotham's phrase. See her book thus titled, Pluto Books, London, 1977.

10 John Dewey, *Experience and Education* (1938), Collier, New York, 1963.

11 S.E.1 People's History Project, 1981.

12 Strong Words, Tyneside, 1977.

13 Vassall Neighbourhood Council, 1980.

14 For information on what is available see: *Writing*, FWWCP, 1978; FWWCP Publications List, 1981; G. T. Gregory, 'Round-ups' of a selection of work produced in 1980 and 1981 in *The English Magazine*, nos. 7, 9, 10.

15 For example, what one encounters in small magazines featuring the work of hitherto unpublished, and chiefly middle-class, writers.

16 By A. S. Jasper, Centerprise, London, 1974.

17 By Ron Barnes, Centerprise, London, 1976. Note also the extensive use of *Our Lives*, ILEA English Centre, 1979.
18 Bristol Broadsides, 1979.
19 Commonplace Workshop, Ealing, 1981.
20 *Taken for a Ride*, Centerprise, London, 1980.
21 'Saturday Night at the Higsons', Scotland Road, Liverpool, in *Voices*, no. 18, Autumn 1978.
22 Fred Eyre, *Kicked into Touch*, Senior Publications, 1981, is an interesting case. An apprentice with Manchester City FC, Eyre failed to make it in the 'big time' and played first in the lower divisions, then for a succession of non-league clubs. What arguably 'legitimates' his autobiography, packed with 'inside' football anecdotes, featuring both big names and the reality of the unglamorous end of football, is that while his football fortunes plummeted, he was becoming an entre- preneur stationery millionaire. (His book is lively and amusing. Eyre now reports on football for the *Observer*.)
23 Some of the understandable confusions around this relationship are illustrated in the readiness of a 16+ group to classify Gorky's *My Childhood* as straight autobiography (on account, presumably, of such features as its title, and general naturalism (of narrative, characterisation, etc.) while the different mode of *Great Expectations*, predictably, guaranteed *its* equally unproblematic classification as novel. (I am indebted to Mike Chapman for this illuminating anecdote.)
24 Note Joyce Crump's point (op. cit.) that there is no need to wait for retirement before reflecting on your life in print.
25 Interview, in Gregory, 1979, op. cit.
26 Quoted in Mike Smith, *The Underground and Education*, Methuen, London, 1977.
27 *Sands of Time*, Word and Action, Dorset, 1981.
28 *I Was a Walworth Boy*, Peckham Publishing Project, 1981.
29 *Shepherd's Bush Memories*, Shepherd's Bush Local History Project, 1981.
30 A good example is Dolly Davey, *A Sense of Adventure*, S.E.1 People's History Project, 1980; see also other publications by this group.
31 Commonword, Manchester, 1981.
32 It should be said, of course, that the publishing world I am here suggesting as a contrast – from Penguin to Pluto, Ginn to Gollancz – is in itself anything but homogeneous in objectives and practices.
33 Scotland Road, Liverpool, in *Writing*, FWWCP, 1978.
34 *Canary Men and Cobblers*, Strong Words, Tyneside, 1975.
35 *Tough Annie*, Stepney Books Publications, 1980.

Index

Index

Index

Index